30 DAYS

TO

GROWING IN
YOUR FAITH

30 DAYS

TO

GROWING IN
YOUR FAITH

ENRICH YOUR LIFE IN

15 MINUTES A DAY

MAX ANDERS

THOMAS NELSON
Since 1798

Published in Nashville, Tennessee, by Thomas Nelson. Thomas Nelson is a registered trademark of HarperCollins Christian Publishing, Inc.

Thomas Nelson titles may be purchased in bulk for educational, business, fundraising, or sales promotional use. For information, please e-mail SpecialMarkets@ThomasNelson.com.

All Scripture quotations, unless otherwise indicated, are taken from the New American Standard Bible®. Copyright © 1960, 1962, 1963, 1968, 1971, 1972, 1973, 1975, 1977, 1995 by The Lockman Foundation. Used by permission. (www.Lockman.org).

Scripture quotations marked ESV are taken from the ESV® Bible (The Holy Bible, English Standard Version®). Copyright © 2001 by Crossway, a publishing ministry of Good News Publishers. Used by permission. All rights reserved.

Scripture quotations marked NIV are taken from The Holy Bible, New International Version®, NIV®. Copyright © 1973, 1978, 1984, 2011 by Biblica, Inc.® Used by permission of Zondervan. All rights reserved worldwide. www.Zondervan.com. The "NIV" and "New International Version" are trademarks registered in the United States Patent and Trademark Office by Biblica, Inc.®

Scripture quotations marked KJV are taken from the King James Version. Public domain.

Scripture quotations marked NKJV are taken from the New King James Version®. Copyright © 1982 by Thomas Nelson. Used by permission. All rights reserved.

Scripture quotations marked NLT are taken from the Holy Bible, New Living Translation. © 1996, 2004, 2015 by Tyndale House Foundation. Used by permission of Tyndale House Publishers, Inc., Carol Stream, Illinois 60188. All rights reserved.

Any internet addresses, phone numbers, or company or product information printed in this book are offered as a resource and are not intended in any way to be or to imply an endorsement by Thomas Nelson, nor does Thomas Nelson vouch for the existence, content, or services of these sites, phone numbers, companies, or products beyond the life of this book.

Library of Congress Cataloging-in-Publication Data

Names: Anders, Max E., 1947- author.
Title: 30 days to growing in your faith : enrich your life in 15 minutes a day / Max Anders.
Other titles: Thirty day to growing your faith
Description: Grand Rapids : Thomas Nelson, 2021.
Identifiers: LCCN 2021003549 (print) | LCCN 2021003550 (ebook) | ISBN 9780310116851 (paperback) | ISBN 9780310116868 (ebook)
Subjects: LCSH: Christian life--Miscellanea. | Spiritual life--Miscellanea. | Spiritual formation--Miscellanea.
Classification: LCC BV4501.3 .A5155 2021 (print) | LCC BV4501.3 (ebook) | DDC 248.4--dc23
LC record available at https://lccn.loc.gov/2021003549
LC ebook record available at https://lccn.loc.gov/2021003550

Printed in the United States of America

21 22 23 24 25 26 27 LSC 10 9 8 7 6 5 4 3 2 1

To my prayer/advisory team:
Ken Axt
Joel Berger
Howard Morrison
David Reeves
Doug Waltz

Anyone would be fortunate to have such
friends praying for and advising them.
It means the world.
Thanks!

CONTENTS

Part 3: Do

THREE REASONS TO READ THIS BOOK

How many times have you heard life-changing truth in a sermon, a conversation, or a book, but afterward you got distracted, forgot about it, and were *never changed* by it?

100 times? 1,000 times?

The reason is because hearing something once is usually not sufficient to change you.

If something is important, it has to be repeated until it changes you. Otherwise, it goes in one ear and out the other.

 ## 1. Because Repetition Is the Gateway to Transformed Behavior

That is why there is a lot of repetition in this book. It is not an accident. It has been carefully designed to drive truth deeply into your brain. This repetition then sinks into your subconscious, changing your fundamental attitudes, values, and behavior.

When this happens, it begins to bring about transformed behavior that is not likely to happen any other way.

If you have been a Christian for a while you may already know some of the information in this book, but you may not have repeated it until it changed you.

Other information in this book is likely new to you. It is very important. It also needs to be repeated until it changes you.

Reading this book will not *complete* the transformation process promised by the truth in it, but it can certainly *begin* it. And, as the truth is reinforced in your *future* learning, the Holy Spirit can complete the process and bring deep, fundamental change to your heart.

2. Because It Is Better to Get All of a Little Rather Than None of a Lot

This information is so super-condensed that I had to leave out a lot of very important information. Even then, I wish there were things I hadn't left out.

Why did I do it? Because *it is better to get all of a little rather than none of a lot.*

But what is left *in* is essential to a balanced and mature Christian life. Knowledge isn't everything, but everything rests on knowledge. You *cannot* live something until you know it, and you *will not* live it until you believe it.

If you are teaching this book, you might feel that something should be added. Feel free to add what you think is missing.

But, *nothing in the book should be left out.*

So, this is not the *most* you need to know about living the Christian life; it is the *least.* It is not the *end* of your learning about living the Christian life; it is the *beginning.*

3. Because It Is Essential to See the Big Picture

Details are only fully understood when seen in relationship to the whole.

For example, if I were to show you a piece of a puzzle and ask you to tell me what things the blue, green, and red colors represent, you wouldn't know. But if I showed you the complete puzzle picture, you would instantly see that the green was grass, the blue was sky, and the red was a barn.

When we see the big picture of anything, it helps us master the details. The same is true with the Christian life. So, this book will give you the big picture of the Christian life, which will help you more effectively master the details.

For this reason, the whole is greater than the sum of its parts.

The methodology in this book is the same as in its companion book, *30 Days to Understanding the Bible* . . . information boiled down to an essential minimum and presented in simple, bite-sized portions, with lots of repetition stirred in. If you see a blank, fill it in! It's there for a reason. It's how the brain works.

If you have not read *30 Days to Understanding the Bible*, I urge you to do so as soon as you have finished this book. The two together will lay a powerful foundation for a lifetime of spiritual growth.

For now, get ready to embark on a journey that has the potential to change your life. Enjoy *30 Days to Growing in Your Faith*.

HOW DO YOU LIVE THE CHRISTIAN LIFE?

First, You Become a Christian

In order to live the Christian life, you must first be a Christian. I wrote this book for Christians, but it is conceivable that someone might begin to read the book without having become a Christian, or not being sure if he or she is a Christian.

As you will see later in the book, Christians are not people who have turned over a new leaf. Rather, by the work of God, they have turned over a new life. The Bible says a Christian is spiritually born again by grace through faith in Jesus, and has become a whole new person. You'll see that explained in chapter 4.

So, you can't earn your salvation by being good or by anything you do for God. It is by believing in and receiving Christ and giving yourself to him.

When a man asks a woman to marry him, he is not looking for anything she can give him. He wants her! The same is true with God. He doesn't want anything we can give him or do for him. He wants us.

If you have not yet become a Christian, or are not sure, I urge you to make that decision now. Please visit www.peacewithgod.net. There you will find full information to guide you in your decision.

Second, You Follow the Scriptural Plan for Spiritual Growth

Shortly after graduating from seminary, I was teaching in a Christian college and had the privilege of leading a young man to Christ.

After he finished praying, he looked up at me in sincerity and trust and asked, "Now what?"

They say that when you have a close brush with death, your whole past flashes in front of you. In this case, my whole future flashed in front of me, because I knew I didn't know the answer to that question. And I wondered why I didn't know the answer, and tried to figure out how I was going to get the answer.

So, I did to him what was done to me. I muttered something about reading your Bible, praying, and going to church.

That was all true and good. But I knew my answer was inadequate, and I didn't know what else to say. That's what the people told me who led me to the Lord. But no one had ever said, "Max, here is how you live the Christian life; here is how you grow in faith as a follower of Jesus." No one ever laid it all out for me.

Many years later, I understand why no one had ever laid it out for me. It's very difficult to do.

Another reason is that the answer has levels of complexity. If you keep it simple, it might be explained in a few sentences. If you make it complex, it might take a small library of books and other resources.

But, because the mind works best when it goes from the simple to the complex, from the general to the specific, I will venture a brief answer, and then I will elaborate more fully in the rest of the book.

Baseline Definition

To grow in your faith, you . . .

- . . . feed your mind the truth (Scriptures and other sources of truth).
- . . . integrate your life with the lives of other solid Christians and learn to imitate their lives as they provide a degree of accountability to you.
- . . . get up each day and try your best to do what is true and right.

You can't believe something until you know it, and you won't live it until you believe it. So, feeding your mind the truth is essential—it is the beginning point. That's why you start with the Bible.

But sometimes the Christian life is more easily caught than taught, so being able to imitate other good examples is a powerful benefit, along with having these examples as a spiritual accountability influence in your life. You can't do it alone.

Finally, you can't be passive. You have to try. You will fail, but you will be better off for trying and failing than if you don't try at all. Then you get up each day and live, as best you are able, the truth you know.

As you do these things, you will learn more truth, and you will try to live that truth with help from others. And God will forgive you, teach you, strengthen you, grow you, and encourage you.

Then you learn more truth, and you try to live that truth with help from others. As you do this, the Holy Spirit will increase your capacity to know, be, and do what you ought in an ever-ascending sweep upward.

Is there more? Of course. But we're trying to establish the baseline. Do you need to pray? Of course. Do you need to learn how to discern God's will? Of course. Do you need to learn how to walk in the Spirit? Of course. And you need to learn that self-effort will not do everything you need. There is an interplay between your responsibility and God's. So, while self-effort is not the only answer, you will never get where you need to go by being passive, careless, or ambivalent.

So, at the baseline,

- You become a truth sponge;
- You become an imitator of other, solid Christians;
- You become a bulldog in pursuit of the truth and the role-modeling you have benefited from so far, believing it will lead to more.

When you are faithful at that level, the Lord will give you more. When you are faithful at that next level, the Lord will give you still more. And so on, for the rest of your life.

Expanded Definition

So, after establishing that baseline, we start adding the things that need to be added, and that is where this book comes in. This book will give you a very simple outline of some of the foundational things you need to learn.

As I said, this book is not the most you need to know—it is the least. It is not the end of your learning about the Christian life; it is the beginning. After you have finished this book, there will still be things you don't know, don't live, and aren't able to do. But you will be closer than you were before. And this book will lay a foundation of information that you can use to build a lifetime of further learning.

Conclusion

There will be people who will feel that I left something essential out. I understand. It was a significant challenge to decide what to put in and what to leave out. As I said earlier, feel free to add anything you think I have left out as you read for yourself and as you teach others.

Overall, this book is a treasure trove of information that I wish I had had when I was just starting out in the Christian life. This is all information that, in the decades since I became a Christian, would have catapulted me faster forward if I had known and understood it from the beginning.

Put another way, this is all information that I would give my life to have known when I was a new believer. In fact, that is what I've done. I've given my life to learning and distilling this information to give you a leg up growing in your faith in an increasingly hostile world.

I have prayed for you that, after you finish this book, the Holy Spirit will guide you to the additional resources you will need to become a more complete Christian. For now, dive into chapter one and begin to "drink in" the wealth of information contained in these pages.

As a complete Christian, you need to:
- Know what you need to know
- Become what you need to be
- Do what you need to do

PART I

KNOW

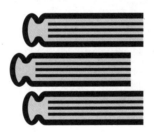

You can't believe
something until
you know it.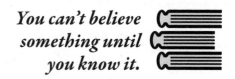

CHAPTER I

THE KEY TO HAPPINESS

You were created *by* God, *for* God, and you will only be truly happy as a Christian who is growing *in* God.

> **CENTRAL PASSAGE:** Matthew 22:37 ESV—"You shall love the Lord your God with all your heart and with all your soul and with all your mind."

1. It is okay for a Christian to want to be happy.

It is okay for a Christian to want to be h_____.

The desire to be happy is the highest desire of the human heart. It is as Blaise Pascal wrote:

> All men seek happiness. This is without exception. Whatever different means they employ, they all tend to this end. The cause of some going to war, and of others avoiding it, is the same desire in both, attended with different views. The will never takes the least step but to this object. This is the motive of every action of every man, even of those who hang themselves.[1]

However, Christians may feel vaguely guilty about wanting to be happy. We may think our highest desire ought to be something loftier, more self-sacrificing, more "spiritual." However, C. S. Lewis suggests:

> If there lurks in most modern minds the notion that to desire our own good and earnestly to hope for the enjoyment of it

3

is a bad thing, I submit that this notion . . . is no part of the
Christian faith. Indeed, if we consider the unblushing promises
of reward and the staggering nature of the rewards promised in
the Gospels, it would seem that Our Lord finds our desires not
too strong, but too weak. We are half-hearted creatures, fool-
ing about with drink and sex and ambition when infinite joy is
offered us, like an ignorant child who wants to go on making
mud pies in a slum because he cannot imagine what is meant by
the offer of a holiday at the sea. We are far too easily pleased.[2]

Hmmm. This opens up possibilities we may not have considered.
Perhaps it might be okay with God for us to want to be happy . . .
perhaps God might have actually even created us with this longing
for happiness.

2. We naturally doubt that God alone is enough for our happiness.

We naturally d_____ that God alone is enough for our happiness.

A problem arises when we don't quite believe that God alone is
our source of true happiness. None of mankind has believed it naturally, ever since Adam and Eve.

Living in the Garden of Eden, *in paradise*, Satan slithered up to
Eve and began a conversation that changed the course of history:

And he said to the woman, "Indeed, has God said, 'You shall not
eat from any tree of the garden'?" The woman said to the serpent,
"From the fruit of the trees of the garden we may eat; but from
the fruit of the tree which is in the middle of the garden, God
has said, 'You shall not eat from it or touch it, or you will die.'"
The serpent said to the woman, "You surely will not die! For God
knows that in the day you eat from it your eyes will be opened, and
you will be like God, knowing good and evil." When the woman
saw that the tree was good for food, and that it was a delight to
the eyes, and that the tree was *desirable* to make one wise, she
took from its fruit and ate. (Genesis 3:1–6, emphasis mine)

Eve saw, she desired, she took. Adam, her husband, followed suit. Satan deceived Eve into doubting God's sufficiently benevolent intentions toward her, and convinced her that in order to be happy she had to take things into her own hands.

It turned out badly.

That is the strategy Satan has used with every one of us since then, because it works so well. We see, we desire, we take.

We, like our first parents, conclude that, in order to be happy, we can take what we want from what God offers us. However, if there are things God's will does not offer us that we think we need for complete happiness and fulfillment, we seek to get those things for ourselves. It turns out badly for us, too.

As believers, it is not that we don't want God. We do. And we want the things he offers us, most notably eternal life. But we also want other things (financial security, good health, respect from others, adequate recreation, friends, good circumstances, an absence of frustration, etc.), and, if the will of God does not give them to us, we are inclined to go outside his will to try to get them for ourselves.

Pascal wrote eloquently of this tendency:

> There was once in man a true happiness of which now remains to him only the mark and empty trace, which he in vain tries to fill from all his surroundings, seeking from things absent the help he does not obtain in things present[.] But these are all inadequate, because the infinite abyss can only be filled by an infinite and immutable object, that is to say, only by God Himself.[3]

3. We must seek our happiness in God.

We must seek our happiness in G____.

God has created us with deep desires because he wants to use them to draw us to himself, the only one who can fulfill those deep desires. Many of the Psalms carry this theme:

1. "Delight yourself in the LORD, and he will give you the desires of your heart" (37:4 ESV).
2. "As the deer pants for the water brooks, so my soul pants for You, O God" (42:1).
3. "How sweet are your words to my taste, sweeter than honey to my mouth!" (119:103 NIV).
4. "In your presence there is fullness of joy; at your right hand are pleasures forevermore" (16:11 ESV).

What deep longings these Psalms express . . . but look to God for their fulfillment. Our desire for happiness and fulfillment is natural and good. The thing we must learn is where to look for these. Real, lasting happiness and fulfillment cannot be found in the things of this world, but only in God.

And think about it: what in this world, by itself, has made you happy for long? A new car, a new home, a new job, a new spouse, a new _____ (fill in the blank)?

Did it keep you happy? Of course not. If we are thinking clearly . . . if we are thinking to the end of the road (death and the afterlife) . . . only God can make and keep his children happy. That's the way we're wired.

Everything God asks of us, he does so to give something good to us, or to keep some harm from us. Therefore, the shortest distance between us and the life we long for is total obedience to Christ.

However, we often resist God's commands because we imagine that they *keep* us from complete happiness rather than *give* us complete happiness. We think that if we give ourselves in total obedience to God, he will make us a pauper missionary and send us to some forsaken part of the globe to waste our lives in third-world futility.

Of course, that's a lie from the pit of hell. But it can be very effective. And while that might not be your specific fear, just substitute your worst fear for "missionary" and "forsaken part of the globe," and "third-world futility," and that's your fear.

We fear that bondage to God will make us miserable (in spite of the scriptural evidences to the contrary), and that we need to be free to follow our hearts.

Just the opposite is true, however. John Piper, in his book *Desiring God*, asserts that the chief end of man is not "to glorify God and enjoy Him forever," as the Westminster Confession states. Rather, he contends that the chief end of man is "to glorify God *by* enjoying Him forever."[4]

He outlines a philosophy of Christian pleasure:

1. The longing to be happy is a universal experience, and it is good—not sinful. In fact, it is a reflection of how God has created us.
2. We should not deny or resist our longing to be happy, but should pursue it.
3. The deepest and most enduring happiness is found only in God.[5]

Elsewhere Piper writes,

The fire of lust's pleasures must be fought with the fire of God's pleasures. If we try to fight the fire of lust with prohibitions and threats alone—even the terrible warnings of Jesus—we will fail. We must fight it with a massive promise of superior happiness. We must swallow up the little flicker of lust's pleasure in the conflagration of holy satisfaction.[6]

Piper's point is, "long" all you want. Long more than you currently do. But go to God to be filled. Piper's zeal in promoting this worldview is rooted in his conviction that a commitment not to pursue the pleasures of the world is *not* sufficient to keep many from succumbing to them.

Piper argues that the only surefire way to resist the pleasures of the world is to be fulfilled in the greater pleasures of God. The highest calling of humanity is not the renunciation of joy but rather the consummation of joy, which can only be experienced in God.

4. Only when we are convinced that our true happiness lies in following God and not sin (anything outside the will of God) will we have the power to fully turn from sin.

Only when we are convinced that our true happiness lies in following G____ and not s____ (anything outside the will of God) will we have the power to fully turn from sin.

So, we see both from Scripture and from observation that we are hardwired by God to desire our own welfare, but this is not a bad thing. And, we see that to follow happiness fully is to follow God completely.

What's more, the genius of God's system is that he asks everything of us in order to give something good to us or to keep some harm from us.

For example, Scripture teaches us that we reap what we sow (Galatians 6:7). If we sow that which is good, we reap that which is good. If we sow that which is bad, we reap that which is bad. So, God instructs us to sow that which is good. Doing so reaps good things and avoids bad things.

When we sow bad actions and attitudes, we reap personal pain, including enmities, strife, jealousy, outbursts of anger, disputes, dissensions, factions, etc., as we read in Galatians 5:20–21. When we sow good attitudes and actions, we reap great personal pleasure, including love, joy, peace, patience, kindness, goodness, faithfulness, gentleness, and self-control, as we see in Galatians 5:22–23.

Which things would you rather have?

When God commands us to live righteous and holy lives, he is intending to spare us from the formidable list of negatives in Galatians 5:20–21: "enmities, strife, jealousy, outbursts of anger, disputes, dissensions, factions" (and much, much more). In its place, he wants to give us "love, joy, peace, patience, kindness, goodness, faithfulness, gentleness, [and] self-control" (Galatians 5:22–23).

Anything wrong with that?

Again, God asks everything of us in order to give something good to us or keep some harm from us. Therefore, the shortest distance between us and the life we long for is total obedience to Christ.

When we come to deeply believe this principle, it helps us make the right decisions. In fact, when we make wrong decisions it is often because we simply don't believe the principle. We might get it right if we had to answer the question on a test, but when it comes to living it out in our daily lives, we prove by our disobedience that we simply don't believe the principle.

If we deeply believe that our true happiness lies in following God and not sin, it puts us on the lookout for opportunities to trust and obey him, and makes us wary of not trusting and obeying him.

As Timothy Keller said, "If you understand what holiness is, you come to see that real happiness is on the far side of holiness, not the near side."[7]

Conclusion

So, do you want to be happy? We all do. We must accept by faith that our true happiness lies in following God and not sin. We must resist the lie of the snake, that God does not have our best interests in mind and that we must take control of things ourselves in order to get what we need to be happy. Rather, we must give ourselves to the pursuit of the one who created us with deep longings (in order to draw us to himself), since he is the only one who can truly and permanently fulfill them.

 REPETITION
Is the Key to Mental Ownership

Chapter Review

1. It is okay for a Christian to want to be h_____.
2. We naturally d_____ that God alone is enough for our happiness.
3. We must seek our happiness in G____.
4. Only when we are convinced that our true happiness lies in following G____ and not s____ will we have the power to fully turn from sin.

The Christian Life in 1,000 Words—Review

If something is important, you must repeat it until it changes you.

You were created *b__* God, *f____* God, and you will only be truly happy as a Christian who is growing *i__* God.

THOUGHT/DISCUSSION
Is the Beginning of Understanding

Answer these questions, either individually by journaling the answers or in a small discussion group.

1. What do you *naturally* think you might need other than (or in addition to) God to be happy in life?
2. What is your greatest fear in giving yourself completely to God?
3. Are you convinced that your true happiness is found in God and not in sin (anything outside the will of God)? If not, why do you think you doubt it?

DECISION TIME
Is the First Step to Change

Answer these questions, either individually by journaling the answers or in a spiritual accountability group.

1. Have you made the decision to follow God completely as the source of true happiness in life?
2. If not, what do you think is the primary reason why? What could you do to bring yourself to the point where you would be willing to make that decision?

RECOMMENDED
Resource

Desiring God, John Piper (especially chapter 1)

You can't believe
something until
you know it.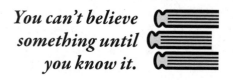

CHAPTER 2

THE NECESSITY OF AN ETERNAL PERSPECTIVE

We must live in this visible, *temporal* world
according to invisible, *eternal* realities.

 CENTRAL PASSAGE: 2 Corinthians 4:18—"We look not at the things which are seen, but the things which are not seen; for the things which are seen are temporal, but the things which are not seen are eternal."

---

1. We must abandon ourselves to an eternal perspective.

We must abandon ourselves to an e_____
p_____.

We live in a physical world, but there are spiritual realities that affect us. If we do not see them or take them into account, life can become very hard.

Scripture teaches that there are two worlds, one we can see and one we cannot see. A great trick of the Christian life is to *live in the physical world according to the overriding spiritual realities.* This is what it means to have an eternal perspective. We must see past the physical present into the spiritual future and live in this world according to the truth and values of the next.

These two worlds—the visible, temporal world and the invisible, eternal world—are in conflict. In the visible world:

- . . . truth is what I say it is.
- . . . emotions are reliable.
- . . . happiness is the highest good.

In the invisible world:

- . . . truth is what God says it is.
- . . . emotions are not reliable.
- . . . holiness is the highest good.

These two sets of beliefs cannot both be true. Therefore, we must choose between them. The overriding truth of the unseen, spiritual, eternal world must be accepted by the Christian as the ultimate reality.

Unless we abandon ourselves to an eternal perspective, we are likely to be disappointed, discouraged, and even defeated by God's unwillingness to bless our temporal plans.

2. We must believe the unbelievable.

We must b_____ the u_____.

To say that we must believe the unbelievable is not really true. The things we must believe that we label "unbelievable" are not *really* unbelievable. They just seem unbelievable to a typical person with a temporal perspective.

In reality, when you think your way out to all four corners of the subject, these things are not only believable; they are the only things that *can* be believed if we are to remain true to reality.

But, as I said, they can *seem* unbelievable to those with a temporal perspective.

First, we must believe that God exists in the absence of scientific proof.

But that is not truly unbelievable, because proof of God is outside the scope of the scientific method. Science cannot speak to God's existence, because God cannot be put into a scientific experiment to prove or disprove the hypothesis of his existence. But, when you leave the laboratory where you were looking for *proof*, and go to the courtroom looking for *evidence*, the ground shifts dramatically. There is plenty of evidence to convince an unprejudiced mind that God exists.

Psalm 19:1–2 (NIV) says, "The heavens declare the glory of God; the skies proclaim the work of his hands. Day after day they pour forth speech; night after night they reveal knowledge."

Romans 1:20 tells us that "since the creation of the world His invisible attributes, His eternal power and divine nature, have been clearly seen, being understood through what has been made, so that they are without excuse."

God intended us to look up in the night sky and say in our hearts, "There must be a God!" So, believing in him only seems unbelievable to someone with a temporal, earthly perspective.

> *We must believe that God e_____ in the absence of*
> *scientific p_____.*

Second, we must believe that God is good in spite of rampant evil in the world.

Those with a temporal perspective often believe the rampant evil in the world is proof that God does not exist. Or, if there is a God, they assume he must be unconcerned about humanity's plight at best or, at worst, lacking in goodness. What kind of God allows people who worship him to be murdered, raped, tortured, or to come to countless other hideous ends?!?

Yet the Bible says that God loves us (John 3:16), that he is good (Psalm 119:68), and that, while he allows evil for reasons hidden in the mystery of his will, its existence in the world doesn't change or detract from who he is.

One reason to believe that God is good in spite of the evil in the world is that God stepped in. God came and paid the price to make it possible for us to be delivered from evil, not fully in all of this world's trials, but absolutely and decisively in the world to come.

What price did God pay? The Father conceived the plan; Jesus willingly complied (John 6:38). Jesus suffered and died to save us from evil. He had the sin of the world placed on him. There was also a price for the Father, however, who had to witness the suffering and death of his Son whom he loved.

So, while God allows evil, he does not exempt himself from suffering under it. Either God is a madman, mindlessly inflicting evil on himself, or else there must be a rationale for allowing evil that is beyond our knowledge, beyond our comprehension, or both.

I do not believe he is a madman because of this fact: in every place where God is taken seriously and followed consistently, goodness, wonderfulness, peace, love, and joy break out, overflow, bubble up, and wash over. Whether on a personal level or a national/historical level, God brings a tsunami of goodness to all who follow him authentically.

Certainly, there are those who have done bad things in God's name. We're not talking about them. We're talking about Christianity being the historical driving force behind literacy, health care for the masses, care for the disabled and disadvantaged, legal justice, and democratic governments on a national/historical level.

Compare that with officially atheistic countries, where the governments of Stalin, Hitler, and Mao were responsible for the senseless and cruel deaths of over 100 million people at the hands of their own countrymen.

On the other hand, there are countless millions who could tell the story of personal, individual goodness brought to their lives by faith in God and Christ, often in the midst of unimaginable suffering.

Wherever God and his Word are taken seriously and followed authentically, goodness, goodness, and more goodness breaks out! All this cannot be the effect of a madman.

We must believe that God is g_____ in spite of rampant e_____ in the world.

Third, we must believe that God loves us in spite of the fact that he does not always make our lives easier.

This is the problem of evil come down from the cosmic level to the personal level. At best, Christians have to admit that when they pray not to have bad things happen to them, sometimes the bad things happen anyway. And, when Christians pray to get good things, sometimes they don't get them. At other times, they get good things they didn't even pray for. There are times when there seems to be so little correlation between prayers and answers that the answers Christians do get could just as easily be chalked up to coincidence.

Sometimes Christians pray for guidance and get none. They ask for help in living the Christian life or for help in overcoming addictions or other troubling personal problems, and get no immediate or perceivable help. They try to be good spouses and sometimes get divorced anyway. They pray for God to help their children grow up to follow him, and some of their children defect from the faith as soon as they leave the home.

Such mixed results are a best-case scenario. At worst, God sometimes allows a missionary to be raped or killed by those very people whose souls he or she came to save. Or his servants get mired down in situations in which people reject what they have to offer, and they seemingly waste their lives trying to help people who, in the end, simply didn't want their help.

"No," atheists conclude, "we don't have sufficient evidence to suggest there is a God, and we wouldn't need him if there were. He simply hasn't earned our trust."

"If you are asking me to believe in your God," the atheists say, "you are asking me to believe the unbelievable."

But, on deeper inspection, there are answers to these objections.

Sometimes the bad things that happen to us are a result of bad decisions we've made. But at other times trouble just seems to seek us out, to hunt us down while we're minding our own business. At such times, if we view our circumstances through a temporal perspective, we typically conclude that there is something wrong.

When you can't seem to make enough money or when health problems, unavoidable financial crises, job losses, or interpersonal conflicts happen, if we look at circumstances from a temporal perspective we will draw wrong conclusions. We will conclude that God has abandoned us, that he doesn't care enough about us to help us succeed, that there is something wrong with us that prevents us from making life work, or that we've simply been dealt such a bad hand that no one could play it well. Coming to these conclusions will make us feel anxious, frustrated, angry, resentful, depressed, or a hundred other things.

If we look at circumstances through an eternal perspective, however, we can take meaning and even joy in what happens to us knowing that things are working out from an eternal point of view.

If we look at things from an eternal perspective, we come to these four reassuring conclusions:

1. We can take joy in these trials, knowing that, if we respond properly, they will make us spiritually complete (James 1:2–4).
2. We can take joy in these trials, knowing that we will receive a disproportionate positive eternal reward for them (Romans 8:18–19).
3. We can take joy in these trials, knowing that they will equip us to make a more effective impact on others' lives (2 Corinthians 1:3–5).
4. We can take meaning in these trials, knowing that they will deepen our relationship with God (Hebrews 12:5–11).

Having an eternal perspective means that whatever losses we feel we have incurred in this life can be counterbalanced by the realization that suffering will be disproportionately compensated in the next life (Romans 8:18). This life is brief. The next life is endless. For the Christian, there is no loss. There is only delay.

We must believe that God l_____ us in spite of the fact that he does not always make our lives e_____.

3. We must choose the undesirable.

We must c_____ the u_____.

When we say, "choose the undesirable," it does not mean that the things we choose are really undesirable. It only means that they seem undesirable to the temporal perspective. In reality, when you think your way out to all four corners of the subject, these choices are not only desirable, but they are the only things that *can* be chosen if we are to remain true to reality.

But, as I said, they can *seem* undesirable to those with a temporal perspective.

First, we must choose God over temporal happiness.

Again, to choose God over temporal happiness only seems undesirable. In fact, choosing God *is* choosing *real* happiness.

C. S. Lewis speaks helpfully to this:

> God made us: invented us as a man invents an engine. A car is made to run on petrol, and it would not run properly on anything else. Now God designed the human machine to run on Himself. He Himself is the fuel our spirits were designed to burn, or the food our spirits were designed to feed on. There is no other. That is why it is just no good asking God to make us happy in our own way without bothering about religion. God cannot give us a happiness and peace apart from Himself, because it is not there.[1]

If we pursue happiness, we will not find God. If we pursue God, we will find happiness.

We must choose God over temporal h_____.

Second, we must choose others over self.

It seems, at first glance, that by choosing others over self, we are sacrificing any hope of happiness. How can one be happy if one abandons any self-life and lives only for the sake of others?!? It seems to be a recipe for becoming a doormat and for sacrificing our happiness in life on the altar of serving others who often do not appreciate it or even recognize it. It seems, at first glance, like a guaranteed recipe for unhappiness.

While God expects us to have our own lives and not simply to give ourselves over to the whims of others, nevertheless, when we give ourselves to others, especially in keeping with scriptural priorities, we get back rich and satisfying relationships in return.

After we surrender to him, God expects us to give ourselves first to our immediate family, then to other Christians, then to the world:

- Husbands, love your wives as Christ also loved the church and gave Himself up for her (Ephesians 5:25).
- Parents, love your children (Ephesians 6:4).
- Christians, do good to all people, but especially those who are of the household of faith (Galatians 6:10).

God has created us as social beings. We need others, and we find joy and meaning in rich relationships with others. As we give ourselves to others, it encourages them to give themselves back to us, creating a bond of unity and harmony.

So, we said that we had to choose *others* over *self.* But that only seems undesirable at first glance. On second glance, it is the only reasonable thing to do. We see that choosing others over self is the way to happiness. It's not that we become doormats, giving ourselves to the world for the world to walk on. Rather, within the will of God and understanding that God has a plan for us, a job for us to do, and gifts we can exercise, we are set free to serve others and so gain the happiness we seek.

We must choose others over s_____.

Third, we must choose the eventual over the immediate.

At first glance, we think it is to our advantage to take a bird in the hand rather than two in the bush. A commercial on television says, *"I want it all, and I want it now."* Modern American culture thinks that having to wait is undesirable. Modern America thinks that following our hearts and choosing whatever we want right now is the way to be happy.

However, one of the marks of emotional maturity is a willingness to make a smaller sacrifice now in order to gain a larger reward later. It is called delay of gratification.

In the well-known Stanford Marshmallow Experiment, children were given the option of being able to eat one marshmallow immediately; alternatively, they could wait and, as a reward, get to eat two marshmallows later.

Researchers recorded the results and followed those children through their early lives. They learned that the children who were willing to delay eating one marshmallow now for the sake of getting two marshmallows later were more successful in life.

The willingness to delay immediate gratification for the sake of a later, larger reward is also a mark of spiritual maturity.

Randy Alcorn, in his book, *The Treasure Principle*, has an excellent illustration of this principle:

> Suppose your home is in France and you're visiting America for three months, living in a hotel. You're told that you can't bring anything back to France on your flight home. But you can earn money and mail deposits to your bank in France.
>
> Would you fill your hotel room with expensive furniture and wall hangings? Of course not. You'd send your money where your home is. You would spend only what you needed on the temporary residence, sending your treasures ahead so they'd be waiting for you when you got home.[2]

This story helps us understand *where* our home is, *when* our reward is, and *how* we live for eternal truth and values over temporal ones.

Christians must choose the undesirable. This means prioritizing the eventual, greater thing over the immediate, lesser thing. Yet we see that that choice is not really undesirable. Not in the long run. It only seems undesirable at first glance. At second glance, we see that the so-called undesirable is a key to our happiness.

*We must choose the eventual over the i*_____.

Conclusion

So, we must abandon ourselves to an eternal perspective. If we do not, we are likely to become disappointed, discouraged, and even defeated because of God's unwillingness to bless our temporal plans. That is because he has greater things for us, and he loves us too much to allow us to settle for less than his best for us . . . for this time and for eternity.

REPETITION
Is the Key to Mental Ownership

Chapter Review

1. We must abandon ourselves to an e_____ p_____.
2. We must b_____ the u_____.
    a. We must believe that God e_____ in the absence of scientific p_____.
    b. We must believe that God is g_____ in spite of rampant e_____ in the world.
    c. We must believe that God l_____ us in spite of the fact that he does not always make our lives e_____.
3. We must c_____ the u_____.
    a. We must choose God over temporal h_____.
    b. We must choose others over s_____.
    c. We must choose the eventual over the i_____.

The Christian Life in 1,000 Words—Review

If something is important, you must repeat it until it changes you.

1. You were created *b__* God, *f____* God, and you will only be truly happy as a Christian who is growing *i__* God.

2. We must live in this visible, t_____ world according to invisible, e_____ realities.

THOUGHT/DISCUSSION
Is a Key to Understanding

Answer these questions, either individually by journaling the answers or in a small discussion group.

1. How completely do you think you have abandoned yourself to an eternal perspective?
2. What is your greatest fear in doing so?
3. Are you prepared to allow God to use trials in your life to convert your perspective from a temporal one to an eternal one?

DECISION TIME
Is a Key to Change

Answer these questions, either individually by journaling the answers or in a spiritual accountability group.

1. Are you prepared to abandon yourself to an eternal perspective now?
2. If not, what do you think is the primary reason why? What could you do to bring yourself to the point that you would be willing to make that decision?

RECOMMENDED
Resources

What You Need to Know about Defending Your Faith, Max Anders
What You Need to Know about Spiritual Growth, Max Anders
Rewriting Your Broken Story, Kenneth Boa

You can't believe
something until
you know it.
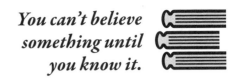

CHAPTER 3

THE NECESSITY OF AN ETERNAL PURPOSE

The main thing *God* gets out of your life is the person you become.
The main thing *you* get out of your life is the person you become.
Therefore, our highest purpose is to *become* the most we can,
in God's eyes, before we die.

 CENTRAL PASSAGE: 1 Corinthians 10:31—"Whether, then, you eat or drink or whatever you do, do all to the glory of God."

1. Who we become is the most important thing in life.

Who we b_____ is the most important thing in life.

A sense of purpose and meaning is essential in life. As far as living a vital Christian life goes, we simply will not have the resolve to get up each morning and take the blows that life will inevitably give us without a clear understanding of why we're doing it, along with the conviction that it is all worthwhile.

Dallas Willard was known for saying that the main thing God gets out of your life is the person you become, and that the main thing you get out of your life is the person you become. God does not want what we can give to him (gifts) or what we can do for him (good works), at least not apart from our love. He wants us! He wants us to love him and to live in close relationship with him.

In return, he promises to bless us with a life of meaning and purpose (John 10:10). The more completely we give ourselves to God and make "becoming" our life purpose, the more God is pleased and the more we are pleased. So, if we establish as our life purpose "becoming the most we can become in God's eyes before we die," we set ourselves up for the fullest life possible.

Notice that the quote doesn't have us *doing* the most we can do before we die, or *achieving* the highest we can achieve before we die, but *becoming* the most we can become. This is a huge distinction, and keeping the difference clear can save us a world of heartache in the end.

On May 25, 1961, President Kennedy announced a staggering national goal: to put a man on the moon and return him safely to earth before the end of the decade. There was a collective gasp among scientists and engineers. Many thought it was impossible and couldn't believe the president's naiveté in announcing it! But, to our national amazement, Kennedy's ambitious vision was achieved on July 20, 1969, when Neil Armstrong stepped onto the moon's surface and then returned safely to earth shortly thereafter.

Does anyone think the United States would've gotten to the moon if Kennedy hadn't set the goal? No. No one thinks so. That's the power of purpose. It focuses the mind, stirs the heart, and strengthens resolve. It is difficult to overstate the power of purpose.

So, accepting the purpose of becoming the most we can become in God's eyes before we die can be our own, personal, spiritual "moon-shot." It can take us further spiritually than we would ever go without it.

2. To become the most they can become, Christians must know what they need to *know*, become what they are meant to *be*, and do what they are gifted to *do*.

To become the most they can become, Christians must know what they need to k_____, become what they are meant to b__, and do what they are gifted to d__.

We must gain the knowledge we need to build a life of purpose.

Becoming the most we can become in God's eyes before we die depends on three things, the first of which is knowledge.

Knowledge isn't everything, but everything rests on knowledge. Jesus said, "You will know the truth, and the truth will set you free" (John 8:32). To the degree that we do not know the truth, we are vulnerable to ignorance and deception. There is some information that is so vital to the Christian life that if you do not know it, you cannot become a complete Christian. By "complete," we do not mean perfect. Rather, we mean mature. Full-grown. Fully developed (Colossians 1:28).

Here are other passages that speak to the importance of knowledge:

- "A wise man is strong, and a man of knowledge increases power" (Proverbs 24:5).
- "Take my instruction and not silver, and knowledge rather than choicest gold" (Proverbs 8:10).
- "The mind of the intelligent seeks knowledge" (Proverbs 15:14).
- "It is not good for a person to be without knowledge" (Proverbs 19:2).
- "Grow in the grace and knowledge of our Lord and Savior Jesus Christ" (2 Peter 3:18).

Whether we go to Scripture, experience, or common sense, we see that knowledge is a good thing, a powerful thing, and something that a Christian must commit himself to acquiring. The fact that you are reading this book is an excellent step in gaining the knowledge you need to build a life of purpose.

We must gain the k_____ we need to build a life of purpose.

We must gain the character we need to build a life of purpose.

Knowledge, however, is never an end in itself. The purpose of knowledge is to provide the impetus for other things, including the development of Christlike character.

Mickey Cohen was a mobster in Los Angeles in the 1940s, involved in illegal gambling. He supposedly got saved at the first Billy Graham crusade there in 1949. When, sometime later, his "salvation" had not resulted in reformed behavior, he was challenged to change his lifestyle to that reflecting his newfound faith.

Mickey replied, "You never told me that I had to give up my career. You never told me I had to give up my friends. There are Christian movie stars, Christian athletes, Christian businessmen. So what's the matter with being a Christian gangster? If I have to give up all that—if that's Christianity—count me out."[1]

Mickey didn't get it. Christians are measured, not so much by what they know or do, but by who they become.

Each of us as Christians has a great challenge to live like who we really are. We are children of God, we're born again, we have the Holy Spirit living within us, we have the Bible to guide us, and we have the challenge to reach the world for Christ. There is something terribly wrong if the people who look at us see an impostor and not the person we really are. Our great challenge is to live consistently with who we are in Christ.

Romans 8:29 tells us that "those whom He foreknew, He also predestined to become *conformed to the image of His Son*" (emphasis mine).

1 John 3:2 tells us, "Beloved, now we are children of God, and it has not appeared as yet what we will be. We know that when He appears, *we will be like Him*, because we will see Him just as He is" (emphasis mine). It is God's intention that we become like Jesus in our character and lifestyle.

As we commit to regular individual and corporate worship, and as we commit to discipleship, mentoring, spiritual accountability, etc., we accelerate our progress toward gaining the character we need to build a life of purpose.

We must gain the c_____ we need to build a life of purpose.

We must gain the skill we need to build a life of purpose.

God gives each person a job to do and gifts with which to do it. Therefore, complete Christians discover and use their spiritual gifts and share their faith with others.

Our "job" was given to us even before we were born. Ephesians 2:10 says, "For we are His workmanship, created in Christ Jesus for good works, which God prepared beforehand so that we would walk in them."

What's more, he gave us gifts with which to do those works. 1 Peter 4:10 says, "As each one has received a special gift, employ it in serving one another as good stewards of the manifold grace of God."

Because God has created us for good works, and because he has gifted us to do them, we will only experience full satisfaction in life as we are using his gifts to do the works he has prepared for us, which includes sharing our faith with others (Matthew 28:19–20).

Christians are never fully satisfied until they are using their spiritual gifts in service to God and sharing their faith in Christ with others. We need a sense of purpose in life, and we will not have it until we are doing what God has gifted and called us to do.

As we get involved doing the things we believe God calls us to do and as we receive training and guidance, we help gain the skill we need to build a life of purpose.

We must gain the s_____ we need to build a life of purpose.

3. To live a life of purpose, Christians need to think big and act small.

To live a life of purpose, Christians need to t_____ b___ and a___ s_____.

We must set a big goal.

One of the principles that needs to guide us on a daily basis is the principle of thinking big but acting small.

That is, when they consider what the Lord might want to do in their lives, Christians need to think as big as possible, to imagine the most that the Lord might want to do in their lives—to shoot for the moon, as we said.

It is commonly said that Henry Ford was once asked if he did market research first, to determine if there was a felt need for the automobile. He said, "No. If I had asked people what they needed, they would have said, 'A faster horse.'" Thinking big often takes us outside the box.

To begin, Christians might ask themselves what, if they knew they would be successful at anything they tried, they would want to do for God? This may not end up being the thing that God eventually wants to do through us, but it gets us started, moving us in the right direction. God delights to lead and steer us as we progress from there.

Your great thing might not be great to someone else, but it's great to you. The things that seem great to me would have seemed small to Billy Graham or other super-achievers. The only thing that matters is if it's great to you.

We must set a b____ goal.

We must be faithful in small responsibilities.

Having said that, doing big things is often a matter of stringing together faithfulness in a lot of little things. In the pursuit of great things, we often get mired in the drudgery of everyday details that must be done if the great thing is eventually to be realized. We must remember, when we're doing the "drudgery" things, that they are just as important to God as the great things.

Mother Teresa founded the Missionaries of Charity, a Roman Catholic religious order of women dedicated to serving "the poorest of the poor." Later, an order of the Missionaries of Charity was founded for men.

One day, one of the men came to Mother Teresa complaining that he was being given too many administrative duties, and that these administrative duties were keeping him from serving lepers— the very cause for which he had joined the order.

"My vocation is to work for lepers," he said. "I want to spend myself for the lepers."

Mother Teresa said quietly, "Brother, your vocation is not to work for lepers; your vocation is to belong to Jesus."[2]

We may want to do great things, to serve the lepers. But in the serving of the lepers there may be times when we simply have to do administrative duties. We have to be faithful in little things in the pursuit of the big thing.

As Helen Keller once reportedly said, "I long to accomplish a great and noble task, but it is my chief duty to accomplish small tasks as if they were great and noble."

The wonderful thing about this is that when we stand before the Lord, the Lord is just as pleased, and we are just as eternally rewarded, when we are faithful in our "small things" in the same way as if we were doing great things.

In the pursuit of our great things, the only thing that matters is faithfulness to what God has given us today.

We must be faithful in s_____ responsibilities.

4. Live with the end in mind.

Live with the e___ in mind.

To live a life of purpose, we live with the end in mind. That is, we go out into the future to determine what our ultimate purpose is, and then we work backward to assess what we must do between now and then to realize our purpose.

One of the gates in the wall of old Jerusalem is called the Damascus gate. That's because if you go out that gate, the road leads you to Damascus. There's another gate that's called the Joppa gate. If you go out that gate, the road leads you to Joppa. If you want to go to Joppa, you don't go out the Damascus gate. It won't take you there.

In the same way, we start living the Christian life with intention and deliberateness when we start living the Christian life with the end in mind. We must start living for the things that will be rewarded when we stand before the Lord. We cannot continue simply living for ourselves. That would be like wanting to go to Joppa but going out the Damascus gate.

The interesting thing, however, is that this adjustment in thinking might not change all the things we're doing. It just might change our motives and our attitudes while doing them.

For example, if you have a job as an electrician, as an engineer, or as a waitress, and you decide you're going to start living your life with the end in mind, that doesn't necessarily mean you quit your job. It might—but probably it won't. You will probably keep doing what you have been doing. But you will keep doing it for the purpose of serving the Lord by doing your job well and by treating others with dignity and respect as you do and sharing your faith when appropriate.

In Colossians 3:22–24, we read:

> Slaves, in all things obey those who are your masters on earth, not with external service, as those who merely please men, but with sincerity of heart, fearing the Lord. Whatever you do, do your work heartily, as for the Lord rather than for men, knowing that from the Lord you will receive the reward of the inheritance. It is the Lord Christ whom you serve.

So, we may continue doing the same thing we have been doing, but we do it with a new motivation—serving the Lord by doing our job well and by treating others with dignity and respect.

Conclusion

There is an order to living life with purpose. First, we must accept that God is good, that he desires our happiness, and that in everything he asks of us, he does so to give something good to us or keep some harm from us. That is the message of chapter 1.

The message of chapter 2 is that we must abandon ourselves to an eternal perspective. Only when we truly believe in God's goodness and good intentions toward us, and only when we completely abandon ourselves to an eternal perspective, will we be prepared to embrace a truly eternal purpose.

Only then will we be willing to abandon our own will for our lives and substitute God's in its place. Only then will we be willing to suffer the loss of our temporal desires for the sake of eternal values.

Only then will we have the perseverance to absorb the blows that life will inevitably give us and keep on pursuing God's will for our lives, rather than giving up and falling back to our desires. Only then will we be able to avoid getting distracted, discouraged, and defeated by God's refusal to bless our will, and we will find the strength to hang in there and receive the full blessing of God, which is the only thing that truly makes life worth living for the complete Christian.

REPETITION
Is the Key to Mental Ownership

Chapter Review
1. Who we b_____ is the most important thing in life.
2. To become the most they can become, Christians must know what they need to k_____, become what they are meant to b___, and do what they are gifted to d__.
   a. We must gain the k_____ we need to build a life of purpose.
   b. We must gain the c_____ we need to build a life of purpose.
   c. We must gain the s_____ we need to build a life of purpose.
3. To live a life of purpose, Christians need to t_____ b____ and a____ s_____.
   a. We must set a b_____ goal.
   b. We must be faithful in s_____ responsibilities.
4. Live with the e____ in mind.

The Christian Life in 1,000 Words—Review
If something is important, you must repeat it until it changes you.
1. You were created b__ God, f____ God, and you will only be truly happy as a Christian who is growing i__ God.
2. We must live in this visible, t_____ world according to invisible, e_____realities.
3. The main thing G____ gets out of your life is the person you become. The main thing y____ get out of your life is the person you become.

Therefore, our highest purpose is to b_____ the most we can become, in God's eyes, before we die.

THOUGHT/DISCUSSION
Is a Key to Understanding

Answer these questions, either individually by journaling the answers or in a small discussion group.

1. Is "who you become" the most important thing in life to you right now?
2. What is the greatest thing you would like to do for God if you knew that you would be successful at anything you wanted to do?
3. As you give yourself fully to the Lord, does it mean you have to change your vocation? Or do you just do your present vocation as unto the Lord?

DECISION TIME
Is a Key to Change

Answer these questions, either individually by journaling the answers or in a spiritual accountability group.

1. Are there any "little things" in which you need to become more faithful?
2. What spiritual goal could you establish for yourself that would be your spiritual "moon shot"?
3. Is this something that excites and motivates you? What could you do now to begin the pursuit of that goal?

RECOMMENDED
Resource

The Me I Want to Be, John Ortberg

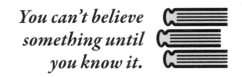

*You can't believe
something until
you know it.*

CHAPTER 4

EMBRACING YOUR TRUE SPIRITUAL NATURE

A Christian is not merely someone who has
turned over a new leaf, but, rather, is someone
who has turned over a new *life*.

 CENTRAL PASSAGE: 1 Peter 1:23 (NIV)—"You have been born
again, not of perishable seed, but of imperishable."

It is vital that we understand who we are. Whether we recognize
it or not, we all act consistently with our beliefs. Our deep beliefs
control everything about us. Therefore, it is essential that we believe
that which is true.

Many Christians do not understand who they are. They do not
understand the difference between who they are now and who they
were before they placed their faith in Jesus. They don't understand
who they have become in Christ. As a consequence, they do not rise
in their behavior to match their true spiritual nature.

*When we understand our true spiritual nature, it can increase our
ability to live consistently with who we truly are.*

One of the most perplexing and persistent problems in helping
people grow in their Christian faith is explaining how Christians
can sin and still be in good standing with God. How much can we
sin? How badly can we sin? Is there a breaking point?

There are places where the Bible says that I am holy and righteous
(Ephesians 4:24; Colossians 3:12). However, I know my own heart

and I can tell you that I am not always holy and righteous in my thoughts, motives, or actions.

So, are we playing word games? Using verbal sleight of hand? Or, do I slip in and out of holiness? And, if so, do I slip in and out of my salvation?

How do I reconcile the presence of sin in the life of a Christian?

I have become convinced that a closer look at Scripture can clear up the muddle and put us on solid ground for understanding how to cooperate with God in the process of spiritual growth and maturation.

And, when we understand our true spiritual nature, it helps us see ourselves more as God sees us. Since we tend to act consistently with our self-perception, seeing ourselves this way also helps us live more righteous lives.

So, let's unpack this.

1. Christians are born again in the likeness of God.

Christians are born again in the l_____ of God.

Our pre-salvation nature: we are truly lost.

The Bible only ever represents us as having one nature or another—there are no in-betweens. We are described as either lost or saved, sinful or holy. Let's look at our pre-salvation/lost state:

- "There is none righteous, not even one" (Romans 3:10).
- "All have sinned and fall short of the glory of God" (Romans 3:23).
- "The wages of sin is death" (Romans 6:23).
- "Remember that you were at that time separate from Christ . . . having no hope and without God in the world" (Ephesians 2:12).

So, we see that our fallen selves are cut off from God because of sin. If left unresolved, sin leaves us destined to an eternity separated from God.

Our post-salvation nature: we are truly redeemed.

"But God . . ." Two of the greatest words in all of language! But God, the Bible says, intervened and paved the way for us to be restored to him. Read one of the greatest, most hopeful passages ever written:

> And you were dead in your trespasses and sins, in which you formerly walked according to the course of this world, according to the prince of the power of the air, of the spirit that is now working in the sons of disobedience. Among them we too all formerly lived in the lusts of our flesh, indulging the desires of the flesh and of the mind, and were by nature children of wrath, even as the rest. But God, being rich in mercy, because of His great love with which He loved us, even when we were dead in our transgressions, made us alive together with Christ. (Ephesians 2:1–5, emphasis mine)

We can see from this passage that we are spiritually reborn by faith in Christ. As Jesus said in John 3:16, "*For God so loved the world, that He gave His only begotten Son, that whoever believes in Him shall not perish, but have eternal life.*"

Another translation says, "He gave His one and only Son, so that everyone who believes in him will not perish but have eternal life" (NLT).

Elsewhere, the apostle John wrote, "*To all who did receive him, to those who believed in his name, he gave the right to become children of God*" (John 1:12 NIV).

Now, we can look more closely at our post-salvation state:

- We were crucified with Christ: "I have been crucified with Christ; and it is no longer I who live, but Christ lives in me; and the life which I now live in the flesh I live by faith in the Son of God, who loved me and gave Himself up for me" (Galatians 2:20).
- We were resurrected with Christ: "Therefore we have been buried with Him through baptism into death, so that as

Christ was raised from the dead through the glory of the Father, so we too might walk in newness of life. For if we have become united with Him in the likeness of His death, certainly we shall also be in the likeness of His resurrection" (Romans 6:4–5).

- We were born again: "Blessed be the God and Father of our Lord Jesus Christ, who according to His great mercy has caused us to be born again to a living hope through the resurrection of Jesus Christ from the dead" (1 Peter 1:3).

- We were given a new self: "Put on the new self, which in the likeness of God has been created in righteousness and holiness of the truth" (Ephesians 4:24).

- This new self has taken on the righteousness of God: "He made Him who knew no sin to be sin on our behalf, so that we might become the righteousness of God in Him" (2 Corinthians 5:21).

- We have taken on the divine nature: "He has granted to us His precious and magnificent promises, so that by them you may become partakers of the divine nature . . ." (2 Peter 1:4).

So, we have been crucified with Christ, resurrected with Christ, and spiritually born again! The result of all this is that we are now holy and righteous; we have become the righteousness of God, having taken on the divine nature. The difference is amazing when all the verses are strung together.

2. Yet Christians still sin.

Yet Christians still s____.

Having said that, we are faced with the seemingly insurmountable conundrum that *we still sin!*

1 John 1:8–9 says, "If we say that we have no sin, we are deceiving ourselves and the truth is not in us. If we confess our sins, He is faithful and righteous to forgive us our sins and to cleanse us from all unrighteousness."

What!?! How can that be? How can we still sin if we have been born again in the likeness of God, holy and righteous?!?

And, supposing this should be true, how can it be that we do not lose our salvation when we sin again and then have to be saved again? And, if that goes on throughout our lives, how is it that we don't have to be saved over and over and over again in the course of a lifetime? What if we die in that split second between the time that we sin and the time we repent and confess in order to be saved again? Are we forever lost, in spite of the fact that we once were saved?

3. It is our outer man that sins, but our inner man is righteous.

It is our outer man that sins, but our inner man is r_____.

How do we reconcile this calamitous conundrum?

First, let's remind ourselves of Ephesians 4:24:

"Put on the new self, which in the likeness of God has been created in righteousness and holiness of the truth."

Another version says, "Put on the new self, created to be like God in true righteousness and holiness" (NIV).

Yet another says, "Put on your new nature, created to be like God—truly righteous and holy" (NLT).

Bottom line: when we were born again, our reborn spirit (the true "us") was created in the likeness of God . . . holy and righteous.

So—again—why/how do we sin?

It is because this holy and righteous spirit, the true "us," is still housed—trapped, as it were—in an unredeemed body, corrupted by sin. It is the outer man that sins, not the inner man.

Paul describes this incongruous duality more fully in Romans 7:15–25, where he uses language that refers to the outer man and the inner man. So, I'll compare the outer man and inner man as I read through the Romans passage:

> [15]For what I am doing, I do not understand; for I (in the outer man) am not practicing what I would like to do (in the inner man), but I am doing (in the outer man) the very thing I hate (in the

inner man). [16]But if I (in the outer man) do the very thing I do not want to do (in the inner man), I agree (in the inner man) with the Law, confessing that the Law is good. [17]So now, no longer am I (in the inner man) the one doing it, but sin which dwells in me (in the outer man). [18]For I know that nothing good dwells in me (in the outer man), that is, in my flesh; for the willing is present in me (in the inner man), but the doing of the good is not (in the outer man). [19]For the good that I want (in the inner man), I do not do (in the outer man), but I practice the very evil (in the outer man) that I (in the inner man) do not want. [20]But if I (in the outer man) am doing the very thing I (in the inner man) do not want, I (in the inner man) am no longer the one doing it, but sin which dwells in me (in the outer man).

[21]I find then the principle that evil is present in me (in the outer man), the one who wants to do good (in the inner man). [22]For I joyfully concur with the law of God in the inner man, [23]but I see a different law in the members of my body (in the outer man), waging war against the law of my mind and making me (in the inner man) a prisoner of the law of sin which is in my members (in the outer man). [24]Wretched man that I am (in the outer man)! Who will set me (the inner man) free from the body of this death (the outer man)? [25]Thanks be to God through Jesus Christ our Lord! So then, on the one hand I myself with my mind (in the inner man) am serving the law of God, but on the other, with my flesh (in the outer man) the law of sin.

This is why Paul said, in Romans 8:1, "Therefore, there is now no condemnation for those who are in Christ Jesus." Because those who are in Christ Jesus are already holy and righteous in the inner man, and all the sin is in the outer man, which is not going to heaven anyway.

So, notice the summary of where Paul puts sin:

1. "Nothing good dwells in me, that is, in my **flesh**."
2. "For I joyfully concur with the law of God in the inner man, but I see a different law in the **members of my body**."

3. "Making me a prisoner of the law of sin which is in my **members**."
4. "Who will set me free from the **body of this death?**"
5. "I myself with my mind am serving the law of God, but on the other, with my **flesh** the law of sin."

So, in the words of Romans 7, sin is

- in the flesh
- in the members of the body
- in my members
- in the body of death
- and in the flesh

John MacArthur said it well in his commentary on Ephesians:

Biblical terminology . . . does not say that a Christian has two different natures. He has but one nature, the new nature in Christ. The old self dies and the new self lives; they do not coexist. It is not a remaining old nature but the remaining garment of sinful flesh that causes Christians to sin. The Christian is a single new person, a totally new creation, not a spiritual schizophrenic. It is the filthy coat of remaining humanness in which the new creation dwells that continues to hinder and contaminate his living."[1]

So, he is saying that the Christian is a single new spiritual person, housed in a still-sinful body.

Then, MacArthur goes on to write that this new spiritual person does not sin:

So righteous and holy is this new self that Paul refuses to admit that any sin comes from that new creation in God's image. Thus, his language in Romans 6–7 is explicit in placing the reality of sin other than in the new self. He said, "Do not let sin reign in your mortal body" (6:12) and "Do not go on presenting the members of your body to sin."

In these passages Paul places sin in the believer's life in the body. In chapter 7 he sees it in the flesh. He says, "No longer am I the one doing it, but sin which indwells me" (v. 17), "nothing good dwells in me, that is, in my flesh" (v. 18), "I am no longer the one doing it, but sin which dwells in me (v. 20), and ". . . the law of sin which is in my members" (v. 23).

In those texts Paul acknowledges that being a new self in the image of God does not eliminate sin. It is still present in the flesh, <u>the body</u>, the unredeemed humanness that includes the whole human person's thinking and behavior. But he will not allow that new inner man to be given responsibility for sin. The new "I" loves and longs for the holiness and righteousness for which it was created.[2]

Because of the fact that the inner man is holy and righteous, when a Christian dies his spirit/inner man goes instantly to be with the Lord (2 Corinthians 5:8). This person, in that nanosecond between leaving the body and being present with the Lord, does not have to be born again, *again!* Nothing has to happen to him between the death of the body and the union with the Lord, because when he was born again he was created in the likeness of God, ready, from that moment, to meet him face to face (Ephesians 4:24).

4. Paul does not condone Dualism.

Paul does not condone D_____.

Yet Paul does not fall into Dualism or Gnosticism, which says that the spirit is righteous and the flesh is sinful. Since the flesh cannot touch the spirit because it would corrupt the spirit, you can do whatever you want with the flesh without affecting the spirit. Consequently, this teaching claims you can sin like crazy in the flesh if you want to.

The Bible does not allow for this dualism, however. After championing the fact that grace is greater than sin at the end of chapter 5 of Romans, Paul begins chapter 6 by asking, "What shall we say then? Are we to continue in sin so that grace may increase?" And then he goes on to answer his own question: "May it never be! How shall we who died to sin still live in it?"

God does not want us to continue to sin; more than that, he holds us accountable for the sinful actions of the outer man. In Galatians 6:7 Paul writes, "Do not be deceived, God is not mocked; for whatever a man sows, this he will also reap."

And in Hebrews 12:5–6 we read, "My son, do not make light of the Lord's discipline, and do not lose heart when he rebukes you, because the Lord disciplines the one he loves, and he chastens everyone he accepts as his son" (NIV).

So, we see that the Lord holds us accountable to "rein in" the sinful desires of the flesh and bring the flesh under the control of the Holy Spirit and the inner man, who both long only to do good. And we pay a price of divine discipline when we don't.

So, we might summarize by saying, "How shall we who died to sin in our inner man still live in sin in our outer man?" When we persist in sin, the Lord brings his chastening hand of discipline into our lives to encourage us to repent.

5. We cannot sin so often or so badly that God will refuse to forgive us.

We cannot sin so o_____ or so b_____ that God will refuse to forgive us.

Because the inner man does not sin, we cannot sin so badly in the outer man that God will refuse to forgive our inner man, causing us to lose our salvation. That cannot happen because the inner man does not sin.

However, we may pay a significant price for the sin as the Lord disciplines us to encourage us to repent (Hebrews 12:5–11). The following examples of the Sinning Saint, the Sinning Son, and the Sinning Celebrants demonstrate that.

The Sinning Saint

We begin by looking at Peter—the Impetuous Apostle—who demonstrated that we cannot sin so often or so badly that God will refuse to forgive us.

First, in Matthew 18:21–22 Peter asked Jesus, "Lord, how often shall my brother sin against me and I forgive him? Up to seven times?" Jesus said to him, "I do not say to you, up to seven times, but up to seventy times seven."

In other words, as often as it happens. And God would not hold us to a higher standard than himself. So, we see in this exchange that you cannot sin so many times that God will refuse to forgive you.

So, the next question is, "Can we sin so badly that God will refuse to forgive us?" Again, Peter comes to the rescue. In Matthew 26:69–75, we see Peter cursing and denying that he ever knew Jesus. How much worse can a sin get?!? Peter paid a dreadful price of shame and regret for this sin, fleeing into the darkness while weeping bitterly.

Yet, we see Peter eating breakfast just a few days later on the shore of the Sea of Galilee with Jesus, in perfect fellowship and harmony with him, clearly forgiven (John 21:15–17).

So, from these examples we see that we cannot sin so often or so badly that God will refuse to forgive us. These sins are in the outer man, not the inner man.

The Sinning Son

In 1 Corinthians 5:3–5, we read a report of a Christian who sins egregiously but is still saved.

A man in the church in Corinth is apparently living with his stepmother (called "his father's wife"). Paul describes a fearful penalty for such blatant sin. He says, "I have decided to deliver such a one to Satan for the destruction of his flesh . . ." Mercy! What a consequence!

But he then goes on to say, ". . . so that his spirit may be saved in the day of the Lord Jesus."

So, we see with the Sinning Son that God brings into his life a fearful discipline for his sin for the purpose of convincing him to repent (Hebrews 12:5–11). But, through it all, the person does not lose his salvation.

The Sinning Celebrants

In yet another example, in 1 Corinthians 11:17–22 we see Christians who are coming to a celebration of communion eating like gluttons, drinking like drunkards, and refusing to repent. Paul responded, "For this reason many among you are weak and sick, and a number sleep" (v. 30). Here we see progressive discipline from the Lord from physical weakness to sickness to death.

However, Paul says that these Christians were judged with divine discipline so that they "will not be condemned along with the world" (v. 32). That is, they are still saved.

So, we cannot sin so often or so badly that God will refuse to forgive us. But if we persist in flagrant sin, God will bring his escalating discipline into the life of the believer—and his outer man will suffer greatly, though his inner man will still be saved, since it was not the inner man that sinned.

I say more about these examples in the next chapter.

Conclusion

So, this is who you are. You are a born-again spirit, "trapped" (as it were) in a still-unredeemed body. For our entire earthly life, the outer man and inner man are locked in a battle for supremacy; one keeps pressing toward sin and death, and the other toward living like Christ. That is what Paul is describing in Romans 7:14–8:1.

In Hebrews 5:8, we see that even Jesus learned obedience from the things which he suffered. He never had to overcome sin, but as a human he had to learn obedience in his walk with the Father. Later, we see in Hebrews 5:14 that we must have our senses trained to discern good and evil.

Our task as Christians is to submit in faithful obedience to the teachings of Scripture (Hebrews 4:12) and to the work of the Lord in our lives (Philippians 2:12–13), so that the Lord may empower us to have increasing dominion over the outer man.

If we do not understand this, we may get confused, discouraged, and even defeated in our Christian walk. But when we understand who we are as Christians and what happened to us when we were born again, this helps us see ourselves more completely as God sees us. And, since we tend to act consistently with our self-perception, this helps us cooperate with God in the process of conforming our behavior into the character and image of Christ. That is why it is important to embrace your true spiritual nature.

We will continue to expand on the implications of this teaching in chapter 5, so read chapters 4 and 5 as a single unit of thought. These two chapters are, perhaps, the most theologically complex chapters in this book. If this is new to you . . . or if you are having to unlearn some things as you process this information, I encourage you to read these chapters more than once to let the verses sink in.

REPETITION
Is the Key to Mental Ownership

Chapter Review

1. Christians are born again in the l_____ of God.
    a. Our pre-salvation nature: we are truly l_____.
    b. Our post-salvation nature: we are truly r_____.
2. Yet Christians still s____.
3. It is our outer man that sins, but our inner man is r_____.
4. Paul does not condone D_____.
5. We cannot sin so o_____ or so b_____ that God will refuse to forgive us.

The Christian Life in 1,000 Words—Review

If something is important, you must repeat it until it changes you.

1. You were created *b*__ God, *f*____ God, and you will only be truly happy as a Christian who is growing *i*__ God.

2. We must live in this visible, t_____ world according to invisible, e_____ realities.

3. The main thing G____ gets out of your life is the person you become. The main thing y____ get out of your life is the person you become. Therefore, our highest purpose is to b_____ the most we can become, in God's eyes, before we die.

4. A Christian is not merely someone who has turned over a new l_____, but, rather, someone who has turned over a new l_____.

THOUGHT/DISCUSSION
Is a Key to Understanding

Answer these questions, either individually by journaling the answers or in a small discussion group.

1. Is this explanation of who a Christian is new to you? Does it contradict anything you previously believed?

2. What difference does it make to you to understand that your inner man does not sin, but your outer man does?

3. Are there any changes you need to make in your life in order to be a more obedient follower of Jesus?

DECISION TIME
Is a Key to Change

Answer these questions, either individually by journaling the answers or in a spiritual accountability group.

1. Have you believed in and received Jesus as your personal Savior?

2. If not, what do you think is the primary reason why? What could you do to bring yourself to the point that you would be willing to make this decision?

3. If so, what is the biggest change you have seen in your life? What is the most important thing you need to do now to be consistent with that decision?

 **RECOMMENDED**
Resource

Lifetime Guarantee, Bill Gillham

You can't believe
something until
you know it.

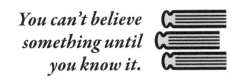

CHAPTER 5

WAGING THE INTERNAL SPIRITUAL WAR

Spiritual growth is the process of the redeemed inner man gaining increasing *mastery* over the unredeemed outer man.

CENTRAL PASSAGE: Ephesians 4:24—"Put on the new self, which in the likeness of God has been created in righteousness and holiness of the truth."

We all struggle with the pull between good and evil in our lives. Who hasn't identified with the cartoon of a person with an angel on one shoulder and a devil on the other, each whispering in the ear of a mortal struggling to make a choice?

But the Bible helps us, as it always does, by clarifying the nature of the internal spiritual war that rages within the life of a child of God.

In Ephesians 4:24, the apostle Paul writes, *"Put on the new self, which in the likeness of God has been created in righteousness and holiness of the truth."*

When Paul says, "Put on the new self..." he is saying, "live out the new self which you received when you were born again."

It is the same idea that we see in Philippians 2:12–13, where we read, "... work out your salvation with fear and trembling; for it is God who is at work in you, both to will and to work for His good pleasure."

Paul did not say in this passage, "work in your salvation," but "work out your salvation."

The point is not that we are to work in order to gain our salvation. Rather, he is saying we are to express, to live out, the salvation we already have. He says that God is working in us, prompting us to "will" his good pleasure, and strengthening us to "work" for his good pleasure. He is doing this for Christians, for his children.

So, to review, when Paul says, in Ephesians 4:24, "Put on the new self," he is saying, "Begin living like the new person you have already become," which is the same point he was making in Philippians 2:12–13.

There are two points of good news about this:

- First, there is a new self. When Christians are born again, they are given a new self, created in the likeness of God. That's who we are.
- Second, while we are still housed in our unredeemed body (the outer man), the new man can gain increasing mastery over the old man and live in a way that is pleasing to the Lord. The battle can be steadily won.

So, let's look at this more closely. If we understand the nature of the internal spiritual war, we stand a greater chance of winning it.

1. The inner man is real, not a metaphor.

The inner man is r_____, not a metaphor.

To begin, we must define terms. In its most basic division, the Bible presents humans as "material and immaterial." The immaterial part of humans is commonly referred to in Scripture as heart, soul, mind, and/or spirit.

A great challenge in understanding what the Bible is teaching in any given passage is that these words are often used interchangeably.

- In one verse, the heart might refer to the "intellect" (Matthew 9:4).
- Other times, it might refer to the "emotions" (Romans 9:2).

- Another time, the "will" (2 Corinthians 9:7).
- Still other times, something else (2 Corinthians 3:2).

The same is generally true of soul, mind, and spirit.

And, to further complicate things, sometimes Scripture refers to the "new self" and the "old self" (Ephesians 4:22–24), as well as the "inner man" and the "outer man" (2 Corinthians 4:16–18), in referring to the immaterial and material parts of humans.

So, in discussing the internal spiritual war we must choose which word or words we are going to use with each specific meaning, and then use the term(s) consistently. I have found the terms "inner man and outer man" most helpful in my thinking and teaching.

So, for this purpose, I will refer to the material part of humans as the "outer man," and will refer to the immaterial part of humans as the "inner man."

- The outer man: the body and brain, the fallen part of a person that will never make it to heaven. The corrupted, fallen, unredeemed brain is the primary "moving force" of the outer man (also sometimes referred to as the "old man").
- The inner man: the essential self, that part of the person who goes to heaven to be with the Lord when the body dies (or the Lord returns).

This new, inner man is not a metaphor. It is not a poetic way of referring to "someone who turned over a new leaf." We've all heard things like:

- . . . he went into the army an 18-year-old boy and he came out a 21-year-old man. He's so much more mature than he used to be. It's like he's a new man.
- . . . he used to be grumpy and silent, but ever since he started dating his new girlfriend, he's come out of his shell. He seems happier and more alive, like a new man.

- . . . ever since she had her baby, she's like a new person—she's so happy.

These "new selves" are metaphorical, referring to a psychological change within a person. But when the Bible talks about a new self, it is not referring to a person who has turned over a new leaf. It's referring to a person who has turned over a new life.

It is a reality. It is the answer, for the Christian, as to who is the real "me."

They say that the cells in your body replace themselves at such a rate that we get a new body every seven years. The first three bodies each get better. The next two bodies hold their own, and every single body thereafter is worse.

But I am not my body. I am greater than—and different from—my body. My present, declining body will not go to heaven. The part of me that goes to heaven is the redeemed, born again, new self—the inner man—and I will get a new body in heaven.

So, when Paul says in Ephesians 4:24, "put on the new self," he is telling us to do something that is real and is possible. He is saying to start living on the outside like who you have already become on the inside. Or, start living in the outer man like who you have already become in the inner man.

2. The inner man is holy and righteous.

The inner man is h_____ and r_____.

As we have noted, the central passage for the redeemed inner man's gaining increasing mastery over the outer man is Ephesians 4:24, "*Put on the new self, which in the likeness of God has been created in righteousness and holiness of the truth.*"

The Greek for "in the likeness of God," is literally, "according to what God is." This is a staggering statement which most of us don't find staggering because we don't understand it or don't believe it. We do not become gods. We are still created beings and are not given the divine attributes of being all-knowing, all-powerful, or all-present. We are not that.

But we *are* holy and righteous. In that way, we are re-created in the likeness of God. It happened the moment we were born again. Peter said that we have become "partakers of the divine nature" (2 Peter 1:4). We have a new nature, a new self, a holy and righteous inner spirit that is fit for the presence of God. There is not one other thing that needs to happen to our new spirit before we can go to heaven.

We must be separated from our old body and given a new body, but that is about the outer man—nothing else has to happen to the inner man. It is ready for the presence of God. When our body dies and we go to heaven, our new self, our inner man, does not have to be born again, *again*. Nothing else has to happen to the new self to get into heaven and stand in the presence of God.

So, the battle between doing right and doing wrong is a battle between the redeemed, righteous inner man and the unredeemed, unrighteous outer man. The outer man still suffers from the leftover power of sin residing in the brain that is still corrupted and programmed to generate and obey wrong desires and impulses.

That corrupted bent is then inflamed by the influence of the world and goaded by the devil. The great task of the Christian life is for the inner man to gain increasing mastery over the outer man. This is a spiritual growth process of the inner man training the outer man to resist and reject the sinful thoughts and impulses of the outer man.

3. The inner man can gain increasing mastery over the outer man.

The inner man can gain increasing m_____ over the outer man.

Here is the good news!!!

Having made the point that we are one nature, and that this nature is created in the likeness of God in holiness and righteousness, the good news is that the redeemed inner man can gain increasing mastery over the unredeemed outer man. It is possible. Because we have a new inner self that is holy and righteous, Paul says "begin living on the outside like who you have already become on the inside."

- "Therefore I, the prisoner of the Lord, implore you to walk in a manner worthy of the calling with which you have been called" (Ephesians 4:1).

  That is, live like who you have become.
- "But solid food is for the mature, who because of practice have their senses trained to discern good and evil" (Hebrews 5:14).

  So, we are, through practice, to discern good and evil. By implication, we increasingly choose to do good.
- "Grow in the grace and knowledge of our Lord and Savior Jesus Christ" (2 Peter 3:18).

  We are to progress from where we are to where the Lord wants us to be.

The unhappy news is that we don't "poof" to spiritual maturity in Christ. We grow; by definition, growing is slower than "poofing." But it is very clear that the Bible expects us to gain increasing dominion over our outer man and even tells us how.

As we said in the last chapter, we have to be sure we don't fall into Gnostic dualism here, concluding that the body and the spirit are totally separate, the body being bad and the spirit being good. In such a view, what happens in one cannot touch the other; therefore, you can let the body sin like crazy if you want to, because the spirit is untouched by it.

This is not an acceptable option for the Christian. This Gnostic heresy was what Paul refuted in Colossians. Though the body and spirit are separate, as Paul teaches, God nevertheless sees us as a unit and holds us responsible to bring the body (outer man) under the dominion of the spirit (inner man).

Paul says in Romans 6:1–2, "What shall we say then? Are we to continue in sin so that grace may increase? May it never be! How shall we who died to sin still live in it?" Then he goes on to say, in verse 4, "as Christ was raised from the dead through the glory of the Father, so we too might walk in newness of life."

So, God calls on Christians to live out their new lives consistently with who they truly are.

I gave the example in the last chapter of the Sinning Son in 1 Corinthians 5:5, who was living in immorality with his stepmother. The apostle Paul says, "I have decided to deliver such a one to Satan for the destruction of his flesh, so that <u>his spirit may be saved in the day of the Lord Jesus</u>" (emphasis mine).

In this example, melding this truth with Romans 7 and Ephesians 4:24, we would say that his sin did not originate in his *inner man*, but his outer man (*body*). As such, his outer man is subject to a potentially lethal discipline by God; not as punishment, but as a discipline to turn him from his sin (Hebrews 12:5–12).

Then, I also gave the example of the Sinning Celebrants in 1 Corinthians 11, where there were believers who were, among other things, drinking all the communion wine and getting drunk. Paul writes, "For this reason many among you are weak and sick, and a number sleep." Again, their bodies are paying the price for their sin. But their spirit has not sinned. Paul goes on to write, "If we judged ourselves rightly, we would not be judged." That is, if we stop sinning by our own volition, God doesn't have to discipline us. Finally, he says, "But when we are judged, we are disciplined by the Lord so that <u>we will not be condemned along with the world</u>" (emphasis mine).

So, both in the case of the sinning son and of the sinning celebrants, their outer man suffered dreadful consequences for their sin, but <u>they did not lose their salvation</u>.

So, being assured through both biblical teaching (Hebrews 12:5–12) and example (1 Corinthians 5 & 11) that prolonged, willful sin will be met with significant divine discipline, there is every motivation, every reason, and every urgency for a person to gain mastery over the outer man.

Conclusion

This distinction between the inner man and outer man does not answer all questions or resolve all issues. Unfortunately, on this complex subject one does not have the option of a position without any questions and unresolved issues. Either we have not been given enough information, or we do not have the capacity to fully understand the information we have, at least not to the point of eliminating all uncertainty.

But, for me, this understanding has been profoundly clarifying and liberating. I now understand who I am. I am a redeemed spirit (inner man) housed in an unredeemed body/brain (outer man).

I am not a two-headed monster, with one good head and one bad head. I am not a spiritual schizophrenic housing both a Dr. Jekyll and a Mr. Hyde. I am not still irrevocably corrupted, wondering how in the world God is ever going to let me into heaven.

I am a redeemed, forgiven, spiritually-reborn person, holy and righteous. I constantly battle my outer man (primarily the brain with its "viruses" and "corrupted hard drive"). My task in life is not to survive as a half-good/half-bad person. My task in life is to give myself in faith and obedience to God, his Word, and the Holy Spirit, thereby gaining increasing mastery over the outer man and, by his grace, beginning to bring my unredeemed outer man into conformity with my redeemed inner man.

The process of gaining mastery over the outer man is not an easy one, and in the chapters ahead we will spend considerable time looking at how this is done. But it is possible. We will never gain absolute mastery over the outer man. It will always be there, waiting for opportunities to assert dominance over us. But, in a life-long, ever-increasing process, we can begin to ever-increasingly "walk in a manner worthy of the calling with which you have been called" (Ephesians 4:1).

We see the overall process described in Romans 12:1–2, which says, "Therefore I urge you, brethren, by the mercies of God, to present your bodies a living and holy sacrifice, acceptable to God, which is your spiritual service of worship. And do not be conformed to this world, but be transformed by the renewing of your mind, so that you may prove what the will of God is, that which is good and acceptable and perfect."

Working the passage backward, we see that we can be living

demonstrations of the fact that God's will is good and acceptable and perfect. However, this can only occur if we are transformed, and we will only be transformed if our minds are renewed. Moreover, our minds will only be renewed if we present our bodies as living sacrifices to God.

(1) We present our bodies as a living sacrifice → (2) our minds are renewed → (3) we are transformed → (4) we become living proof that God's will is good and acceptable and perfect.

Like a snake sheds its skin, like a cicada sheds its outer body, like a butterfly sheds its cocoon, we (our true selves, our redeemed inner men) will each one day shed our outer man and rise to heaven. There, we will be given a new body that is uncontaminated by sin, and we will fellowship with the Lord, unimpeded by sin forever. Until that time, we are to put off the outer man and put on the inner man—that is, to cooperate with God in the process of having our inner man gain increasing mastery over our outer man. This is the process of sanctification, or spiritual growth.

As I mentioned, the rest of the book is a study in how to do this. Then, as we understand this, we can make greater progress in our spiritual growth and become God's best version of us.

REPETITION
Is the Key to Mental Ownership

Chapter Review

1. The inner man is real, not a m_____.
2. The inner man is h_____ and r_____.
3. The inner man can gain increasing m_____ over the outer man.

The Christian Life in 1,000 Words—Review

If something is important, you must repeat it until it changes you.

1. You were created *b*__ God, *f*____ God, and you will only be truly happy as a Christian who is growing *i*__ God.

2. We must live in this visible, t_____ world according to invisible, e_____ realities.

3. The main thing G____ gets out of your life is the person you become. The main thing y____ get out of your life is the person you become. Therefore, our highest purpose is to b_____ the most we can become, in God's eyes, before we die.

4. A Christian is not merely someone who has turned over a new l_____, but, rather, someone who has turned over a new l_____.

5. Spiritual growth is the process of the redeemed inner man gaining increasing m_____ over the unredeemed outer man.

THOUGHT/DISCUSSION
Is a Key to Understanding

Answer these questions, either individually by journaling the answers or in a small discussion group.

1. Explain in your own words what you think it means that a Christian is not someone who has turned over a new leaf, but rather someone who has turned over a new life.

2. Explain in your own words what you think the inner man is, and what you think the outer man is.

3. What is your greatest challenge in "living like who you have become?"

DECISION TIME
Is a Key to Change

Answer these questions, either individually by journaling the answers or in a spiritual accountability group.

1. Are you currently experiencing things in life because you have done something wrong that has brought negative consequences into your life? If so, have you repented of it? Is there anything else you might need to do to restore yourself?

2. Are there additional steps you need to take in "living like who you have become"?

3. Have you taken the first step in the Romans 12:1–2 process of becoming a living demonstration of the fact that God's will is good and acceptable and perfect: presenting your body as a living sacrifice to God? If not, are you prepared to do so now?

RECOMMENDED
Resource

What You Need to Know about Spiritual Warfare, Max Anders

*You can't believe
something until
you know it.*

CHAPTER 6

THE CENTRALITY OF MENTAL RENEWAL TO SPIRITUAL GROWTH

For our lives to be *transformed*, our minds must be *renewed*.

 CENTRAL PASSAGE: Romans 12:2—"Do not be conformed to this world, but be transformed by the renewing of your mind, so that you may prove what the will of God is, that which is good and acceptable and perfect."

One of the secrets of the Christian life—a secret that is lying in plain sight throughout Scripture, but which is not well known or understood—is that, in order for our lives to be transformed, our minds must be renewed. We introduced this idea in the last chapter, and want to elaborate on it in this one.

We are not transformed when angel dust is sprinkled on us. We are not transformed as a reward for trying to be good. We are transformed when our minds are renewed.

Romans 12:2 says, "Do not be conformed to this world, but be transformed by the renewing of your mind, so that you may prove what the will of God is, that which is good and acceptable and perfect."

When we work this passage backward, we see that we can be living demonstrations of the fact that God's will is good and acceptable and perfect, but only if we are transformed. And we will only be transformed if our minds are renewed.

So, mental renewal is a "make-or-break" issue in the Christian life. If your mind is not renewed, your life will not be transformed. And, renewing the mind is a bigger challenge than we often realize. Therefore, it is critical that we understand the principles of mental renewal.

1. We must believe what is true.

We must believe what is t_____.

Being changed by truth presupposes that we believe what is true. That is not always the case. The brain does not necessarily believe what is true. It believes what it is told often enough. Because we are continuously getting bad "truth" from culture around us, we often believe it simply because we have heard it so often.

If we believe something that is not true and then act on that belief, the results can often be very unpleasant.

A book titled *Up to No Good: The Rascally Things Boys Do*, is a compilation of stories recalling the childhood years of men who grew up to be "perfectly decent."

One story recalled, "Lou was playing with some friends and decided to try flying. So they climbed up onto the roof of the barn, and Lou strapped some heavy wooden boards onto his brother's arms. Then they counted down, and he jumped. He was lying on the ground, groaning in pain with several broken bones, and Lou yelled down, "Hey Shorty! You forgot to flap your wings!"[1]

You see, Lou's brother, Shorty—momentarily persuaded by Lou—*believed* he could fly. Based on that belief, Shorty jumped off the roof of the barn. But what he believed was untrue, and he paid the price.

What we believe controls everything about us. If we believe we can fly, we jump off the barn. If we don't believe we can fly, we don't jump off the barn.

Even more to the point, if we say we have changed and that we no longer believe we can fly but we keep jumping off of barns, a reasonable person can assume that somewhere, deep down, a part of us still holds to the false belief.

So, clearly, what we believe is important; very important. Big things happen in life based on what we believe. In fact, the course of our very lives is shaped by what we believe. So, we must manage very carefully what we believe!

Jesus said, "You will know the truth, and the truth will make you free" (John 8:32). To the degree that we do not know the truth, or to the degree that we do not believe it, we are vulnerable to ignorance and deception.

So, the first step in mental renewal is making sure that what we believe is actually true so we don't just absorb "bad" truth from culture around us. That takes discernment, guidance from others, and feeding our minds things we know are true. We can gain these qualities by becoming serious students of Scripture. If this is new to you, I encourage you to read my companion book *30 Days to Understanding the Bible*.

2. We must fill our minds with truth.

We must fill our m_____ with truth.

After we have taken care that what we believe is true, we must fill our minds with that truth.

A few years back, our neighbors got an Old English Sheepdog puppy. It was the most adorable little gray and white ball of fur you have ever seen. It romped and played and wagged furiously where its tail should have been, and was a full-blown number 10 on the puppy "Cute Scale."

They kept "Daisy" inside, and I didn't see Daisy for months after that. One day, as I was driving home I looked into our neighbor's yard, and there stood this huge, hulking gray and white canine mammoth lumbering through the yard.

Because the last time I had seen the puppy it was a small size, and then it was a big size the next time I saw it, it was as though Daisy had instantly "poofed" from little puppy into big dog.

I was flabbergasted! My first thought was, "How in the world did that puppy get so huge?" My next thought was, "Where did all that bulk come from?" This dog was now probably 40 pounds heavier than when I saw it last.

And, right on the heels of those questions was the realization, "from a dog food bag." As we know, nothing comes from nothing. That forty pounds of bulk came from dog food bags! The puppy ate dog *food* and digested it; the body assimilated it—molecularly rearranging it—turning it into *dog*.

It was the most dramatic realization I had ever had that we become what we put into our bodies.

It was also a compelling illustration to me of a parallel idea: we also become what we put into our brains. So, we must take great care of what we put into our brains, because whatever goes into them becomes part of who we are as people. In fact, in a very real way, what we put into our minds determines who we become.

That is why the Scriptures are so persistent in urging discrimination in what we allow into our minds:

Jesus said in Matthew 22:37, "You shall love the Lord your God with all your heart, and with all your soul, and with all your *mind*" (emphasis mine).

Philippians 4:8 says, "Finally brethren, whatever is true, whatever is honorable, whatever is right, whatever is pure, whatever is lovely, whatever is of good repute, if there is any excellence and if anything worthy of praise, dwell on these things."

Second Corinthians 10:5 says, "We are destroying speculations and every lofty thing raised up against the knowledge of God, and we are taking every thought captive to the obedience of Christ."

This challenge is great because the world today is a more dangerous place for the mind than, perhaps, at any other time in history. The constant bombardment of the mind with secular values through entertainment, education, social media, and culture is so formidable that many Christians are losing the battle without even realizing they are in a battle.

Neuroscience adds current scientific observations to Scripture to help Christians understand how we can begin to win that battle.

The brain always changes in the direction of what we put into it. Therefore, what we put into our brains shapes the very course of our lives. As Dr. Caroline Leaf wrote:

> When you understand the power of your thought life . . . you truly begin to get a glimpse of how important it is to take responsibility for what you are thinking. . . . God was so serious about us capturing our thoughts and renewing our minds that he gave us science as an encouragement.[2]

Whatever you think about the most will grow, so the more you think a particular thought, the stronger it grows. Dr. Leaf continues, "You can't just apply a thought once and think change has happened. It takes repeated work for [it] to take effect."[3]

Therefore, an urgent task of the Christian is to fill the mind consistently with truth. The more we think about truth, the more that truth becomes part of us.

3. We must repeat truth until it changes us.

We must r_____ truth until it changes us.

However, as we saw, we "can't just apply a thought once and think change has happened." Rather, we must repeat truth until it changes us.

To understand how and why this happens, we must understand the power of the subconscious.

Recognize the power of the subconscious.

The conscious brain gets most of our attention in life, but the non-conscious brain is where the real power is. The non-conscious brain is something like a million times more powerful than the conscious brain. The conscious brain processes about 2000 bits of information per second. The non-conscious brain processes about 400 billion bits of information per second. The conscious brain operates with a very short-term memory span, generally limited to 20 seconds or less. The non-conscious brain remembers everything it experiences forever. The non-conscious brain is responsible for the majority of our thinking.

We are aware of a tiny fraction of the thinking that goes on in our minds, and we can control only a tiny part of our conscious thoughts. The vast majority of our thinking efforts goes on subconsciously.[4]

We're finding that we have these unconscious behavioral guidance systems that are continually furnishing suggestions through the day about what to do next, and the brain is considering and often acting on those, all before conscious awareness. Sometimes those goals are in line with our conscious intentions and purposes, and sometimes they're not.[5]

Because of this, there is great significance to the Christian in understanding the role and power of the subconscious mind in spiritual behavior. As the *New York Times* article states, our subconscious attitudes, values, and behavior are often at odds with our conscious attitudes, values, and behavior.

For example, on a conscious level, we may think we agree with the passage in Philippians that says, "My God will supply all your needs according to His riches in glory in Christ Jesus" (4:19). But, subconsciously, we are not so sure.

Or, we may believe this on one level, but be concerned that God may not meet all our needs on the level to which we've become accustomed. The result is that when we are threatened on a major level with financial loss, it is usually accompanied by stampeding anxiety. Why? Because what we believe consciously is at variance with what we believe subconsciously.

So, a key to bringing our conscious values in line with our subconscious values is repeating truth over and over again, driving that truth into our subconscious where it begins to replace our true unbiblical beliefs, bringing us into harmony and allowing us to live out truly biblical values. After a period of repeated thinking about a choice over and over, the new thought moves into the subconscious level, where it becomes part of our internal perception. It is at this level that we are deeply changed.[6]

Recognize the power of directing our thinking.

Again, neuroscience tells us:

> When we direct our rest by introspection, self-reflection, and prayer; when we catch our thoughts; when we memorize and quote Scripture; and when we develop our mind intellectually, we enhance the default mode network that improves brain function and mental, physical, and spiritual health.[7]

So, neuroscience tells us that when we . . .

1. repeat truth over and over,
2. direct our thinking,
3. develop our mind intellectually,

. . . it improves our brain function, our mental health, and our spiritual health. Amazing!

Repetition of truth would include memorization of Scripture and other important information/truth.

Directing our thinking would include meditation (not emptying the mind *a la* Eastern meditation, but filling the mind with truth *a la* biblical meditation), affirmations, and regular spiritual mental-renewal exercises, etc.

Developing our mind intellectually would include going to church, listening to sermons, participating in Bible studies, reading good books, watching good movies, spending time with good friends, taking online and other courses, spending time alone in nature, teaching/mentoring/helping others, hobbies that feed you, etc.

When we do those three things:

- We get smarter and have better memory (*develops our mind*).
- We get more mature (*improves mental health*).
- We get spiritually stronger (*improves spiritual health*).

So, we see that the course of the Christian life is determined by three great challenges/opportunities:

1. Believing what is true
2. Filling our minds with truth
3. Repeating truth until it changes us

Conclusion

When we give ourselves over to those three challenges/opportunities, four remarkable, life-changing things happen:

1. **Conscious Change:** The truth comes to the surface of our conscious thought, affecting our decisions and emotions. For example, it enables us, when we get angry or fearful, to recall verses and truth about anger and fear that we have fed into our minds and to use that information to help us keep from acting in anger or fear.
2. **Subconscious Change:** Through repetition, that truth sinks deeply into our subconscious where it lodges as controlling beliefs and begins to alter our basic attitudes, values, and behavior. When this happens, it takes spiritual growth to whole new levels. Consequently, instead of merely enabling us on a conscious level not to act on anger or fear, this truth now, on a subconscious level, changes us so that we don't get angry or fearful in the first place!
3. **Greater Awareness:** The truth triggers our Reticular Activating System, the part of our brain that chooses what to let into the brain and what to keep out. As a result, we start seeing things we didn't see before, we start connecting dots, and we

start getting a clue! We start perceiving truth that escaped us before. It helps feed new insights, revises estimates of importance, and sees relative significance, making us more aware, more insightful, and more in command of our lives.

4. **Increased Capacity:** Finally, the subconscious bubbles this mental gold back up to the conscious level, where we begin to go through this same cycle again but at an even higher level. *We feed our subconscious, and then our subconscious feeds us.*

Who wouldn't want to get caught up in this remarkable upward spiral of spiritual growth?!?

We can love the Lord our God with all our mind by taking the three steps to renewing our mind: (1) believing truth, (2) filling our minds with truth, and (3) repeating truth until it changes us, releasing the remarkable power of mental renewal to transform our lives.

REPETITION
Is the Key to Mental Ownership

Chapter Review

1. We must believe what is t_____.
2. We must fill our m_____ with truth.
3. We must r_____ truth until it changes us.

Conclusion: When we give ourselves over to these three challenges/opportunities, four remarkable things happen:

1. C_____ Change.
2. S_____ Change.
3. Greater A_____.
4. Increased C_____.

The Christian Life in 1,000 Words—Review

If something is important, you must repeat it until it changes you.

1. You were created *b*__ God, *f*____ God, and you will only be truly happy as a Christian who is growing *i*__ God.

2. We must live in this visible, t_____ world according to invisible, e_____ realities.

3. The main thing G____ gets out of your life is the person you become. The main thing y____ get out of your life is the person you become. Therefore, our highest purpose is to b_____ the most we can become, in God's eyes, before we die.

4. A Christian is not merely someone who has turned over a new l_____, but, rather, someone who has turned over a new l_____.

5. Spiritual growth is the process of the redeemed inner man gaining increasing m_____ over the unredeemed outer man.

6. For our l_____ to be transformed, our m_____ must be renewed.

THOUGHT/DISCUSSION
Is a Key to Understanding

Answer these questions, either individually by journaling the answers or in a small discussion group.

1. Can you think of a time when you acted on something you thought was true, and it turned out not to be true? How did that turn out? Do you suspect that you have bought bad "truth" from culture around you that you need to change?

2. How successful do you think you have been at filling your mind with truth? How careful have you been at protecting your mind from harmful input?

3. Is the concept of repeating truth until it changes you new to you? How often have you heard life-changing truth, but then went on with life and a year later were unchanged by it?

DECISION TIME
Is a Key to Change

Answer these questions, either individually by journaling the answers or in a spiritual accountability group.

1. How careful have you been in the past of making sure that what you believe is true? How passive have you been about simply accepting as truth what the culture around you says is true? What do you think you might need to do in the future to be more careful about believing what is actually true?

2. What have you been filling your mind with lately? Is it going to get you where you want to go spiritually? What do you need to change?

3. What truth do you think is most important now in your life to repeat until it changes you? Are you memorizing Scripture that speaks to that need? If not, are you prepared to begin?

 **RECOMMENDED**
Resource

Brave New Discipleship, Max Anders (especially chapters 1, 2, 16, 17)

*You can't believe
something until
you know it.*

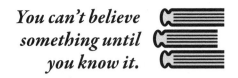

CHAPTER 7

UNDERSTANDING THE COMPONENTS OF SPIRITUAL GROWTH

Spiritual growth requires a balance of God's part and our part.

> **CENTRAL PASSAGE:** Philippians 2:12-13—". . . work out your salvation with fear and trembling; for it is God who is at work in you, both to will and to work for His good pleasure."

In the broadest strokes, there are five components of the spiritual growth process that must be in place if a person is to become spiritually mature. If all five of these components are in place, the Christian will become as spiritually mature as the will of God allows. If even one of these components is not in place, the Christian will not become spiritually mature.

Therefore, it is essential that we understand these five components, and cooperate with God in the process of growing spiritually. The five components are:

1. The Work of God
2. Personal Commitment
3. The Word of God
4. Other Believers
5. Time and Trials

These five components in sufficient measure will enable a Christian to become as spiritually mature as the will of God allows.

To help us remember them, we can reduce these elements to a spiritual maturity equation: The Work of God + Personal Commitment + the Word of God + Other Believers + Time & Trials = Spiritual Maturity.

We can reduce this further to: WG + PC + WG + OB + T&T = SM.

Let's look at each one more closely.

The first component of the spiritual maturity equation is the Work of God (WG).

The first component of the spiritual maturity equation is the W_____ of G___ (WG).

The spiritual growth process begins with God. He is the one who gives us the desire to do his will along with the increasing ability to do his will. The central passage for this is Philippians 2:12–13 ("work out your salvation with fear and trembling; for it is God who is at work in you, both to will and to work for His good pleasure").

I will never forget, many years ago, hearing one of my seminary professors say:

God does the work of God.
    Man does the work of Man.
    Man cannot do the work of God.
    God does not do the work of Man.

Of course, when we say "Man," in this context, it means both male and female.

That truth has been very valuable to me over the years. I have noticed, in my own life as well as in others, what havoc is wreaked when we *try* to do the work of God, as well as when we *fail* to do the work of Man. Life only works when we stick to our job and let God do his.

The Philippians passage introduces the concept of reciprocal involvement between God and Man. In the course of fully living out our salvation, God initiates, prompts, and "works in us" to do something. Our task is to reciprocate and do that which he prompts us to do.

As we do, he prompts again for our next step. We are to reciprocate. As this process plays itself out, the result is progress toward spiritual maturity.

Here is a small but representative list of the things that God does to initiate spiritual progress in our lives:

- God has sovereign control over all circumstances.

    "Whatever the LORD pleases, He does, in heaven and in earth" (Psalm 135:6).

- God convicts of sin and calls to righteousness.

    "And He, when He comes, will convict the world concerning sin and righteousness and judgment" (John 16:8).

- He causes us to be spiritually born again.

    "Blessed be the God and Father of our Lord Jesus Christ, who according to His great mercy has caused us to be born again to a living hope through the resurrection of Jesus Christ from the dead" (1 Peter 1:3).

- God illumines our minds to the truth of Scripture.

    "Now we have received, not the spirit of the world, but the Spirit who is from God, so that we may know the things freely given to us by God, which things we also speak, not in words taught by human wisdom, but in those taught by the Spirit" (1 Corinthians 2:12–13).

- God changes us into the character image of Jesus, giving us the fruit of the Spirit.

    "The fruit of the Spirit is love, joy, peace, patience, kindness, goodness, faithfulness, gentleness, self-control" (Galatians 5:22–23).

Humans cannot do any of these divine things. Our job is to respond.

The second component of the spiritual maturity equation is Personal Commitment (PC).

The second component of the spiritual maturity equation is
P_____ C_____ *(PC)*.

We, then, must respond to this work, as Philippians 2:12 tells us, to work out our salvation. We are not passive in the spiritual growth process. We cannot generate our own spiritual growth, but neither will God grant us spiritual growth unless we are pursuing it. Francis Schaeffer called this "active passivity." We cannot do it, but God will not do it unless we are pursuing it.

As a side note, some have interpreted this passage from Philippians as teaching that we must do good works in order to earn our salvation. Yet this interpretation does not stand up to the overall teaching of Scripture.

A well-known rebuttal to this interpretation is, "It says '*work out*' our salvation, not '*work in*' our salvation." That is correct, but let's expand the idea a little.

If one did not have a mature understanding of overall New Testament truth, he or she might be excused for misinterpreting this passage, thinking that it was teaching that we had to do good works in order to earn our salvation.

However, one of the fundamental principles of interpreting the Bible is, "Interpret unclear passages in light of clear passages." And while this passage might possibly be interpreted in more than one way, there are other passages that are so clear they can only be interpreted one way.

One of those passages is Ephesians 2:8–9, which says, "For by grace you have been saved through faith; and that not of yourselves, it is the gift of God; not as a result of works, so that no one may boast."

Then there is, "He saved us, not on the basis of deeds which we have done in righteousness, but according to His mercy" (Titus 3:5).

So, there we have it in black-and-white. Salvation is not a result of works. It is by grace through faith in Jesus. So, we take these unambiguous passages and read them back into the ambiguous passage, and comfortably conclude that Philippians is telling us to work out the salvation we already possess, not to try to work into a salvation we do not yet possess.

Having made that point, let us return to the topic of the work we are to do in response to God's work in us. Here is a small but representative list of the things we are to do:

- We can believe in Jesus.

    "For God so loved the world, that He gave His only begotten Son, that whoever believes in Him shall not perish, but have eternal life" (John 3:16).

- We can love God.

    "'You shall love the Lord your God with all your heart, and with all your soul, and with all your mind.' This is the great and foremost commandment. The second is like it. 'You shall love your neighbor as yourself'" (Matthew 22:37–39).

- We can trust God.

    "Trust in the LORD with all your heart and lean not on your own understanding; in all your ways submit to him, and he will make your paths straight" (Proverbs 3:5–6 NIV).

- We can obey God.

    "If you love Me, you will keep My commandments" (John 14:15).

- We can love others.

    "Love is patient, love is kind. It does not envy, it does not boast, it is not proud. It does not dishonor others, it is not self-seeking, it is not easily angered, it keeps no record of wrongs. Love does not delight in evil but rejoices with the truth. It always protects, always trusts, always hopes, always perseveres. Love never fails" (1 Corinthians 13:4–8a NIV).

- We can be good examples of Christianity to others.

    "Do to others as you would have them do to you" (Luke 6:31 NIV).

These are all things we can do, and things which God has commanded us to do.

The third component of the spiritual maturity equation is the Word of God (WG).

The third component of the spiritual maturity equation is the W_____ of G___ (WG).

The Word of God is essential to the spiritual growth process. In John 17:17, Jesus prayed, "Sanctify them in the truth; Your word is truth."

Hebrews 4:12 says, in the New Living Translation, "For the word of God is alive and powerful. It is sharper than the sharpest two-edged sword, cutting between soul and spirit, between joint and marrow. It exposes our innermost thoughts and desires."

Second Timothy 3:16–17 adds to the centrality of the Scriptures to the spiritual growth process: "All Scripture is inspired by God and profitable for teaching, for reproof, for correction, for training in righteousness; so that the man of God may be adequate, equipped for every good work."

The Psalms say, "Your word is a lamp to my feet and a light to my path" (119:105), and "I have hidden your word in my heart, that I might not sin against you" (119:11 NLT).

Beyond this, Psalm 1:2–3 says of the spiritually mature person, "But his delight is in the law of the LORD, and in His law he meditates day and night. He will be like a tree firmly planted by streams of water, which yields its fruit in its season and its leaf does not wither; and in whatever he does, he prospers."

These passages make it clear that without the Word of God, we cannot grow to spiritual maturity.

The fourth component of the spiritual maturity equation is Other Believers (OB).

The fourth component of the spiritual maturity equation is O_____ B_____ (OB).

The Christian life was not meant to be lived alone. God intends us to be Three Musketeers, not Lone Rangers. We cannot make it alone. We need others, and others need us.

The Bible refers to Christians, collectively, as a body, indicating that, just as individual members of a body (arm, leg, eye, ear) cannot make it alone, so individual members of the body of Christ cannot make it alone (Romans 12:5).

Ephesians 4:11 tells us that God has given the church gifted individuals, including evangelists, pastors, and teachers, without whom we cannot grow to spiritual maturity.

In Ephesians 4:16, the apostle Paul tells us that as each individual member of the body of Christ makes its contribution to the whole, the whole body grows to maturity.

The Bible is filled with things we are supposed to do with/for one another. Here is a small sample:

- Be devoted to one another in brotherly love (Romans 12:10).
- Admonish one another (Romans 15:14).
- Serve one another in love (Galatians 5:13).
- Bear one another's burdens (Galatians 6:2).
- Encourage one another and build each other up (1 Thessalonians 5:11).

Unless Christians are integrated into a body of believers, making their contribution to the "whole," and allowing the "whole" to make its contribution to them, they will not grow to spiritual maturity.

The fifth component of the spiritual maturity equation is Time and Trials (T&T).

The fifth component of the spiritual maturity equation is T_____ and T_____ (T&T).

The process of growing to spiritual maturity, involving the Work of God + Personal Commitment + the Word of God + Other Believers must take place over time and include trials.

First Peter 2:2 says, "Like newborn babies, long for the pure milk of the word, so that by it you may grow in respect to salvation." Just as a physical baby must grow to physical maturity over time, so a spiritual baby must grow to spiritual maturity over time. You cannot become holy in a hurry.

In addition to time, it takes trials to grow to spiritual maturity. The apostle James wrote, "Consider it all joy, my brethren, when you encounter various trials, knowing that the testing of your faith produces endurance. And let endurance have its perfect result, so that you may be perfect and complete, lacking in nothing" (1:2–4).

In a strikingly similar passage, the apostle Paul wrote, "We also exult in our tribulations, knowing that tribulation brings about perseverance; and perseverance, proven character; and proven character, hope; and hope does not disappoint, because the love of God has been poured out within our hearts through the Holy Spirit who was given to us" (Romans 5:3–5).

Just as strenuous physical effort brings the athlete to peak physical condition, so trials are used by God to bring the Christian to peak spiritual condition.

Conclusion

We will deal with all five of these components in greater detail elsewhere in this book. But it is valuable to have the bird's eye view, to see the "whole," so that the details, when we look at them, will take on greater significance.

For now, we simply want to overview the five components and make the point that when each element of the spiritual maturity equation is present in sufficient measure, the Christian can become spiritually mature. If even one element is not present in sufficient measure, the Christian will not be spiritually mature.

REPETITION
Is the Key to Mental Ownership

Chapter Review

1. The first component of the spiritual maturity equation is the W_____ of G___.

2. The second component of the spiritual maturity equation is
P_____ C_____.

3. The third component of the spiritual maturity equation is the
W_____ of G___.

4. The fourth component of the spiritual maturity equation is
O_____ B_____.

5. The fifth component of the spiritual maturity equation is T_____
and T_____.

The Christian Life in 1,000 Words—Review

If something is important, you must repeat it until it changes you.

1. You were created *b___* God, *f____* God, and you will only be truly
happy as a Christian who is growing *i___* God.

2. We must live in this visible, t_____ world according to
invisible, e_____ realities.

3. The main thing G_____ gets out of your life is the person you become.
The main thing y_____ get out of your life is the person you become.
Therefore, our highest purpose is to b_____ the most we can
become, in God's eyes, before we die.

4. A Christian is not merely someone who has turned over a new
l_____, but, rather, someone who has turned over a new l_____.

5. Spiritual growth is the process of the redeemed inner man gaining
increasing m_____ over the unredeemed outer man.

6. For our l_____ to be transformed, our m_____ must be
renewed.

7. Spiritual growth requires a balance of G_____ part and o____ part.

THOUGHT/DISCUSSION
Is a Key to Understanding

*Answer these questions, either individually by journaling the answers or in
a small discussion group.*

1. Did any of these five components surprise you? Which one,
and why?

2. Which of the five components were you least surprised about? Which one, and why?

3. Which one do you like the best? Which one do you like the least?

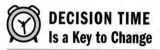

DECISION TIME
Is a Key to Change

Answer these questions, either individually by journaling the answers or in a spiritual accountability group.

1. Have you given yourself as completely as you need to master the Word of God? Are there any changes you need to make?

2. Are you as integrated into the lives of other believers as you ought to be in order to benefit from that component of spiritual growth? Do you regularly attend church? Do you fellowship with Christian friends? Are there any changes you need to make?

3. What is your response to the Time and Trials component? Have you had enough time to be spiritually mature? Are you as spiritually mature as you think you ought to be, given the length of time you have been a Christian? Are there any adjustments you need to make in light of this?

*You can't believe
something until
you know it.*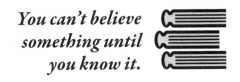

CHAPTER 8

THE THREE ENEMIES OF THE CHRISTIAN

There are three enemies of the Christian:
the *world*, the *flesh*, and the *devil*.

 CENTRAL PASSAGE: 2 Corinthians 10:3-5—"For though we walk in the flesh, we do not war according to the flesh, for the weapons of our warfare are not of the flesh, but divinely powerful for the destruction of fortresses. We are destroying speculations and every lofty thing raised up against the knowledge of God, and we are taking every thought captive to the obedience of Christ."

Theologians talk of the three enemies of the Christian: the world, the flesh, and the devil.

These enemies are formidable, of course. Christians often find themselves, knowingly or unknowingly, in battles with these enemies that leave them feeling anywhere from disappointed and discouraged to defeated.

And not just any battle plan will work. The apostle Paul wrote, in 2 Corinthians 10:3–5, "For though we walk in the flesh, we do not war according to the flesh, for the weapons of our warfare are not of the flesh, but divinely powerful for the destruction of fortresses. We are destroying speculations and every lofty thing raised up against the knowledge of God, and we are taking every thought captive to the obedience of Christ."

Rule #1 in any war is, "know your enemy." So, while we will

spend a good deal of time in subsequent chapters dealing with the specifics of how to wage war against these enemies, the purpose of this chapter is to define them so we can know what we are up against.

1. The first enemy of the Christian is the world.

The first enemy of the Christian is the w_____.

The "world" in the New Testament means the attitudes, values, and behavior of the non-Christian world.

In 1 John 2:15, we read, "Do not love the world nor the things in the world. If anyone loves the world, the love of the Father is not in him."

Then John goes on to enumerate specific things of the world that are to be rejected: "the lust of the flesh and the lust of the eyes and the boastful pride of life" (2:16).

This harmonizes well with what Paul said in Romans 12:2: "Do not be conformed to this world, but be transformed by the renewing of your mind, so that you may prove what the will of God is, that which is good and acceptable and perfect."

One of the great tasks, and one of the great battles of life, is to resist the gravitational pull of modern culture (the world).

Culture naturally has great power.

We all tend to conform to culture around us. This is the way we were created. It helps us tremendously if the culture around us is positive. It hurts us tremendously if the culture around us is negative.

When I grew up, if you conformed to culture around you, you didn't violate any of the 10 Commandments. Now, if you conform to culture around you, you violate most of the 10 Commandments.

Christian polls for the last 30 years have recorded the inexorable decline of both belief and behavior in the Christian world and the United States. This parallels, of course, the inexorable decline of our culture, which was founded on biblical principles but which has eroded in the last 50 years to be a mere shadow of its former self.

In 1948, George Orwell wrote a dystopian novel titled *1984*, in which he envisioned a very bad future for us based on the fact that everything we wanted was going to be *withheld* from us by a totalitarian government. Big Brother is watching you!

A few years earlier, Aldous Huxley wrote a dystopian novel titled *Brave New World*, in which he envisioned a very bad future for us based on the fact that everything we wanted would be *given* to us! Nothing we wanted would be withheld from us! And because we did not have the strength of character to rise to the higher things that were available, we all began to sink to the lowest level.

Of these two contrasting visions of the future, the brave new world began presenting the most immediate danger to Christians in America beginning in the 1960s. This has been followed in recent years by a move toward censorship and government control which is beginning to resemble Orwell's *1984*. Now, like two wings of an airplane, the values of both *Brave New World* and *1984* are flying us into a future deeply hostile to the Christian faith.

Regarding the values of *Brave New World*, a quick review of cable television and movies reveals a preoccupation with unrestrained and perverted violence and sex, a preoccupation with the demonic and paranormal, and voyeuristic explorations into deviant and bizarre lifestyles. Cable television and movies are showing us the future, and it is not a pretty sight. Culturally, we are losing ground in the United States at an alarming rate.

Regarding the values of *1984*, cultural opposition to Christian values along with governmental censorship and encroachment on basic freedoms bring additional threats to religious liberty. Because everything that affects culture also affects the Christians living in that culture, this retrogression is having its effect on the church in America. As we enter the brave new world of the 21st century, *Christians must learn new ways of standing against this downward trend if we hope to not be neutralized by a mind meld with modern culture or to be driven into exile by a hostile culture.*

The values of both *Brave New World* and *1984* are powerfully promoted by electronic media. In a dramatic instance of the impact of this media, I was presenting workshops at a discipleship conference in England a number of years ago. Delegates were there from all over the world. In one of my workshops, there was a delegation from central Africa, and after the session was over we sat around talking about discipleship issues. This delegation said that their mission was to try to reach the rural villages in central Africa with the Gospel before the village got electricity, because before a village got electricity their interest in spiritual things was very high. After a village got electricity, however, their interest in spiritual things dried up almost overnight. This was because electricity brought not only light bulbs and refrigeration, but also television, movies, music, and the internet. These things captured the minds of the villagers and made them almost impervious to the Gospel. Like trying to save people from a coming tsunami, this delegation was trying to save rural central Africans from the coming tidal wave of electrification.

That's the power of media, and media shapes our culture.

Culture naturally has great p_____.

There are three problems created by modern media.

Because of the presence, power, and corruption of modern media, it may be generally more difficult to live the Christian life in the 21st century than at any other time in history. Music in elevators, monitors in gas pumps, smart phones, tablets, computers, electronic games, smart watches, televisions everywhere in restaurants, and televisions in our homes (that often go on first thing in the morning and stay on until the last thing at night) all leave our minds awash in input from electronic media. And, because we naturally *"become what we behold,"* we are dramatically impacted by the pervasive presence of electronic media.

This creates three serious problems:

First, it gives the mind no down time, no solitude, and no time for reflection, planning, evaluating, or thinking.

It keeps us from thinking about the higher things of life. The result is that it is very difficult to conceive of higher things, to rise above wherever we are at the moment. We get trapped in the present with little hope for the future because we give no thought to it.

Second, the input that we receive is often godless.

By godless, we mean two things: On the one hand, it may be an affront to the truth and moral standards of God. The input may include violence, hatred, greed, and sexual immorality.

On the other hand, even if the input is not an obvious affront to God, media typically represents life and values that do not include God or accurately reflect him. So, even if a given program on television is not morally reprehensible, it still tends to teach us to think and live without God, because an accurate and authentic relationship with God is virtually never modeled. All we ever learn by example is how to live without him.

Third, electronic media is more powerful than other media.

It impacts the mind more than spoken or written communication. Have you ever tried to read a book while the television was on? You usually wind up watching television. The power of electronic media takes over the mind. That is why it is so powerful.

Therefore, because electronic media (1) keeps us from thinking about the higher things of life, (2) because much of the input is godless, and (3) because electronic media has a greater power over the mind than spoken or written communication, the typical mind in Western culture is held captive by electronic media. As a result, it is held captive to secular values and thinking. Unfortunately, this is true of the Christian mind as well as the non-Christian mind.

Therefore, the serious Christian must take seriously the power of modern culture and the problems created by modern media, and must guard his heart and mind against this power lest he be easily defeated by the world, this first enemy of the Christian.

There are three problems created by modern media.

1. First, the mind has no d_____ t_____.
2. Second, the input is often g_____.
3. Third, electronic media is more p_____ than other media.

2. The second enemy of the Christian is the flesh.

The second enemy of the Christian is the f_____.

It is very difficult to define the "flesh" in the theological sense. In studying for this book, I consulted any number of resources looking for definitions of the "flesh," and found no two that were alike. Some were similar, but not exactly alike.

However, there is general agreement on the broad strokes: God created Adam as both a material (body) and immaterial (spirit) being. When Adam sinned, both his body and spirit became corrupted by sin and cut off from God. The body became given over to disease and death, and the spirit became given over to self-direction, so that it could no longer *not* sin. The decision to choose self over God was the fundamental "sin" which corrupted the spirit, the essential self, so that it was now given over to an endless succession of "sins."

When a person becomes a Christian, his spirit is born again, and is "created to be like God in true righteousness and holiness" (Ephesians 4:24 NIV).

But the spirit is still housed in a physical body contaminated by sin. The body, of course, includes the brain, which is corrupted by sin and is naturally governed by a bent toward sin.

Paul wrote of the flesh in Romans:

1. "For I am not practicing what I would like to do, but I am doing the very thing I hate" (7:15).
2. "I know that nothing good dwells in me, that is, in my flesh" (7:18).
3. "If I am doing the very thing I do not want, I am no longer the one doing it, but sin which dwells in me" (7:20).

As I said, the "flesh" is a very complex and broad subject in which there is great diversity and even disagreement among biblical scholars. Thus, for our purposes, we must narrow its definition to prevent this topic from overwhelming this chapter.

For the purpose of this chapter, we will define the flesh as:

"The corrupted and unredeemed part of the Christian (the earthly physical body, including the brain), in which sin is entrenched and pulls the Christian's behavior toward sin."

As such, the flesh is one of the enemies of the Christian that wages war against a Christian's attempt to live in righteous behavior. We will deal with many of the implications of the Christian's battle against the flesh in subsequent chapters of this book.

3. The third enemy of the Christian is the devil.

The third enemy of the Christian is the d_____.

The devil, of course, is the highest formerly-good angel, who sinned against God and became the personification of evil and the chief enemy of God.

His will is to become like God and to raise himself above God. His goal in our lives is to deceive, discourage, and defeat Christians . . . even destroy us, if he can. For this reason, we will give considerable time in subsequent chapters to dealing specifically with the devil. Therefore, we will not say any more about him in this chapter. Our goal now is simply to identify him as one of the three enemies of our soul and place him alongside the other two for greater overall understanding of the battles the Christian faces.

Conclusion

I remember one of my professors in seminary saying that the spiritual warfare in which we all find ourselves ("our struggle is not against flesh and blood" [Ephesians 6:12]) involves the world and the flesh, but it is also likely that the devil (and his minions, the demons) use the world and our flesh simultaneously to deceive and defeat us. So, properly understood, it is likely that we often fight all three enemies simultaneously.

Therefore, Christians must take their three enemies seriously. Not to do so is to be naïve and to place oneself in greater danger than necessary.

REPETITION
Is the Key to Mental Ownership

Chapter Review

1. The first enemy of the Christian is the w_____.
    a. Culture naturally has great p_____.
    b. There are three problems created by modern media.
        First, the mind has no d_____ t_____.
        Second, the input is often g_____.
        Third, electronic media is more p_____ than
        other media.
2. The second enemy of the Christian is the f_____.
3. The third enemy of the Christian is the d_____.

The Christian Life in 1,000 Words—Review

If something is important, you must repeat it until it changes you.

1. You were created *b__* God, *f____* God, and you will only be truly happy as a Christian who is growing *i__* God.
2. We must live in this visible, t_____ world according to invisible, e_____ realities.
3. The main thing G____ gets out of your life is the person you become. The main thing y____ get out of your life is the person you become. Therefore, our highest purpose is to b_____ the most we can become, in God's eyes, before we die.
4. A Christian is not merely someone who has turned over a new l_____, but, rather, someone who has turned over a new l_____.
5. Spiritual growth is the process of the redeemed inner man gaining increasing m_____ over the unredeemed outer man.
6. For our l_____ to be transformed, our m_____ must be renewed.
7. Spiritual growth requires a balance of G_____ part and o____ part.
8. There are three enemies of the Christian: the w_____, the f_____, and the d_____.

THOUGHT/DISCUSSION
Is a Key to Understanding

Answer these questions, either individually by journaling the answers or in a small discussion group.

1. How careful have you been in guarding your mind against the values of the world? How significantly do you think your values have been shaped by the world?

2. How significantly do you think your values have been shaped by the flesh (desire of the flesh, desire of the eyes, desire of pride)?

3. How alert have you historically been to the fact that the devil is a constant adversary in your life, using the world and the flesh to deceive and defeat you?

DECISION TIME
Is a Key to Change

Answer these questions, either individually by journaling the answers or in a spiritual accountability group.

1. What is the most important thing you think you should do to intensify your resistance to the world? Are you prepared to do it now? If so, when and how? If not, why not?

2. What is the most important thing you think you should do to intensify your resistance to the flesh? Are you prepared to do it now? If so, when and how? If not, why not?

3. What is the most important thing you think you should do to intensify your resistance to the devil? Are you prepared to do it now? If so, when and how? If not, why not?

You can't believe
something until
you know it.
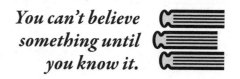

CHAPTER 9

THE POWER OF A PROTECTED MIND

A *protected* mind will be spared the *downward* pull of negative input and be released to the *upward* pull of positive input.

CENTRAL PASSAGE: Colossians 3:2—"Set your mind on the things above, not on the things that are on earth."

Over a hundred years ago Auguste Rodin created a sculpture called *The Thinker*. It sits at the Rodin Museum in Paris, and is one of the most famous and widely recognized sculptures in the history of art.

People have wondered for years what the thinker is thinking about. Some have speculated he is trying to remember where he put his car keys or what he came into the room to get. But others know that he was created as a symbol for Dante, who wrote the classic work *The Divine Comedy*, and who is apparently pondering the fate of those who enter the infernal halls.

But whatever he has been thinking about for the last hundred years, it is going to make a big impact on him when he moves to action, because we become what we think about.

This fact caused nineteenth-century English poet William Blake to write, "We become what we behold."[1] This phrase was picked up and popularized by culture guru Marshall McLuhan in the 1960s, and is verified powerfully by the modern study of the brain. Impressions travel along pathways in the brain to various destinations in the brain. The more often an impression travels the pathway, the deeper that pathway becomes; and the more powerful the impression, the deeper the pathway.

That is why we have to repeat a phone number several times in order to remember it, or why we have to go over and over a poem or Bible verse before we can remember it. And that is why extremely good things and extremely bad things are often remembered vividly without repetition.

The need to protect the mind is important for everyone, but it is particularly obvious for Christians.

- The Bible teaches us to "set [our minds] on the things above, not on the things that are on earth" (Colossians 3:2).
- The apostle Paul wrote that he did not lose heart because he focused "not at the things which are seen, but at the things which are not seen" (2 Corinthians 4:18).
- He also wrote of our need to "[take] every thought captive to the obedience of Christ" as a key strategy in waging spiritual warfare (2 Corinthians 10:5).

There is power in the protected mind, and if we want to control life, rather than having life control us, we have to govern what we think about.

1. We must guard our minds against three dangers.

We must guard our minds against three d_____.

We must guard our minds against false teaching.

We need to watch out for doctrinal errors that can divert us from the true gospel. Scripture encourages us to earnestly contend for "the faith which was once for all delivered to the saints" (Jude 1:3 NKJV). God's revelation to us was delivered once and for all. That means nothing is going to be added to it.

And that means the message has been around for a while. Someone has said, "If it's new, it's not true"—because the biblical faith we believe is the one that was handed down from "the saints" two thousand years ago.

How do we guard our minds against false teachings? By mastering the truth. Jesus said, "You will know the truth, and the truth will make you free" (John 8:32). If we do not know the truth, we are vulnerable to ignorance and deception. If, on the other hand, we have tasted the truth and then come into contact with a lie, we more easily detect that it's counterfeit. So, as Christians, we learn the truth, and the truth will guard our minds against false teaching.

We must guard our minds against false t_____.

We must guard our minds against temptation.

Psalm 101:3 says, "I will set no worthless thing before my eyes." That's a good verse to put on your television. When was the last time you switched channels because what you were seeing was worthless?

If we're going to guard our minds, we have to be careful about what we watch because it causes temptation. The Bible says very clearly in James 1:14 that sin starts with a thought. You've probably heard the old American proverb: "You sow a thought, you reap an action. You sow an action, you reap a habit. You sow a habit, you reap a character. You sow a character, you reap a destiny."

Our destiny begins in our thoughts. The mind is a strategic battlefield, and if Satan can get your thought life, he's going to get you. So, those harmless thoughts are not harmless at all. Guard your mind against temptation.

We must guard our minds against _____.

We must guard our minds against spiritual deception.

Those who don't do this can either end up in a cult or go wobbling after someone who's leading them out into left field. The Bible says, "Do not believe every spirit, but test the spirits to see whether they are from God, because many false prophets have gone out into the world. By this you know the Spirit of God: every spirit that confesses that

Jesus Christ has come in the flesh is from God; and every spirit that
does not confess Jesus is not from God" (1 John 4:1–3). Galatians 1:8
says that even if an angel tells you something different than what the
Word of God says, don't believe it. Scripture tells us that the devil
disguises himself as an angel of light (2 Corinthians 11:14). So we
must guard our minds against spiritual deception.

We must guard our minds against spiritual d_____.

2. We must guard our minds with three safeguards.

We must guard our minds with three s_____.

We must guard what we let into our minds.

You've seen the old magician's trick where he puts a silk handker-
chief in a top hat and then, presto, pulls out a rabbit. What he gets
out is not the same as what he put in. Well, that's a trick, and it's not
true. You can only get out of something what you put into it.

There is an old computer programming proverb: GIGO = garbage in, garbage out. Related to computers, it's saying that what you
get out of your computer can be no better than what you put in it.

The same is true with the mind. You get out of it what you put
into it. So, if we want good or helpful things out of our minds, we
must put good and helpful things into our minds. If we put bad and
unhelpful things into our minds and then go to our minds later for
good and helpful things, it doesn't work. So, we have to guard what
we let into our minds.

We must guard what we let i_____ our minds.

We must guard what we let our minds create.

Second, we have to guard what we let our minds create. Our minds
are affected not only by what we put into them but also by what we
let our minds create. When we imagine things, we are creating things
mentally inside of ourselves that can be just as good or just as bad as
letting outside things into our minds. For example, someone asked

Thomas Edison how he ever came up with the idea for the electric light bulb. He reportedly said, "By thinking about it all the time." So, he let his mind dwell on ideas for the electric light bulb and consequently helped change the course of history. That is an example of something good that can happen when we let our minds create good things.

On the other hand, if we think about bad things, or inappropriate things, it leads to bad results. Jesus said in Matthew 5 that not only should we not murder or commit adultery, we should not even nurture anger or look inappropriately on a woman. Why? Because we can sin in our hearts long before we sin with our actions. And, if we nurture sinful thoughts long enough, they inevitably lead to sinful actions. So, we must guard what we let our minds create.

We must guard what we let our minds c_____.

We must guard what we let our minds dwell on.

Finally, we need to be careful about letting our minds dwell on bad or negative thoughts. Philippians 4:8 says, "Whatever is true, whatever is honorable, whatever is right, whatever is pure, whatever is lovely, whatever is of good repute, if there is any excellence and if anything worthy of praise, dwell on these things."

Why? Because if we dwell on hurts, if we dwell on anger or resentment, or if we dwell on failure or other negative things, those things grow, dominate our thinking, affect our emotions, and begin to control who we are and what we do. But, on the other hand, if we dwell on positive things, then those positive things begin to dominate our thinking and affect our emotions and actions.

We must guard what we let our minds d_____ on.

So, we guard our minds in three ways:

- We guard what we let into our minds.
- We guard what we let our minds create.
- We guard what we let our minds dwell on.

3. We must guard our minds with two weapons.

We must guard our minds with two w_____.

We must guard our minds with Scripture.

Listen to what the Bible says about the power of Scripture:

- It will make you free (John 8:32).
- It will give you insight for your life (Psalm 119:105).
- It will make you adequate and equipped (2 Timothy 3:16–17).
- It will make you spiritually successful (Joshua 1:8).
- It will make you spiritually prosperous (Psalm 1:1–3).

What a litany of power is available to us in Scripture! Especially if:

- We deeply memorize key passages of Scriptures.
- We ponder the meaning of them, turning the verses over and over again in our minds.
- We rehearse them when we get up, when we go to bed, and when we are driving or waiting.
- We go to them whenever we are in need.

The Bible is not magic . . . but it *is* powerful. It is the foundation on which a life of peace and power can be built.

We must guard our minds with S_____.

We must guard our minds through prayer.

As we are memorizing and meditating on Scripture, we stay in conversation with God, asking him to help our efforts to grow to completeness in him. In Philippians 4:6–7, the apostle Paul wrote, "Be anxious for nothing, but in everything by prayer and supplication with thanksgiving let your requests be made known to God. And the peace of God, which surpasses all comprehension, will *guard your hearts and your minds* in Christ Jesus (emphasis mine)."

This passage tells us that grateful prayer will guard our hearts and minds. Again, prayer is not magic . . . but it is powerful. We will spend an entire chapter on prayer later, but for now we need to make the point that through Scripture and through prayer we can guard our minds.

We must guard our minds through p_____.

Conclusion

In Gary Smalley's book, *Change Your Heart, Change Your Life*, he shares some of his personal testimony. He said that a big change occurred in his life when he had a heart attack. His emotions were in shambles. Facing major heart surgery, he was scared. He knew he could die. He knew that he would go to heaven, but it didn't comfort him emotionally. He lay in the hospital bed in a panic.

He had known the importance of memorizing and meditating on Scripture, and it had even helped some. But not enough. He needed something on a deeper level than he had ever experienced before.

He chose one of the super-passages of Scripture, Romans 5:3–5 (NLT):

> We can rejoice, too, when we run into problems and trials, for we know that they help us develop endurance. And endurance develops strength of character, and character strengthens our confident hope of salvation. And this hope will not lead to disappointment. For we know how dearly God loves us, because he has given us the Holy Spirit to fill our hearts with his love.

Those verses told him that he should make the best of trials, because if he did they would make him into a different person . . . one with character and hope, and who enjoyed the ongoing blessings of God in his life. Again, he already knew this, but it hadn't helped.

As he read the passages over and over, the truth began to penetrate his mind . . . deeply . . . on a level he had never experienced before. He memorized the verses and reviewed them over and over, day after day. He pondered their deepest meaning.

As he did, the passages began, as he described it, "to seep into his heart." Their meaning began to become more than distant principles, turning into deep beliefs thoroughly embedded in his heart. Within a few weeks, Smalley writes, "most of my fears slipped away." His new, deeply-understood, and deeply-embraced beliefs conquered his negative and fearful emotions.[2]

It is no secret that our consistent thoughts become our beliefs, and our beliefs control everything about us. The key is to reinforce good beliefs until they replace bad beliefs. Every time you think a thought, it wears a slight path in your mind. Week after week or month after month, as that same thought is repeated over and over again, the path becomes a road. And as the thoughts are repeated still more, the road becomes a four-lane freeway. "When our key beliefs are set within our hearts like four-lane freeways, they control everything about us."[3]

So, there is power in a protected mind. The power to be who we long to be is determined by how we guard our minds. Guard yours well, and become who you long to be.

REPETITION
Is the Key to Mental Ownership

Chapter Review

1. We must guard our minds against three d_____.
   a. We must guard our minds against false t_____.
   b. We must guard our minds against t_____.
   c. We must guard our minds against spiritual d_____.
2. We must guard our minds with three s_____.
   a. We must guard what we let i_____ our minds.
   b. We must guard what we let our minds c_____.
   c. We must guard what we let our minds d_____ on.
3. We must guard our minds with two w_____.
   a. We must guard our minds with S_____.
   b. We must guard our minds through p_____.

The Christian Life in 1,000 Words—Review

If something is important, you must repeat it until it changes you.

1. You were created *b__* God, *f____* God, and you will only be truly happy as a Christian who is growing *i__* God.
2. We must live in this visible, t_____ world according to invisible, e_____ realities.
3. The main thing G____ gets out of your life is the person you become. The main thing y____ get out of your life is the person you become. Therefore, our highest purpose is to b_____ the most we can become, in God's eyes, before we die.
4. A Christian is not merely someone who has turned over a new l_____, but, rather, someone who has turned over a new l_____.
5. Spiritual growth is the process of the redeemed inner man gaining increasing m_____ over the unredeemed outer man.
6. For our l_____ to be transformed, our m_____ must be renewed.
7. Spiritual growth requires a balance of G_____ part and o____ part.
8. There are three enemies of the Christian: the w_____, the f_____, and the d_____.
9. A p_____ mind will be spared the d_____ pull of negative input and be released to the u_____ pull of positive input.

◯ THOUGHT/DISCUSSION
Is a Key to Understanding

Answer these questions, either individually by journaling the answers or in a small discussion group.

1. To which of the three dangers are you the most vulnerable? How would you state, in your own words, specifically what your danger is?
2. Which of the three safeguards most addresses your greatest vulnerabilities? How would you state in your own words specifically what your danger is?
3. Which of the two mind-protecting weapons is your stronger weapon? Why do you think it is your stronger weapon?

DECISION TIME
Is a Key to Change

Answer these questions, either individually by journaling the answers or in a spiritual accountability group.

1. Are you adequately guarding your mind against false teaching? Are you adequately guarding your mind against temptation? Are you adequately guarding your mind against spiritual deception? What changes must you make in each of these areas?

2. Are you adequately guarding what you let into your mind? Are you adequately guarding what you let your mind create? Are you adequately guarding what you let your mind dwell on? What changes must you make in each of these areas?

3. Are you adequately guarding your mind with Scripture? Are you adequately guarding your mind with prayer? What changes must you make in each of these areas?

RECOMMENDED
Resources

Brave New Discipleship, Max Anders (especially chapters 1, 2, 16, and 17)
Change Your Heart, Change Your Life, Gary Smalley

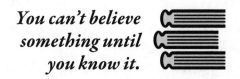
CHAPTER 10

THE CHALLENGE OF PAIN, SUFFERING, AND EVIL

We must make peace with the difficult fact that God is *good* and, at the same time, his children *suffer*.

 CENTRAL PASSAGE: Psalm 34:8 (NKJV)—"Oh, taste and see that the LORD is good; blessed is the man who trusts in Him!"

If there were a silver bullet that could be used against God, it would be the problem of pain, suffering, and evil in the world.

It is the most serious problem in the world (hereafter sometimes referred to only as "evil"). It is also the one serious objection to the existence, nature, and character of God. Perhaps more people have rejected Christianity because of the problem of evil than for any other reason, and it is certainly the greatest test of the Christian faith.

Atheists commonly point to evil as justification for rejecting God. In a YouTube video that went viral, the British comedian Stephen Fry delivered a vicious, scathing attack on the Judeo-Christian God when asked what he would say if it turned out, after he died, that God did in fact exist. He called this God a "maniac," pointing to the large amount of unnecessary suffering in the world which he, by default, created and allows.[1]

What kind of God, atheists ask, has created a world in which innocent children die in floods, starve to death, or die in agony from malaria? What kind of God allows his own children who worship him to be murdered, raped, tortured, beheaded, and come to countless other shocking ends?

Atheists argue that the existence of suffering is an impossible problem for those who believe in an all-good, caring God to solve. According to atheists, even if those people try to argue that without some suffering there can be no love and compassion, or that people who do wrong are eventually punished, they cannot justify the suffering of innocent children, atrocities against sincere believers, or disaster on a horrific scale among people who did not deserve such retribution.

Atheists and agnostics were in full cry early in this century when a massive tsunami killed more than 250,000 people around the rim of the Indian Ocean. Afterward, newspapers and magazines were full of letters and articles asking, "where was God?"

Atheists contend that a God who is benevolent and loving, as they are told the Christian God is, would never create the world we live in. Believing in him requires either ignoring an ominous dark side or excusing it.

The classic problem of pain is this: If God is all-good, and if God is all-powerful, then why is there pain, suffering, and evil?

The implication is that either God is not all good and he doesn't care that evil exists, or that he isn't all-powerful and can't do anything about it, or that God doesn't exist at all.

A Christian needs to have assurances about these implications. Pain, evil, and suffering are, indeed, serious problems for any thinking person, Christians included. So, let's take these implications in reverse order.

1. God exists in spite of suffering.

God e_____ in spite of suffering.

It is not uncommon for people to conclude that the existence of evil proves that God doesn't exist. The reasoning is that a good God would not allow the senseless suffering that has dominated human history.

Initially, this seems reasonable. However, looking at things more deeply, we would have to ask ourselves where we got the idea of senseless and pointless suffering. Evolution does not suggest that suffering is morally wrong. Acute and senseless suffering dominates nature. Just try watching a PBS special on African animals gorging on one another on the grasslands of the Serengeti. So, evolution doesn't suggest that pain and suffering are morally wrong—it only says they are part of the natural order.

Or, if we are mere products of evolution, consider Hitler, who thought that causing Jews and Christians to suffer was good and proper. If there is no God, on what authority would that be considered wrong?

Or, a similarly prejudiced person who hates people not of his own ethnic origin might rejoice in the 250,000 people killed in a tsunami in the Indian Ocean in the early part of this century. It rid the world of a significant population burden. It wiped out not only the 250,000 but the millions who would have come from those 250,000!

So, one person thinks that suffering is unjust, and another thinks it is just. Who is right?

If there is no God, neither is right. Or, both are right. As Dostoevsky said in *The Brothers Karamazov*, "If there is no God, all things are permissible."[2]

You say something is right. I say it is wrong. We are both humans and we are equal, so we cancel each other out. If there is no God, there is only personal preference; there can be no categorical right and wrong, good and bad, or just and unjust.

Only if there is a transcendent, supernatural Being who is above humans, who is the source of truth, who defines what is just and unjust, right and wrong, and good and bad, can those categories exist.

So, denying the existence of God does not solve the problem of pain, suffering, and evil. Instead, the fact that people think things are senseless and wrong suggests that they indeed hold to moral values about such things, not from the natural world championed by atheists/evolutionists, but from the world that God created and the value system that has come from that origin.

2. God is all-powerful, in spite of suffering.

God is a____-p_____, in spite of suffering.

A second conclusion people commonly come to is that, even if there is a God and he is good, he is still unable to correct the suffering of human existence.

Again, it's easy to see how a surface consideration of the issues might lead one to this conclusion, but the option disappears once we begin thinking more deeply about the subject.

Just because God doesn't do something doesn't mean he cannot. It only means he has not, or has not yet.

If there is a God, he created the universe and all that is in it. Think of the expanse of space—think of galaxies, supernovas, and black holes. Think of the balance of gravity and centrifugal force in the universe that is so precise that the universe does not fly apart on the one hand, nor collapse on itself on the other hand. Surely, if God did this, he could eliminate evil if he chose.

No, the issue cannot be that God cannot eliminate evil. It must be that he has chosen not to.

3. God is good, in spite of suffering.

God is g_____, in spite of suffering.

So, the real issue appears to settle in on whether or not God is good in spite of the fact that he has allowed evil and has not eliminated it.

The Bible insists that God is good.

Against all atheistic/agnostic reasoning, the Bible insists that God is good:

1. "Oh, give thanks to the LORD, for He is good! For His mercy endures forever" (1 Chronicles 16:34 NKJV).
2. "Good and upright is the LORD" (Psalm 25:8 NKJV).
3. "Oh, taste and see that the LORD is good; blessed is the man who trusts in Him!" (Psalm 34:8 NKJV).

4. "You are good and do good" (Psalm 119:68).

5. "No one is good except God alone" (Mark 10:18).

The Bible insists that God is _____.

God will ultimately resolve the problem of evil.

So, how can we reconcile the goodness of God with the presence of rampant evil in the world?

First, we must admit that we do not know what was in the mind of God when he allowed evil in the first place. For reasons that we either have not been told or cannot comprehend, he allowed evil to begin, and allows it to continue.

Second, God has promised eventually to resolve the problem of pain, evil and suffering. Revelation 21:1 and 4 (NIV) say, "I saw a new heaven and a new earth . . . there will be no more death or mourning or crying or pain, for the old order of things has passed away."

God will ultimately resolve the problem of e_____.

Until then, we rest in His sacrificial love for us.

But one might ask, "what about all the suffering that will be experienced before God sets everything right? How do we resolve God's goodness with that?"

Well, we must admit that this presents a challenge. But *pressing ahead toward God rather than retreating from him,* we consider that even though God allows evil for the present time, he nevertheless stepped into it and allowed the consequences of evil to touch him. He did not, and does not, leave us here to suffer alone (Hebrews 4:15–16).

First, Jesus, God's Son, died to deliver us from evil (Romans 5:8).

So, how is God good in spite of the presence of evil? Well, while God allows evil, he stepped into it and allowed the consequences of evil to touch him. Jesus had to die to conquer evil. And he didn't just die; he first suffered. It would be one thing if he had been guillotined. That is a painless way to die. But he was crucified . . . a terribly painful and distressing way to die. Furthermore, he was separated from God the Father, which appears to have been the most distressing thing for Jesus ("My God, My God, why have you forsaken me?" [Matthew 27:46]). And he didn't have to die! He chose to. John 10:18 says, "No one takes (my life) from me, but I lay it down of my own accord" (NIV). So, why did he? Because he loved us and was willing to pay whatever price was required to redeem us and pay for our sin so that we would not have to. That is not the act of a maniac.

Indeed, that is the act of a man of towering moral courage and character. That supreme act of love ("Greater love has no one than this, that one lay down his life for his friends." [John 15:13]) demonstrates that, while we may not be able to explain why God allowed evil in the first place, if he did not exempt himself from it there must be a reason that we do not currently understand. And because there are many things in this world that we accept even though we do not understand, we now have a rational basis for not rejecting God because of evil in the world.

Second, the Father also stepped into this evil for our sake.

The Father made the decision to send Jesus to die for us. Jesus willingly came down from heaven, but it must have been a terribly painful decision for the Father to ask him to do so ("I have come down from heaven, not to do My own will, but the will of Him who sent Me" [John 6:38]).

Then, the Father *witnessed* the suffering and death of his Son, something any loving parent would recognize as an agonizing thing to do. Even more, the Father loves all of us . . . all the people who have ever lived. And, he has had to witness all the pain and suffering of all people in all places for all time.

It is an agonizing experience for anyone to witness the suffering of someone they love, let alone all people of all places for all time. Why does God endure this? Love seems the only conceivable answer (John 3:16).

Until then, we rest in his s_____ love for us.

We conclude that God is not a maniac, because everything he touches turns to goodness.

So, God allows evil but does not exempt himself from it. Therefore, either God is a maniac (creating a system of senseless suffering that even he has to endure), or there is a rationale that is beyond our knowledge or comprehension.

I do not believe God is a maniac, as Stephen Fry suggested. I look at evidence that points to just the opposite:

1. Love can explain his actions, rather than insanity (John 3:16).
2. His teachings are of the highest order.
   - Love your neighbor as yourself (Matthew 22:37–39).
   - Do unto others as you would have others do unto you (Luke 6:31).
   - Love does no wrong to a neighbor; therefore, love is a fulfillment of the law (Romans 13:10).
3. Faithful obedience to his teachings produces the fruit of the Spirit in the life of his followers: peace, love, and joy (Galatians 5:22–23).

These teachings are not the marks of a maniac! Everywhere God is followed authentically, goodness, peace, love, and joy break out, overflow, bubble up, and wash over.

This is true both on a historic level and a personal level. Regarding history, in his book *What If Jesus Had Never Been Born?*, D. James Kennedy wrote that these things happened as a result of Jesus's life and teachings:

1. Literacy has been taken to the world, allowing people to learn and grow and make a better living, making a middle class possible.
2. Health care for the masses was unknown before Jesus. After Jesus, Christianity is responsible for establishing healthcare for the masses around the world.

3. Help for the disabled and disadvantaged was unknown before Jesus. As a result of his life and teaching humanitarianism has spread worldwide, but only in the countries affected by Christianity. In other countries, not so much. The United States gives more money to humanitarian causes than any other nation, and, compared to China which has three or four times the number of people, gives vastly more money because of our Christian heritage.

4. Before Jesus, the common man could not expect legal justice. Now, because of the Magna Carta and the Constitution of the United States (documents born out of Christian principles and biblical values) and the influence these documents have had in history, justice is established on Christian values for the common man.

5. Governments founded on Christian principles allow people to be protected from the excesses of tyrannical governments or other powers. The governments of Stalin, Hitler, and Chairman Mao were hostile to Christianity and were responsible for the deaths of over 100 million people—not by war, but mostly by the hands of their own countrymen. The Crusades are often brought up as a bad example of Christianity. However, while they may be nothing for Christianity to be proud of, the evil of the Crusades (which were a distortion of Christianity, not a valid expression of it) pales in comparison to the evil of these tyrannical governments.[3]

This tight summary gives a striking overview of the impact Christianity has made throughout history. None of this would have happened if Jesus had not been born.

Furthermore, many attribute the dramatic rise of the United States as the dominant superpower of the modern world directly to its original foundation on Christian principles. Wherever God and his Word are taken seriously and followed carefully, goodness, goodness, and goodness breaks out. Because God *is* good.

And this is not only true on a historic level, but also on a personal level. Multiplied millions testify to the profound positive change God has made in their lives when they gave themselves to Jesus . . . even those in terribly trying circumstances. Corrie ten Boom testified to God's goodness in the darkness of a concentration camp. Joni Eareckson Tada testifies to God's goodness in the pain and restriction of physical paralysis and chronic pain. Countless believers in areas of persecution today testify to the sufficient, sustaining grace of God even in the face of terrible tragedy.

We conclude that God is not a maniac, because everything he touches turns to g_____ .

Conclusion

So, why did God create a world in the first place in which evil would be present and innocent people would suffer terribly?

The fact is, we don't know. The answer is either something we have not been told, or something that, having been told, we do not yet comprehend.

However, the previous reasons confirm that we can believe that God exists, is all-powerful, and is good in spite of the pain, suffering, and evil in the world.

So, we see that there is no silver bullet against God. While challenging issues will always create a need for clear and deep thinking . . . when we do think clearly and deeply, God is revealed to be just who he says he is . . . one who *is* good and who *does* good (Psalm 119:68).

 **REPETITION**
Is the Key to Mental Ownership

Chapter Review
1. God e_____ in spite of suffering.
2. God is a____-p_____ , in spite of suffering.
3. God is _____ , in spite of suffering.
    a. The Bible insists that God is g_____ .
    b. God will ultimately resolve the problem of e_____ .

c. Until then, we rest in his s_____ love for us.

d. We conclude that God is not a maniac, because everything he touches turns to g_____.

The Christian Life in 1,000 Words—Review

If something is important, you must repeat it until it changes you.

1. You were created b__ God, f_____ God, and you will only be truly happy as a Christian who is growing i__ God.

2. We must live in this visible, t_____ world according to invisible, e_____ realities.

3. The main thing G____ gets out of your life is the person you become. The main thing y____ get out of your life is the person you become. Therefore, our highest purpose is to b_____ the most we can become, in God's eyes, before we die.

4. A Christian is not merely someone who has turned over a new l_____, but, rather, someone who has turned over a new l_____.

5. Spiritual growth is the process of the redeemed inner man gaining increasing m_____ over the unredeemed outer man.

6. For our l_____ to be transformed, our m_____ must be renewed.

7. Spiritual growth requires a balance of G_____ part and o____ part.

8. There are three enemies of the Christian: the w_____, the f_____, and the d_____.

9. A p_____ mind will be spared the d_____ pull of negative input and be released to the u_____ pull of positive input.

10. We must make peace with the difficult fact that God is g_____ and, at the same time, his children s_____.

THOUGHT/DISCUSSION
Is a Key to Understanding

Answer these questions, either individually by journaling the answers or in a small discussion group.

1. Has suffering, including psychological and emotional suffering, ever caused you to conclude that God doesn't exist, or isn't good?

If not, what has given you stability? If so, what most helps you recover your stability?

2. Explain in your own words how Jesus's suffering for us helps us believe that God loves us, in spite of the fact that he doesn't make our lives go better?

3. What goodness have you seen in your own life, or perhaps observed in others, that helps persuade you that God is good?

DECISION TIME
Is a Key to Change

Answer these questions, either individually by journaling the answers or in a spiritual accountability group.

1. Has your confidence in God's existence been shaken because of evil in the world? Do you need to recommit yourself to his existence?

2. What is the most important thing you think you should do to prepare yourself to share this important truth with others who may question God's existence or goodness because of evil in the world?

RECOMMENDED
Resources

Where Is God When It Hurts?, Philip Yancey

A complete Christian needs to:
- Know what you need to know
- Become what you need to be
- Do what you need to do

PART 2

B E

*You won't
live it until
you believe it.*

CHAPTER 11

UNDERSTANDING WHY THE CHRISTIAN LIFE DOESN'T WORK ANY BETTER THAN IT DOES

God wants *faith* and *love* over anything else we might offer him.

 CENTRAL PASSAGE: Matthew 22:37—"You shall love the Lord your God with all your heart, and with all your soul, and with all your mind."

Have you ever wondered why the Christian life doesn't work any better than it does?

Have you ever wondered why, when you've tried and when you've done your best, you still don't have the character, the spiritual strength, or the ministry impact you thought you should have?

Have you ever wondered that if you have the Holy Spirit living within you, why he doesn't make a greater difference?

Have you ever wondered why progress is so slow, and why the results are so unremarkable?

Has the thought ever struck you that there must be something wrong with you, something wrong with God, or something wrong with the system?

Why doesn't the Christian life work any better than it does?

If you have never wrestled with these questions, you are blessed. But for those of us who have, we would like to explore some answers.

1. God has a different timetable than we do.

God has a different t_____ than we do.

In his book *When God Doesn't Make Sense*, James Dobson has a section which could be entitled, "Four Days Late."[1] It alludes to the fact that, after having been summoned by Mary and Martha because of the serious illness of their brother, Lazarus, Jesus arrived after Lazarus had already been dead for four days. It looked as though Jesus was four days late.

There are a host of other examples in the Scriptures in which, from a human perspective, it seems that God is late.

- Abraham was promised a son, but the promise was not fulfilled for another 25 years until he was 100!
- Joseph was given a promise from God that he would be a great ruler, but it was another 15 or so years before the promise was fulfilled, and Joseph spent that time as a slave and in prison!
- David was anointed by the prophet Samuel to be the next king over Israel. But instead of having an inauguration ceremony the next day, David spent much of the next 13 years or so of his life dodging Saul, the current king, and trying to keep Saul from lopping his head off.

Yes, God's timetable is typically much longer than ours. And when God doesn't move as quickly in our lives as we think he should, it is easy for us to have the same reaction that Israel did . . . to fear that God has forgotten about us, and to assume he is someplace else in the universe doing something more interesting with someone more important.

So, what can we conclude when God moves so slowly in our lives that our minds begin to fill with doubts and questions and concerns?

1. We don't know why God seems to have woven "slowness" into his system, but he has. 2 Peter 3:8–9 says, "With the

Lord one day is like a thousand years, and a thousand years like one day. The Lord is not slow . . ." It just seems, from our perspective, that God is slow. But he has his plan, he is not slow, and his promises never fail. So, our task is to accept this, grow in our understanding of his system, and cooperate with his plan.

2. God has a number of things he has chosen to accomplish by his "slowness."

   o *To bring glory to God.* Jesus explained that Lazarus's death created greater glory to God (John 11:40). Many came to Christ as a result of Lazarus's resurrection (John 12:10–11).

   o *To strengthen our faith.* God was testing Abraham's faith by delaying the birth of Isaac. Scripture says that Abraham believed God, and it was credited to him as righteousness (Romans 4:3).

   o *To mature our character.* James 1:2–4 tells us that trials (and God's "slowness" can be a real trial) make us perfect and complete, lacking in nothing, if we go through them in faith.

   o *To increase our eternal reward.* Romans 8:18 tells us that the sufferings of this present time are not worthy to be compared with the glory that will be revealed to us.

   o *To increase our eternal position.* Luke 19:11–19 tells us that when we are faithful at little things, God will give us greater things.

So, slowness is baked into God's plan for his purposes, some of which we can understand and some we can't. But there's nothing wrong with God, nor us, nor the system when things move slowly. We may not prefer that system, but it is what it is, and God is good, and he causes all things (including slowness) to work together for good to those who love God and are called according to his purpose (Romans 8:28). It is our task to accept this and work within it.

2. God has different criteria for success than we do.

God has different c_____ for success than we do.

If you are a Christian, the Holy Spirit lives in you ("do you not know that your body is a temple of the Holy Spirit who is in you?" [1 Corinthians 6:19]). Why doesn't it make a greater difference?

If you were going to write a science fiction movie and you were going to have a Greek god inhabit your hero, wouldn't it make a big difference? Wouldn't your hero suddenly take on the superpowers of the god who now inhabits your hero? Wouldn't he/she be stronger and smarter, with extraordinary abilities? Wouldn't it be obvious to everyone who sees the movie that your hero was inhabited by a god?

So why doesn't it make a greater difference that the Holy Spirit inhabits us?

1. Why don't we have bedazzling power when we speak and minister to others?
2. Why don't we live life with all the right, deep, and unflagging convictions?
3. Why don't we stand resolute against temptation, laughing in the face of enticement?
4. Why don't we have limitless enthusiasm for the priorities of God and fading enthusiasm for the world's?
5. Why don't we show the world unfailing peace, love, and joy in the face of difficult circumstances and challenging people?

Why doesn't the world see our super-abilities and stand in awe that we are inhabited by God? Is there something wrong with us? Is there something wrong with God? Is there something wrong with the system? No, it is all as it should be. And here is why:

God Is Not Interested in Superhero Abilities

God doesn't want anything we can *give* him. He wants us. He wants our love. Therefore, God is not interested in giving us superhero powers. That would not impress him (after all, he is omnipotent). If we had superhero powers, it would likely bring glory to us in the eyes of the world, not him. When God does choose to do miracles, he does so in a way that brings glory and credit to him, not us.

We Have Been Dramatically Diminished by the Fall

Our capacities might be feebler than we think they should be or wish they could be, because they are coming from such a weakened and corrupted fallen vessel.

Our brains have been so corrupted by the "fall," our wills so poisoned by the world, and our hearts so blinded by the enemy, that our response to God's love is sapped, like a skeletal, disease-ravaged athlete trying to become an Olympic gold-medalist.

But God is not limited by our limitations. God does not want us on divine steroids. And while our imperfect response of love to God and our awkward giving back of trust and obedience are not bedazzling to the world, it is what God wants from us.

God Just Wants Our Love

As an example, our son, in a craft class when he was small, painted a plastic plate with a picture of a basketball in the center, and then an arch of letters above the basketball that said: "Greatest Mom!" He gave it to my wife for Mother's Day.

It is not well-drawn. It is not skillfully lettered. But it was a sincere expression of his love and appreciation for his mother. At the time, he was giving his mom his best. So, the skill didn't matter. The only thing that mattered was the love behind it.

If, while he was making the plate, my wife had taken hold of his hand, and by her greater power and artistic ability caused him to draw a better basketball than he could normally draw and write better lettering than he could normally write, it would not have enhanced the gift. In fact, it might have diminished the gift because it would not have been a 100% expression of his love alone.

My wife didn't *need* a plate with a basketball painted on. She didn't *want* (previously) a plate with a basketball painted on it. She hadn't been *looking* for one to buy.

But she did want our son's love. And our son painted the plate as a sincere expression of love for his mother. As a result, the plate is a life treasure even though it is not a work of fine art.

In the same way, God doesn't want to come over us and enable us to "leap tall buildings in a single bound" as Superman did, or be "faster than a speeding bullet, more powerful than a locomotive" (additional Superman abilities). He doesn't need those humanly exceptional abilities. He doesn't need or want any *thing* like this that we can give him.

Rather, he wants to create in us the miracle of the spiritual birth and spiritual transformation in the face of the great obstacles against it (the world, the flesh, and the devil), and to use us as his instruments to further the same with others.

So, when we do something for the Lord (preach a sermon, share our faith, raise money for ministry), it's always done with less excellence than if God did it himself (anything we can do, God can do better), but if it's a gesture of sincere love to him, he is pleased.

In times past, I have been tempted to conclude that there was something terribly wrong with me since the indwelling Holy Spirit has not made a greater difference in me. I thought I should be walking on water, always absorbing life's blows with unruffled grace, and performing miracles for others.

But I underestimated the diminishment of my capacities in humanity's Fall, and overestimated God's desire to have me manifest superhero abilities to the world. *He* can be in charge of the *miracles*. He wants *me* to *love* him.

So, in love, I trust him and obey him as best I can, waiting for the day when I will worship him in heaven, knowing more, being more, and doing more than I ever imagined . . . thrilled with my (finally) bedazzling resurrection body and abilities. I will be enraptured by the reality that, once again, God is pleased because our shared love— and all that flows out of that love—is all he ever wanted from me and for me.

3. God insists that we do things his way rather than our way.

God insists that we do things h____ way rather than our way.

There is another reason why the Christian life doesn't seem to work as well as we think it should; we don't do a very good job of being faithful to the biblical process for growth. Instead, we're trying to do it our way. This might flow from two possible causes:

Ignorance

God's way is always best. Our way is always less than best. And because God loves us and wants the best for us, he insists that we do things his way. That is the third reason why the Christian life does not always work as well as we think it should: we are trying to do it our way.

Sometimes this is out of ignorance. We grow in grace and knowledge (2 Peter 3:18). Inherent in that principle is the concept that there are some times in which we simply don't know the things that would be helpful. As a result, we may do things "our way" out of ignorance. We just don't understand the system yet.

I spent years of my Christian life not understanding the fundamental principles of spiritual growth. I was relatively committed and disciplined in my faith habits, but because I didn't understand how spiritual growth worked, I floundered. It is this experience that has driven me to want to share principles for growing faith and gaining comprehensive spiritual truth with others.

This book is designed to address that shortcoming, to try to guide and accelerate spiritual growth by providing an essential foundation for further spiritual growth.

This is also why it is to our advantage to become serious students of Scripture. It reduces the number of problems we bring down on our own heads because of ignorance.

- Yes, you study the Bible to learn more about God and walk closer with him.
- Yes, you study the Bible to learn how to minister to others.
- Yes, you study the Bible to help others come to Christ.

But you also study the Bible to cut down on the amount of pain you bring into your own life because of ignorance!

Disobedience

Other times, we try to do things "our way" out of prideful disobedience. We know what God wants us to do, but we don't want to do it. So, we do it our way.

We will deal with this theme more fully in another chapter, but for now let me just make the fundamental point: if we believe God, we trust him and obey him. If we don't believe God, we follow our own will. Correctly understood, the opposite of obedience is not disobedience. It is unbelief.

Many Christians don't believe that following God fully is the shortest distance between us and the life we long for. As a result, we imagine we can take from God what we want (eternal life and basic principles for a good life), and then scheme to acquire, by our own efforts, whatever else we think we need to be fully happy.

God, of course, objects to this strategy—again because of his love for us—and allows us to pay a negative price for it, encouraging our repentance and spurring our return to full obedience in him.

Thus, we see that sometimes the Christian life does not work as well as we think it ought to because we are half-hearted in our pursuit. And half-hearted measures always yield half-hearted results.

Conclusion

So, why doesn't the Christian life work as well as we think it should?

- Because God has a different timetable than we do.
- Because God has different criteria for success than we do.
- Because God insists that we do things his way, rather than our way.

REPETITION
Is the Key to Mental Ownership

Chapter Review

1. God has a different t_____ than we do.
2. God has different c_____ for success than we do.
3. God insists that we do things h____ way rather than our way.

The Christian Life in 1,000 Words—Review

(Only the last ten chapters will be displayed)

If something is important, you must repeat it until it changes you.

2. We must live in this visible, t_____ world according to invisible, e_____ realities.

3. The main thing G____ gets out of your life is the person you become. The main thing y____ get out of your life is the person you become. Therefore, our highest purpose is to b_____ the most we can become, in God's eyes, before we die.

4. A Christian is not merely someone who has turned over a new l_____, but, rather, someone who has turned over a new l_____.

5. Spiritual growth is the process of the redeemed inner man gaining increasing m_____ over the unredeemed outer man.

6. For our l_____ to be transformed, our m_____ must be renewed.

7. Spiritual growth requires a balance of G_____ part and o____ part.

8. There are three enemies of the Christian: the w_____, the f_____, and the d_____.

9. A p_____ mind will be spared the d_____ pull of negative input and be released to the u_____ pull of positive input.

10. We must make peace with the difficult fact that God is g_____ and, at the same time, his children s_____.

11. God wants f_____ and l_____ over anything else we might offer him.

THOUGHT/DISCUSSION
Is a Key to Understanding

Answer these questions, either individually by journaling the answers or in a small discussion group.

1. Can you think of times in your life when you have been frustrated by God's slow timing? How did it make you feel?
2. Have there been times in the past when you were puzzled by how little difference it seemed to make that the Holy Spirit lived within you? What did you conclude was the reason?
3. In your experience, has it been ignorance or disobedience that was the greater cause for lack of spiritual progress in your life?

DECISION TIME
Is a Key to Change

Answer these questions, either individually by journaling the answers or in a spiritual accountability group.

1. In the past, have you been more inclined to give God your "best efforts" or to give God your faith and love?
2. What decisions do you think you need to make in order to overcome any spiritual ignorance in your life?
3. What decisions do you think you need to make in order to overcome any disobedience in your life?

RECOMMENDED
Resource

Rewriting Your Broken Story, Kenneth Boa

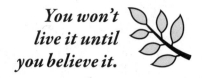

You won't
live it until
you believe it.

CHAPTER 12

THE ROLE OF TRIALS IN CHRISTIAN GROWTH

God will often *deliver* us in a manner that seems,
initially, to *destroy* us.[1]
—Daniel Defoe

 CENTRAL PASSAGE: James 1:2-4—"Consider it all joy, my brethren, when you encounter various trials, knowing that the testing of your faith produces endurance. And let endurance have its perfect result, so that you may be perfect and complete, lacking in nothing."

Chapter 10 was titled, "The Challenge of Pain, Suffering, and Evil." It dealt with the issue of suffering on a philosophical level.

Now we have to deal with suffering on a personal level. After I have wrestled with why God allows suffering at all, I have to wrestle with why he allows suffering in *my* life—and you do, too! It is one thing to come to grips with suffering on a cosmic level, and another to come to grips with suffering on a personal level.

The reality is that some personal suffering transcends normal purposes. For example, some Christians have suffered terribly in concentration camps for a short time and were then mercilessly killed. There is no doubt that the meaning and purpose of such suffering is resolved in God's mind, but these things simply may not be resolvable in human minds; they must be wrestled with on a deeply personal level and often lead us into places shrouded by deep mystery. Believers who have endured such struggles have tread on holy ground and wrestled with immense things about the deepest nuances of God's love and sovereignty.

However, the purpose of this chapter is to look at a more normal level of suffering in the believer's life that has the opportunity of being transformational and formative.

We naturally desire a pleasant, comfy life, and typically struggle when life is hard. The more unpleasant life is, the more we tend to struggle. But if we understand the role of trials in Christian growth, it can help us maintain our perspective in the midst of the suffering and strengthen us spiritually, rather than weakening us.

There are four components to understand when gaining perspective on personal suffering:

1. God gives his children life dreams.

God gives his children l_____ d_____.

The beginning point for mastering this idea is found in Ephesians 2:10 where we read, "For we are His workmanship, created in Christ Jesus for good works, which God prepared beforehand that we should walk in them" (NKJV).

From this, we learn 3 things:

1. God has created us for good works.
2. He did so before we were even born.
3. He intends that we should "walk in them."

Knowing this, we return to Philippians 2:12–13, which we looked at in Chapter 7: "Work out your salvation with fear and trembling; for it is God who is at work in you, both to will and to work for His good pleasure."

This passage tells us that God is at work in us, both to will and to work for his good pleasure and that, as a result, we respond to this prompting by being faithful to that divine work in our lives.

So, putting Ephesians 2:10 together with Philippians 2:12–13, if God has created us for good works and if he is at work in us to "will" his good pleasure, then it seems reasonable to conclude that he will give us the leading, prompting, and desire to do the good works he wants us to do.

This, then, becomes our "life dream." We each have something that we would like to do to serve God. When we understand what that is, it can give us a major sense of purpose in life.

As we walk in these good works, our lives take on the meaning, the fulfillment, and the sense of purpose that gets us out of bed in the morning, ready to face the day and willing to take the beatings that life gives us, all for the sake of a higher calling.

2. Between the giving of the dream and the fulfillment of the dream is often a long, dark valley.

Between the giving of the dream and the fulfillment of the dream is often a long, dark v_____.

Job said, "Man is born for trouble, as sparks fly upward" (Job 5:7).

The apostle Peter wrote, "For you have been called for this purpose, since Christ also suffered for you, leaving you an example for you to follow in His steps" (1 Peter 2:21).

The fact is, for many of us, at least from time to time, life is going to be hard. It's a given. It's harder for some than for others, but it is hard for everyone at one time or another. During our dark valleys, we tend to lose sight of God's work in our lives and his intention to use us for his glory. We often feel stuck in the backwater of life, feeling forgotten by God or unimportant to him. We may see little benefit and great detriment to our suffering, and it can cause us to lose confidence in our relationship with God.

3. The purpose of the valley is not to keep you *from* your dream, but to prepare you *for* your dream.

The purpose of the valley is not to keep you f____ your dream, but to prepare you f___ your dream.

During the dark valleys, many of which can last a very long time, it is not uncommon to conclude that the suffering we're going through is proof that our dream is dead, that God is not going to use us, that we are not important or useful to God, and that we are left on our own to muddle through life.

Nothing could be further from the truth.

The reality is that the suffering is part of the process for fulfilling the dream. It is part of the process of making us into the kind of people through whom the dream can be fulfilled.

The apostle James wrote, "Consider it all joy, my brethren, when you encounter various trials, knowing that the testing of your faith produces endurance. And let endurance have its perfect result, so that you may be perfect and complete, lacking in nothing" (James 1:2–4).

In the same vein, the apostle Paul wrote, "We also exult in our tribulations, knowing that tribulation brings about perseverance; and perseverance, proven character; and proven character, hope; and hope does not disappoint, because the love of God has been poured out within our hearts through the Holy Spirit who was given to us" (Romans 5:3–5).

If we are going to be *able* to fulfill the dream that God gives us, we must be transformed. Who we become is more important than what we do. In fact, what we do is always built on who we become! God only "does" as much through us as we have "become." As a general rule God changes us first, and uses us second. In some special mountaintop seasons of spiritual growth, he may even do both simultaneously, causing doing and being to fuel each other in a catalytic way. However, God patently refuses to allow us to "do" things for him apart from spiritual transformation, and transformation usually comes in the valley.

Our Enemy, Satan, wants to use the valley to keep us from our God-given dream. He is the deceiver (Revelation 20:3) and the destroyer (the meaning of Abaddon/Apollyon in Revelation 9:11), and he wants to deceive us concerning God's intentions for us and destroy the dream. He wants to convince us that we are unimportant to God, that we are not worthy or capable of fulfilling a God-given dream, and that it would be foolish for us to even try.

4. Those who see their dream realized are the ones who do not give up on God in the valley.

Those who see their dream realized are the ones who do not g_____ u_ on God in the valley.

The apostle Paul wrote, "For I consider that the sufferings of this present time are not worthy to be compared with the glory that is to be revealed to us" (Romans 8:18).

He also wrote, "Therefore we do not lose heart, but though our outer man is decaying, yet our inner man is being renewed day by day. For momentary, light affliction is producing for us an eternal weight of glory far beyond all comparison, while we look not at the things which are seen, but the things which are not seen; for the things which are seen are temporal, but the things which are not seen are eternal" (2 Corinthians 4:16–18).

We see, then, that suffering is part of God's will for us. It is the refiner's fire that he uses to separate us from the things that hold us back from our full spiritual potential. The suffering he allows into our lives is not designed to keep us from our dreams, but to prepare us for our dream.

A. W. Tozer once wrote, "It is doubtful whether God can bless a man greatly until He has hurt him deeply."[2]

It sounds almost cruel to state this so bluntly, but it harmonizes with many of the passages of Scripture we have looked at.

When God has done his work in us during the valley, he then takes us from the valley and uses us for the purposes he determined before we were even born.

Your Personal Example

So, now we come to the issue of your God-given dream. In what good works do you believe God wants you to walk? You might be given a big life dream—or a series of smaller life dreams. Or, most likely, a combination of the two.

His dream for you may be very specific: He wants you to build a home for orphans in Guatemala. Or it may be very general: that he wants you to help prisoners believe that God loves them. It may be big: He wants you to get one million Bibles to China. Or it may be very small: He wants you to help your grandchildren learn about Jesus.

What the dream is doesn't matter. What matters is that you take meaning and purpose in life by following the dream God gives you, and that you gain strength to endure the blows of life because you are living for a higher purpose than personal comfort.

And, sometimes, there is more than one valley. There may be multiple valleys as God works out his will in your life and as he prepares you, one level at a time, for subsequent good works.

Conclusion

The "Sit-Stay" command is the hardest command to teach dogs in obedience training. They must sit and stay for usually around 3 minutes while their trainer and the judge go behind a screen of some kind, out of sight. The dogs think their handlers are not doing anything with them, and they assume they have been forgotten.

But the dogs *are* doing something. They are sitting and staying, obeying the single most difficult command, bringing glory to themselves and to their trainers if they are faithful. And they are *not* at all forgotten. In fact, all the judges, trainers, and owners are holding their breaths in hopes their dogs will keep faith until the end. The moment at which they feel most forgotten—about 2 minutes and 45 seconds in—is the moment they are least forgotten and when they are most at the center of the judges' attention.

So it is with you. God is trying to make some-<u>one</u> out of you. Then he will do some-<u>thing</u> with you.

During the dark valleys, we are often in the sit-stay position. When we are there, we are doing something. We are sitting and staying. We are not forgotten. We are being scrutinized by all of heaven to see if we will be faithful. Believing this can give us great hope, comfort, and strength, enabling us to be faithful to the end and allowing God to fulfill his great purposes in us.

REPETITION
Is the Key to Mental Ownership

Chapter Review

1. God gives his children l_____ d_____.
2. Between the giving of the dream and the fulfillment of the dream is often a long, dark v_____.
3. The purpose of the valley is not to keep you f_____ your dream, but to prepare you f____ your dream.
4. Those who see their dream realized are the ones who do not g____ u__ on God in the valley.

The Christian Life in 1,000 Words—Review

(Only the last ten chapters will be displayed)

If something is important, you must repeat it until it changes you.

3. The main thing G____ gets out of your life is the person you become. The main thing y____ get out of your life is the person you become. Therefore, our highest purpose is to b_____ the most we can become, in God's eyes, before we die.
4. A Christian is not merely someone who has turned over a new l_____, but, rather, someone who has turned over a new l_____.
5. Spiritual growth is the process of the redeemed inner man gaining increasing m_____ over the unredeemed outer man.
6. For our l_____ to be transformed, our m_____ must be renewed.
7. Spiritual growth requires a balance of G_____ part and o____ part.
8. There are three enemies of the Christian: the w_____, the f_____, and the d_____.
9. A p_____ mind will be spared the d_____ pull of negative input and be released to the u_____ pull of positive input.
10. We must make peace with the difficult fact that God is g_____ and, at the same time, his children s_____.
11. God wants f_____ and l_____ over anything else we might offer him.

12. God will often d_____ us in a manner that seems, initially,
to d_____ us.

THOUGHT/DISCUSSION
Is a Key to Understanding

*Answer these questions, either individually by journaling the answers or in
a small discussion group.*

1. Is it news to you that God has good works he wants you to do?
   Do you have some idea of what your life dream might be?
2. In your experience, has there been more than one valley? How many
   can you think of?
3. What are some of the lessons you have learned in past valleys?
   How have they prepared you for good works?

DECISION TIME
Is a Key to Change

*Answer these questions, either individually by journaling the answers or in
a spiritual accountability group.*

1. Are you in a valley now? Are you tempted to give up? What do you
   think you need to do now to remain faithful if you are in a valley?
2. What do you think are areas in your life that might need to be
   transformed in order to prepare you for future good works? Are
   there things you can do now to begin working on those areas so
   God may not have to take you through a valley for the change?
3. What is the greatest thing you would like to do for God, if you
   could do anything you wanted to and knew that you would succeed?
   What area of change do you think you would need to have in order
   to do this?

RECOMMENDED
Resource

Disappointment with God, Philip Yancey

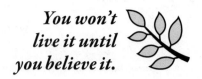

CHAPTER 13

GOD'S GAME PLAN WITH HUMANITY

God's blessing in the Old Testament was the "fruit of the *vine*"; in the New Testament, it is the "fruit of the *Spirit*."

> **CENTRAL PASSAGE:** Galatians 5:22-23—"The fruit of the Spirit is love, joy, peace, patience, kindness, goodness, faithfulness, gentleness, self-control . . ."

A "game plan" is a carefully thought-out strategy; people make them for athletics, politics, or for any other pursuit in which a specific outcome is desired.

God has a game plan for humanity. He has a carefully thought-out strategy that he uses to achieve his desired outcome with us.

Just as in athletics or politics, if we understand the game plan it is often easier for us to understand the big picture of what is being attempted, and it can also be easier to understand and interpret details.

1. God's game plan with humanity has four parts.

God's game plan with humanity has f_____ parts.

Reveal truth: God makes known his truth to humanity. In the earliest days, he often did this directly through prophets, dreams, visions, or direct contact. However, he also oversaw the writing down and preservation of his revelations so that his primary means of revelation today is the Bible (2 Timothy 3:16–17). This revelation includes *facts* (people, places, events) to be known, *doctrines* to be believed, and *principles* to be lived.

Reveal t_____.

Require faith: Many of the things that God asks of humanity in the Bible take us 180 degrees in the opposite direction of our natural inclinations. Therefore, Christians will only respond appropriately if we trust God and believe him. The test of our willingness to trust God is our obedience (John 14:15).

Require f_____.

Reward obedience: If we believe God and trust in him, we will do as his revelation requires. If we do not believe God and trust in him, we reject his revelation and pursue our natural inclinations. We reap the consequences of our faith or lack thereof (Galatians 6:7). If we follow God in faithful and trusting obedience, God rewards us. If we do not, God disciplines us to encourage repentance and righteousness (Hebrews 12:5–11).

Reward o_____.

Reproduce disciples: When others look at a trusting and obedient disciple and see the blessing that comes to her as a result of her faith, others are drawn to want to know God because of what they see of him in the life of his disciple (John 13:34–35).

Reproduce d_____.

This is God's fourfold game plan. Now, we'll see how it works itself out in the Old and New Testaments . . .

2. God's blessing in the Old Testament was the fruit of the vine.

God's blessing in the Old Testament was the fruit of the v____ .

Revelation of truth: In Old Testament times, revelation was through prophets, visions, and dreams, along with the Old Testament Scriptures. Today, all that remains of that system for Christians is the part that was recorded in the Old Testament. This revelation asked people to act in ways opposite to their natural inclinations.

- For example, they were not to amass horses as military resources (Deuteronomy 17:16), but rather were to rely on the Lord to use only an army of citizen soldiers to protect them from military threat.
- They were to refrain from labor or commerce every seventh day (Exodus 20:10), and every seventh year they were to let their land lie uncultivated for the entire year (Leviticus 25:4). God promised to bless them sufficiently in six years to provide for them in the seventh.
- They were to give a substantial portion of their income for tithes and offerings in worship to the Lord, in addition to (and before) the taxes they paid to run the affairs of government. God promised that if they were faithful in this, he would bless them so much that they would never lack for sufficient wealth (Malachi 3:10).

Requirement of faith: If you believed that an invisible God would protect you from enemies, you would be willing to forego the development of cavalry and chariot warfare. If you did not trust God to protect you, you would ignore God and raise all the horses, chariots, and even godless foreign allies you could to protect yourself.

If you believed that an invisible God would prosper your farming so greatly that you could raise in six years all you needed with enough left over for an entire seventh year of rest, then you would forego planting crops the seventh year. If you did not believe, you would ignore God and plant every seventh year to raise all the crops you could and provide for yourself.

If you believed that God would prosper you financially so that you could more than afford to give around 30 percent (all totaled) for national security and religious purposes, you would give your tithes and offerings joyfully. If you didn't trust God to prosper you sufficiently, you would ignore God, cheat on taxes, and hoard as much money as possible to fund your personal needs and plans.

These are just three examples of how God's revelation took people in the opposite direction of their natural inclinations. We are no different today than they were then—our natural inclination is still to protect ourselves and provide for ourselves. Faith requires that we believe God and trust him enough to act against our inclinations; in doing so, we obey him. If we believe, we obey. If we do not obey, it is because we do not believe.

Reward of blessing: God promised Israel, in an astonishing passage in Deuteronomy 28, that if they obeyed all his commandments fully, the blessings on their nation would be staggering. In an ominous counterpart to this promise, he also warned that he would curse them beyond measure if they didn't.

The story of the Old Testament, as recorded in Judges, 1 & 2 Samuel, 1 & 2 Kings, 1 & 2 Chronicles, Ezra, and Nehemiah, reveals the irrefutable evidence that God was utterly faithful to his Word. When the judges, chieftains, and kings of Israel and Judah led the nation in righteousness, God blessed them with financial and military prosperity. When these leaders steered the nation into unrighteousness, they suffered in both areas.

Reproduction of disciples: God did not choose Israel to the exclusion of all the other nations of the world. Rather, he chose Israel in order to reach all the other nations of the world. God fully desired to save the Gentile nations, but he intended to do it through Israel.

In Psalm 67 we read, "God be gracious to us and bless us, and cause his face to shine upon us—that Your way may be known on the earth, Your salvation among all nations . . . God blesses us, that all the ends of the earth may fear Him" (verses 1–2, 7).

God's plan was to bless Israel so fully that the other nations of the world would see the supernatural nature of the blessing and desire to know the God of Israel because of what they saw of him in the nation of Israel. We see an example of this happening in 1 Kings 10 during the reign of King Solomon, whose prosperity was almost unimaginable, having been built on the prosperity and faithfulness of his father, David, and increased by Solomon's dependence on God's wisdom.

As a result of the astonishing wealth of Israel, the Queen of Sheba wanted to see it all with her own eyes. So, she came to Jerusalem for a closer look. Solomon displayed to her his palace, the city of Jerusalem, and the Lord's temple, one of the most glorious buildings ever built.

After the queen had seen everything, the Bible says in verse 5, "there was no more spirit in her." Apparently, she practically swooned. One translation says she was "overwhelmed" (NIV). She said that she couldn't believe what she had heard about Solomon's wealth and wisdom and had to see it for herself. Having seen it, she said, "You exceed in wisdom and prosperity the report which I heard" (v. 7). Then, she broke out in spontaneous eulogy to God: "Blessed be the LORD your God" (v. 9).

Notice that she did not break out in eulogy to Solomon. She broke out in eulogy to God.

This is the way it was supposed to work. The people of the world would see the splendor of Israel, and their attention would be drawn to the God of Israel. The idea was that they would want to know the God of Israel because of all they had seen him do for, in, and through the people of Israel.

This was physical blessing—the blessing of the "fruit of the vine."

3. God's blessing in the New Testament is the fruit of the Spirit.

God's blessing in the New Testament is the fruit of the S_____.

In the Old Testament, God's dealings with the nation of Israel were very much physical and were designed to picture, or foreshadow, the spiritual truths in the New Testament.

- The Old Testament sacrificial system was intended to picture the spiritual work that would be done by Christ on the cross in the New Testament.
- The beauty of the Temple was designed to be a smaller picture of the glory of God and the true Temple in heaven.
- The physical blessings of protection and food were designed to picture the spiritual protection and nourishment that is ours in Christ.

In the Old Testament, fundamental reality was "seen." In the New Testament, fundamental reality is "unseen." In the Old Testament, people lived primarily for the present world. In the New Testament, Christians live primarily for the next world. The blessings of the Old Testament were conspicuously material and physical . . . the fruit of the vine. The blessings of the New Testament are conspicuously spiritual . . . the fruit of the Spirit.

Revelation of truth: The revelation of New Testament truth is, in essence, the same as in the Old Testament, but is spiritual in nature. Whereas the Old Testament took people in the opposite direction of their natural inclinations with physical issues, the New Testament takes us in the opposite direction of our natural inclinations with spiritual issues.

Because Jesus fulfilled the law, we no longer need to sacrifice animals. Nor do we need to refrain from amassing horses or from planting in every seventh year. Since Jesus's kingdom is not of this world, these things are not the most relevant arena for faith and obedience anymore.

But we are still required to function contrary to our natural inclinations:

- If we would keep our lives, we must lose them.
- If we are to be strong, we must be gentle.
- If we want to receive, we must give.
- If we want to be first, we must be last.
- If we want to be great, we must become servants to others.

In the Old Testament, people often killed their enemies. In the New Testament, we are instructed to love, feed, and pray for our enemies. In the Old Testament, obedience was rewarded with material blessing. In the New Testament, material blessing is often deferred or rejected in order to pursue spiritual blessing.

Requirement of faith: Much New Testament revelation seems opposite of our natural inclinations, and it requires great faith to live a blessed life in New Testament times, just as it did in Old Testament times. It all boils down to the same thing: If we believe God, we obey what he teaches and commands (Galatians 2:20). If we don't believe God, we don't obey. Our disobedience is linked to a lack of faith.

Reward of blessing: In the New Testament, God blesses faithful obedience with the fruit of the Spirit rather than the fruit of the vine. We are given supernatural growth and endurance in the fruit of the Spirit: love, joy, peace, patience, kindness, goodness, faithfulness, gentleness, and self-control (Galatians 5:22–23).

If you ask people what they want out of life, they will typically say that they just want to be happy. The blessing which is promised to the faithful child of God in New Testament times is so much greater than that! The fruit of the Spirit includes lasting inner peace, genuine love, deep joy, etc.

Reproduction of disciples: In the Old Testament, God promised to raise Israel higher than other nations around them by bestowing on them material abundance. In the New Testament, he promises to raise individual Christians higher than the world by bestowing on them spiritual abundance.

The strategy in the Old Testament was that other nations would look at the material abundance of Israel and desire to know God because of his blessings on Israel. The strategy in the New Testament is that other individuals would look at the spiritual abundance of believers and desire to know Jesus because of his blessings on both the individual Christian and the Church.

We see this working in 1 Thessalonians 1:5–7 where Paul wrote:

. . . our gospel did not come to you in word only, but also in power and in the Holy Spirit and with full conviction; just as you know what kind of men we proved to be among you for your sake. You also became imitators of us and of the Lord, having received the word in much tribulation with the joy of the Holy Spirit, so that you became an example to all the believers in Macedonia and in Achaia.

- Paul appealed to the quality of his life (you know what kind of men we proved to be among you).
- The Thessalonians liked what they saw and became imitators of Paul and the Lord (you also became imitators of us and of the Lord).
- This resulted in the Thessalonians taking on the life qualities of Paul and the Lord, and, as a result, becoming an example to others (you became an example to all the believers).

The Thessalonians changed because of Paul's example, becoming in return a change-inspiring example to others. That's the way spiritual blessing is supposed to work. It encourages the reproduction of disciples.

Conclusion

The great challenge, then, for New Testament believers is to cultivate an eternal perspective, living for Christ's invisible Kingdom instead of any visible, earthly kingdom.

We read God's revelation to us, and we obey because we believe; as a result, we are enabled to bear the fruit of the Spirit.

Others, then, desire to know Jesus because of what they see of him in us.

This is God's game plan for us, and when we understand it, it makes it easier for us to deny our natural inclinations in favor of faithful obedience to God's revelation.

REPETITION
Is the Key to Mental Ownership

Chapter Review

1. God's game plan for humanity has four parts.
   - a. Reveal t_____.
   - b. Require f_____.
   - c. Reward o_____.
   - d. Reproduce d_____.
2. God's blessing in the Old Testament was the fruit of the v_____.
3. God's blessing in the New Testament is the fruit of the S_____.

The Christian Life in 1,000 Words—Review

(Only the last ten chapters will be displayed)

If something is important, you must repeat it until it changes you.

4. A Christian is not merely someone who has turned over a new l_____, but, rather, someone who has turned over a new l_____.
5. Spiritual growth is the process of the redeemed inner man gaining increasing m_____ over the unredeemed outer man.
6. For our l_____ to be transformed, our m_____ must be renewed.
7. Spiritual growth requires a balance of G_____ part and o____ part.
8. There are three enemies of the Christian: the w_____, the f_____, and the d_____.
9. A p_____ mind will be spared the d_____ pull of negative input and be released to the u_____ pull of positive input.
10. We must make peace with the difficult fact that God is g_____ and, at the same time, his children s_____.
11. God wants f_____ and l_____ over anything else we might offer him.
12. God will often d_____ us in a manner that seems, initially, to d_____ us.
13. God's blessing in the Old Testament was the "fruit of the v_____"; in the New Testament, it is the "fruit of the S_____."

THOUGHT/DISCUSSION
Is a Key to Understanding

Answer these questions, either individually by journaling the answers or in a small discussion group.

1. Explain what, to you, is the most helpful thing about understanding God's game plan.
2. Explain in your own words what it means that the blessing in the Old Testament was the fruit of the vine.
3. Explain in your own words what it means that the blessing in the New Testament is the fruit of the Spirit.

DECISION TIME
Is a Key to Change

Answer these questions, either individually by journaling the answers or in a spiritual accountability group.

1. The great challenge of cooperating with God in executing his game plan is the necessity of obedience. How prepared are you to believe God in all things?
2. Have the lifestyles of other Christians been a significant encouragement to your Christian life? Do you think your lifestyle is an encouragement to others in their Christian lives? Are there changes you need to make to improve in this area?
3. Would you prefer God's blessings to be the fruit of the vine or the fruit of the Spirit? Since you live in New Testament times, you (of course) do not have this choice, but if you had love, joy, and peace (the first three fruits of the Spirit), would you want anything else? How fully does that motivate you to be obedient to God from the heart in all things?

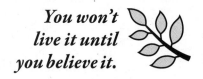

CHAPTER 14

THE PRIMACY OF LOVE

We are all born for *love*. It is the principle
of *existence*, and its only end.[1]
—*Benjamin Disraeli*

 CENTRAL PASSAGE: Matthew 22:37, 39—"You shall love the
Lord your God with all your heart, and with all your soul,
and with all your mind . . . You shall love your neighbor
as yourself."

Benjamin Disraeli, Prime Minister of the United Kingdom in the
mid-19th century, said it well in his novel *Sybil*: "We are all born
for love. It is the principle of existence, and its only end."

Love is, perhaps, the most important force in human existence.
This is because God himself is love and because he created us to love
him and others in return. To the degree that we do this, wonderful
goodness breaks out all over. To the degree that we fail to do this,
terrible evil breaks out all over.

A Christian's mind will never be properly oriented toward reality
until he understands the primacy of love.

1. Divine love is a motivating characteristic, not an emotion.

Divine love is a motivating characteristic, not an e_____.

Having said this, we must understand what love is, and what it is
not. There are four different words for "love" in biblical Greek (the
original language of the New Testament):

1. *Storge'*, which is fondness.
2. *Eros*, which is physical or romantic love.
3. *Phileo*, which is familial and friendship love.
4. *Agape'*, which is divine, sacrificial love.

When we talk about the primacy of love, we are talking about *agape'* love, the sacrificial, divine love.

- When the Bible says that God is love, it is talking about *agape'* (1 John 4:8).
- When the Bible says we are to love God and our neighbor, it is talking about *agape'* (Matthew 22:37–39).
- When the Bible says love is to be a defining characteristic of a Christian, it is talking about *agape'* (John 15:12).

The primary quality of *agape'* is that it gives itself for the welfare of another (all emphases in the following list are mine).

- In John 3:16 we read, "For God so *loved* the world, that He *gave* His only begotten Son."
- In Galatians 2:20 we read, "the life which I now live in the flesh I live by faith in the Son of God, who *loved* me and *gave* Himself up for me."
- In Ephesians 5:2 we read, "walk in love, just as Christ also *loved* you and *gave* himself up for us."
- In Ephesians 5:25 we read, "Husbands, love your wives, just as Christ also *loved* the church and *gave* Himself up for her."

We see in these passages that the primary characteristic of *agape'* love is that it "*gives*" itself for the welfare of another.

2. God is love.

God is l____.

The primary personal attribute of God is that he is "love," and that he loves each of us individually and personally.

While it's true that God is omnipotent, omniscient, and omnipresent, if he were only those three things he might be just an all-powerful, all-knowing, everywhere-present celestial machine . . . like a divine supercomputer.

But that is not what God is like. Over those and all his other characteristics is the umbrella of his love. 1 John 4:8 says, "God is love." So, we conclude from this that love is the motivating attribute of everything God does. "Love" is what he does.

This love, then, is directed toward his creation. John 3:16 says, "For God so loved the world, that He gave His only begotten Son, that whoever believes in Him shall not perish, but have eternal life."

God Loves the World: We see from this that God loves the world. But does that mean that he also loves me personally? God *must* love me, at least in a philosophical sense. But does he love me personally, individually, for who I am?

For example, after a politician wins a smashing political victory, he/she meets with close supporters after the polls have closed, to declare victory. The politician says, "This is a victory for all of us. This could not have happened without you! I love you all!"

And while the politician might "love" everyone there in a philosophical sense, he or she doesn't even know every single individual in the room on a personal level. Is that how God loves us?

God Loves Individuals: As we probe this question more deeply, we see that God loves each of us as an individual.

In Luke chapter 15, Jesus tells the parable of a shepherd who has 100 sheep. He discovers that one of them is missing, so he leaves the 99 and goes searching for the missing sheep until he finds it. Then, when he does find it, he doesn't just haul it back to the rest of the flock. Rather, he puts it on his shoulders, carries it home, and throws a party.

Then Jesus said, "I tell you that in the same way, there will be *more* joy in heaven over one sinner who repents than over ninety-nine righteous persons who need no repentance" (Luke 15:7).

So, from this we conclude two monumental things. First, that if no one else on earth had ever sinned, and I was the first and only one who had sinned, Jesus would have died for me . . . the one lost sheep. Mercy! What a thought! That tells me that my sin put Jesus on the cross, regardless of your sin; it tells me the lengths to which God was prepared to go to demonstrate his love for me, the individual.

This thought is bolstered by Romans 5:8, which says, "But God demonstrates his own love toward us, in that while we were yet sinners, Christ died for us."

The second thing we conclude from this parable is that Jesus cares about each of us personally . . . individually. We each matter to Jesus as individuals, not just as members of a larger group that he cares about. (Try going back and plugging your own name into that verse in place of the words "us," and "we." What an uplifting and affirming thought!)

God's love is also personal and heartfelt. When Jesus finished telling the parable of the lost sheep, he said that there is "more joy in heaven over one sinner who repents . . ." So, his love for me is heartfelt. He felt "joy" over my having been "found."

Also, in Psalm 103:13–14, we read, "Just as a father has compassion on his children, so the LORD has compassion on those who fear Him. For He Himself knows our frame; He is mindful that we are but dust."

Well, if we fear him, he has compassion on us, taking into account our individual weaknesses and imperfections!

God feels joy at our having been found, and feels compassion for our weaknesses. His love for us is heartfelt.

3. Christians are to love God.

C_____ are to love God.

One of the defining characteristics of Christians is that we are meant to reciprocate God's self-giving and love him in return. God's Grand Gesture to us is that he loves us; all he wants from us is to return the Gesture—to love him in return.

Jesus said, "You shall love the Lord your God with all your heart, and with all your soul, and with all your mind. This is the great and foremost commandment" (Matthew 22:37–38).

But one might ask oneself, if love is not an emotion and if God doesn't need anything we might give him, "What does it mean to love God?"

Scripture comes to the rescue in understanding this. Jesus said in John 14:15, "If you love Me, you will keep My commandments."

But it's a little more nuanced than that. For example, the Pharisees in Jesus's time kept the law rigorously. Yet Jesus called them hypocrites. He said, "This people honors Me with their lips, but their heart is far away from Me" (Matthew 15:8). So, it is possible to obey God without loving him.

To that end, Paul spoke of being obedient from the heart (Romans 6:17). That's what God wants. Not cold-hearted obedience. Not obedience with gritted teeth, clenched fists, and squinted eyes. Rather, obedience from the heart.

Hebrews 11:6 helps us further. It says, "Without faith it is impossible to please Him, for he who comes to God must believe that He is and that He is a rewarder of those who seek Him."

This passage tells us that when we trust God, that's what pleases him. God is not pleased with legalistic obedience. But when we trust him, when we believe him, and then when we do what he says based on our confidence in his character, this pleases God. That is what Jesus meant when he said, "If you love Me, you will keep My commandments."

We can keep his commandments without loving him, but we cannot love him without keeping his commandments.

So, obedience from the heart is how we demonstrate our love for God. If this is what governs our overall attitude in our Christian life, we will automatically get many, many of the smaller things right.

4. Christians are to love our neighbors.

Christians are to love our n_____.

After Jesus gave us, in Matthew 22, the greatest commandment to love God, he also gave us the second greatest commandment:

to love our neighbors. "The second is like it, 'You shall love your neighbor as yourself'" (Matthew 22:39).

But again, we might ask ourselves, "What does it mean to love our neighbor as ourselves?"

Unsurprisingly, Scripture again comes to the rescue. After calling people to sincere demonstrations of love in 1 Corinthians 13:4–8, the apostle Paul describes the right heart attitude behind these acts:

> Love is patient, love is kind and is not jealous; love does not brag and is not arrogant, does not act unbecomingly; it does not seek its own, is not provoked, does not take into account a wrong suffered, does not rejoice in unrighteousness, but rejoices with the truth; bears all things, believes all things, hopes all things, endures all things.
>
> Love never fails.

So, if these characteristics govern the hearts of Christians, we will get many, many of the other things in life right.

Conclusion

We began by saying that love is the most important/powerful force in human existence. This is because God is love. He created us in his image to love and be loved. Christians may rest in God's love for them, both collectively and personally, and they are to love God and others in return. To the degree that this happens, wonderful goodness breaks out all over. To the degree that this does not happen, terrible evil breaks out all over.

This all rests on the character of God (God is love—1 John 4:8) and on his unconditional love for us.

Parents have a tender love for their newborn babies. But one might ask, "What has that baby ever done to make her parents love her?" The answer: nothing! In fact, the infant may have already done some things that might—on the face of it—*keep* her parents from loving her: crying uncontrollably, randomly soiling her diapers, and generally being totally self-absorbed and utterly inconsiderate of the inconvenience she was creating.

But the parents love their infant anyway. Why? Because the love comes from the heart of the parents and the worth and dignity they inherently bestow upon her, not from any performance of the child herself.

So it is with God. Love for us comes freely and willingly from the heart of God, not from our performance.

When we begin to grasp that God loves us on a personal level (because of who we are), not merely on a professional level (because we are members of the human race), it helps us love him more fully and more personally in return. It deepens and strengthens our bond with him, ushers us into a more satisfying relationship with him, and enables us to faithfully love others, too, bringing a small taste of heaven to earth.

REPETITION
Is the Key to Mental Ownership

Chapter Review

1. Divine love is a motivating characteristic, not an e_____.
2. God is l_____.
3. C_____ are to love God.
4. Christians are to love our n_____.

The Christian Life in 1,000 Words—Review
(Only the last ten chapters will be displayed)
If something is important, you must repeat it until it changes you.

5. Spiritual growth is the process of the redeemed inner man gaining increasing m_____ over the unredeemed outer man.
6. For our l_____ to be transformed, our m_____ must be renewed.
7. Spiritual growth requires a balance of G_____ part and o____ part.
8. There are three enemies of the Christian: the w_____, the f_____, and the d_____.

9. A p_____ mind will be spared the d_____ pull of negative input and be released to the u_____ pull of positive input.

10. We must make peace with the difficult fact that God is g_____ and, at the same time, his children s_____.

11. God wants f_____ and l_____ over anything else we might offer him.

12. God will often d_____ us in a manner that seems, initially, to d_____ us.

13. God's blessing in the Old Testament was the "fruit of the v_____"; in the New Testament, it is the "fruit of the S_____."

14. We were born for l_____. It is the principle of e_____, and its only end.

 ## THOUGHT/DISCUSSION
Is a Key to Understanding

Answer these questions, either individually by journaling the answers or in a small discussion group.

1. How convinced are you that God loves you personally, individually? Do you take comfort and meaning in this fact?

2. How consistent are you in loving others (in the sense of *agape'* love)? How "in tune" with this concept do you think American culture is? How in tune with this concept are you?

3. Has this chapter changed your understanding of what it means to love God? Describe in your own words what you think it means to love God.

 ## DECISION TIME
Is a Key to Change

Answer these questions, either individually by journaling the answers or in a spiritual accountability group.

1. Do you find it easy to accept God's love for you, or do you struggle with feeling "unlovable"? How does reflecting on your love for others encourage you to accept God's love for you?

2. How consistent are you in loving God? Are there areas of your life that need to change to love him as he desires to be loved?

3. How well does 1 Corinthians 13:4–8 govern your relationships with others? What changes do you think you might need to make in this area?

 **RECOMMENDED**
Resource

The Difficult Doctrine of the Love of God, D. A. Carson

You won't
live it until
you believe it.
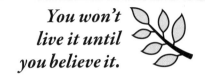

CHAPTER 15

THE NECESSITY OF SELF-DISCIPLINE

To be free to *sail* the seven seas, you must
make yourself a slave to the *compass*.

 CENTRAL PASSAGE: 1 Corinthians 9:27—"I discipline my body
and make it my slave, so that, after I have preached to others,
I myself will not be disqualified."

Someone once said, "In order to be free to sail the seven seas, you must make yourself a slave to the compass."

This is because every freedom has a corresponding bondage, and every bondage has a corresponding freedom. You can be free from the toothbrush and a slave to cavities, or you can be a slave to the toothbrush and free from cavities. But you cannot be free from the toothbrush and free from cavities. That kind of absolute freedom doesn't exist, because all actions have consequences.

So, we must choose our freedoms well, for from them come our bondages; and we must choose our bondages well, for from them come our freedoms.

Clearly seen, then, self-discipline is the key to personal freedom.

Self-discipline is the ability to make oneself do what is right when it would be easier not to. Many of us identify with Oscar Wilde, who famously said through his character Lord Darlington, "I can resist everything but temptation."[1] But temptation needs to be resisted. That's where self-discipline comes in.

Admittedly, it seems backward: discipline = freedom! But much in the Bible seems backward: To save your life, you must lose it. To be first, you must be last. To receive, you must give.

So, it is consistent with the "backwardness" of what we find in the Bible that freedom comes only through self-discipline. This truth is important to everyone for many reasons, but it is especially important to the Christian if we are to become God's best version of ourselves.

The freedom to achieve our greatest potential in life depends on self-discipline. In this context, self-discipline has two facets.

- *Delaying something pleasant*: The ability to delay an immediate gratification for the sake of a greater long-term reward. For example, you might not take a one-week vacation this summer so you can accumulate your vacation days and take a two-week vacation next summer.
- *Enduring something unpleasant*: The ability to endure something unpleasant in the short term for the sake of a greater reward in the long term. For example, you might get up early and exercise now so you can be in shape to hike the Grand Canyon next October.

1. The Bible teaches that we should be self-disciplined.

The Bible teaches that we should be s____-d_____.

- "Do not be deceived, God is not mocked; for whatever a man sows, this he will also reap" (Galatians 6:7).
- "I discipline my body and make it my slave, so that, after I have preached to others, I myself will not be disqualified" (1 Corinthians 9:27).
- "Therefore I urge you, brethren, by the mercies of God, to you present your bodies a living and holy sacrifice, acceptable to God, which is your spiritual service of worship" (Romans 12:1).
- "The fruit of the Spirit is . . . self-control" (Galatians 5:22–23).

These passages tell us that self-discipline is essential for a meaningful, purposeful, and vital Christian life, and that it is a fruit of the Holy Spirit. Not everyone who is self-disciplined is filled with the Spirit, but everyone who is filled with the Spirit is self-disciplined.

2. Self-discipline guards us against disaster.

Self-discipline guards us against d_____.

Proverbs 25:28 declares, "Like a city that is broken into and without walls is a man who has no control over his spirit." If we have no control over our spirit, we are vulnerable to whatever temptations Satan might place in our paths *to sabotage us.*

Matadors know that bulls cannot resist charging a dangling cape. So, to demonstrate their skill and bravery, they dangle the cape in front of the bull knowing it will charge every time. They toy with the bull for a while, and then kill it. Regardless of how you feel about the sport of bullfighting, the parallels to our journey toward self-discipline are striking!

Christians are in a perpetual spiritual war, and if Satan knows that we have no self-discipline against anger, pride, lust, fear, materialism, or alcohol, then all he has to do to sabotage us is to dangle something sufficiently tempting in front of us—like a matador dangling a cape in front of the bull—knowing that we will not resist!

If bulls could expand their thinking to understand what's going on, they might say to themselves, "When my friends charge the cape, bad things happen to them. So, I'm not going to charge the cape this time and see what happens." In doing so, they would save themselves from disaster and discover a new path to freedom and longer life.

If Christians can expand their thinking to understand what's going on, we might say to ourselves, "When I respond to the temptations that Satan puts in front of me, bad things happen. So, I'm not going to respond to those temptations anymore." In doing so, we would save ourselves from painful consequences and also enjoy new breakthroughs of spiritual freedom and abundant life!

3. Self-discipline reaps cause/effect rewards.

Self-discipline reaps c_____/e_____ rewards.

As we saw earlier, the apostle Paul wrote in 1 Corinthians 9:27, "I discipline my body and make it my slave, so that, after I have preached to others, I myself will not be disqualified." We can easily grasp this in the realm of athletics. The more disciplined an athlete is in his training, the faster he can run, the higher he can jump, and the more weight he can lift.

We are often not as quick to recognize this principle in our daily lives. But even in the secular world, self-discipline is being increasingly recognized as the key to life success. Books, magazines, and internet articles/sites are awash with tips on self-discipline and motivational information on the wisdom of being self-disciplined.

> For every disciplined effort, there are multiple rewards. That's one of life's great arrangements. If you sow well, you will reap well. Life is full of laws that both govern and explain behaviors, but the law of sowing and reaping may well be the major law we need to understand: For every disciplined effort, there are multiple rewards.[2]

Yes, self-discipline is a core character issue in life. Self-discipline will keep us from self-inflicted disasters and will enable us to achieve our potential in life.

4. Self-discipline helps us achieve our potential.

Self-discipline helps us achieve our p_____.

There are a couple sayings about self-discipline commonly attributed to two well-known figures. First, breakthrough Olympic gold medalist Jesse Owens remarked, "We all have dreams. But in order to make dreams come into reality, it takes self-discipline."[3]

Next, President Theodore Roosevelt also reinforced this idea when he said, "With self-discipline, most anything is possible."[4]

Most of us would all like to have more self-discipline, but the trick is, "how to get it!"

We began this chapter by looking at what the Scriptures have to say about self-discipline. Self-discipline is a fruit of the Spirit ("the fruit of the Spirit is . . . self-control"—Galatians 5:22–23), but it is also a principle that can be exhorted and nurtured ("Like a city that is broken into and without walls is a man who has no control over his spirit" [Proverbs 25:28]; "I discipline my body and make it my slave . . ." [1 Corinthians 9:27]).

And while everything in the Bible is true, not everything that is true is in the Bible. For Christians who want to take seriously the biblical principle of self-discipline, we will do well to feed our minds with Scripture and nurture our spiritual life, while at the same time accepting Solomon and Paul's instruction and example to be more disciplined as a sensible act of faith and obedience. To this end, we can find information beyond the Bible to help us in our quest.

Here are 5 well-researched and time-tested methods for nurturing self-discipline:

Set a goal and envision the future.

"Don't concentrate on the willpower; concentrate on the 'prize.' The lack of discipline is really a lack of vision."[5] So spoke Rory Vaden, author of the *New York Times* bestseller *Take the Stairs: Seven Steps to Achieving True Success*.

Unless we see clearly where we want to go, we will have no idea what the intermediate steps are to get there, nor will we have the motivation and the discipline to get there. Plus, when the brain has a goal it begins to see information, resources, and opportunities that it didn't see before, moving us toward our goal.

A goal clearly identified and regularly reinforced has a powerful neurological ability to move us toward the goal.

Take appropriate steps toward the goal.

Once we have set the goal in our minds and visualized the change we want, we must then figure out what intermediate steps are needed to reach the goal and achieve the vision.

To do this, there are three sub-steps to take:

- Get help figuring out your plan, if necessary: books, courses, the internet, counselors, friends, etc.
- Set realistic goals. Unrealistic goals guarantee failure. Counselors and friends can help determine if goals are unrealistic.
- Take extreme ownership of the process. This means no excuses for the past. Own up to it. And no excuses for failure in the future. If we try one thing and it doesn't work, we change the plan and try again. If that doesn't work, we change the plan and try again. We don't take "no" for an answer. There is no one else to blame.[6]

Create a supportive environment.

Our environment is a key element of success for building greater self-discipline. As we structure our environment to make it easier to do the right thing (we stock apples and peanut butter in the fridge) and harder to do the wrong thing (we don't stock ice cream in the freezer), then our environment will make it easier to make right choices.

Also, we must be aware that self-discipline is a resource that can be depleted. When we are tired, sick, frustrated, or tempted, we can burn through the reserve of self-discipline we have very quickly and run out. We don't want to *unnecessarily* expose ourselves to things that require self-discipline so that we will not run out of this reserve when we need it.

So, we guard our environment to protect ourselves from tempting or frustrating companions, tempting or frustrating circumstances, tempting or frustrating activities, and tempting or frustrating surroundings.

Now, the reality is that we cannot always protect ourselves from tempting or frustrating things, but when we can we need to do so. And clutter is a major enemy. Research shows that clutter in our surroundings encourages clutter in our minds.

Research shows that creating the optimal environment is more than half the battle in nurturing self-discipline.[7]

Guard the people and places around you.

The people around us have a major effect on us, so we have to be alert to two things:

First, we have to be alert to choose our friends wisely. Our actions are significantly influenced by the people we choose to be around.[8] The Bible, of course, reinforces this idea: "Bad company corrupts good morals" (1 Corinthians 15:33).

Second, we must be alert to choose our locations wisely. Sometimes it's not only the people with whom we surround ourselves, but it's also where we go to be with those people. So, we must also stay away from places that strip us of willpower.

This most likely would include places where we have engaged in negative behavior in the past, as that environment will make it feel more natural to sin once again. If a believer wants to maintain an evangelistic contact with former drinking buddies, for example, the best thing to do would be to meet someplace other than a bar and to include believing friends in the mix to help change up the dynamics and increase accountability.

Then, we may need to get an accountability partner or partners. These might be people who are trying to achieve the same goal we are. Or they might just be helpful individuals who can encourage us along the way. The Bible expands on this idea, saying, "two are better than one," because they can help each other in life's various needs (Ecclesiastes 4:9–12).

Repeat the truth until it changes you.

Finally, and this is a powerful final point, we must renew our minds with repetition of truth and ideas that support self-discipline.

If something is important, it needs to be repeated over and over again. This repetition does two things. First, it creates deep neurological pathways in the brain allowing us to "own" that truth on a conscious level.

Second, it drives that information into the subconscious, where the subconscious links it to other things that we know and where the brain begins to see things it didn't see before. This creates powerful changes in our attitudes, values, and behavior.

Use the power of spiritual resources.

In addition to these 5 "wisdom" principles for increasing our self-discipline, we also look to the Scriptures, the Lord, prayer, and any other biblically permissible and beneficial sources we can find, knowing that all real truth is God's truth:

- Absorb what Scripture has to say about discipline.

  The passages we have referred to previously would be powerful resources to nurture self-discipline. Memorizing these passages, reviewing them daily, and meditating on them have both a neurological and spiritual value. It recognizes the role of the brain while at the same time bringing to bear the power of the Word and the Holy Spirit:
    - "The fruit of the Spirit is love, joy, peace, patience, kindness, goodness, faithfulness, gentleness, self-control" (Galatians 5:22–23).
    - "Like a city that is broken into and without walls is a man who has no control over his spirit" (Proverbs 25:28).
    - "I discipline my body and make it my slave, so that, after I have preached to others, I myself will not be disqualified" (1 Corinthians 9:27).
- Pray for discipline as you work out your salvation (Philippians 2:12–13).
- Engage in general mental-renewal strategies regarding discipline (Romans 12:11–12).
- Nurture Christian friendships that support and reinforce self-discipline goals (Proverbs 13:20).

Attending a strong Bible-teaching church, reading helpful books, listening to helpful audiobooks, attending classes or seminars (either online or in person), watching inspiring movies, spending time in nature, and spending time with enriching friends are all additional things that will take nurturing thoughts through our minds, renewing our minds and transforming our lives.

As we submit our hearts to the Scriptures, to truth, and to the ministry of the Holy Spirit, and as we use wisdom principles to increase our self-discipline, the Lord will build self-discipline, a fruit of the Holy Spirit, into our lives.

Conclusion

Angela Duckworth wrote an acclaimed book entitled *Grit*, in which, after studying success and successful people, she determined that grit was the one characteristic that was common to all successful people. She defined grit as "passion and perseverance for long-term goals."[9]

Yes, self-discipline is widely recognized as an essential ingredient in life success.

Mischa Elman, one of the greatest violinists of the twentieth century, was walking through the streets of New York City one afternoon when a tourist approached him. "Excuse me, sir," the stranger began, "could you tell me how to get to Carnegie Hall?" Elman reportedly sighed deeply and replied, "Practice, practice, practice."[10]

We smile because the tourist was referring to physical directions, whereas Elman was speaking from personal experience and referring to the self-discipline required to perform at Carnegie Hall.

But the principle is a parallel to success in the Christian life—or all of life, really. How do you achieve your greatest potential? "Self-discipline, self-discipline, self-discipline!"

REPETITION
Is the Key to Mental Ownership

Chapter Review

1. The Bible teaches that we should be s_____-d_____.

2. Self-discipline guards us against d_____.

3. Self-discipline reaps c_____/e_____ rewards.

4. Self-discipline helps us achieve our p_____.

The Christian Life in 1,000 Words—Review

(Only the last ten chapters will be displayed)

If something is important, you must repeat it until it changes you.

6. For our l_____ to be transformed, our m_____ must be renewed.

7. Spiritual growth requires a balance of G_____ part and o____ part.

8. There are three enemies of the Christian: the w_____, the f_____, and the d_____.

9. A p_____ mind will be spared the d_____ pull of negative input and be released to the u_____ pull of positive input.

10. We must make peace with the difficult fact that God is g_____ and, at the same time, his children s_____.

11. God wants f_____ and l_____ over anything else we might offer him.

12. God will often d_____ us in a manner that seems, initially, to d_____ us.

13. God's blessing in the Old Testament was the "fruit of the v_____"; in the New Testament, it is the "fruit of the S_____."

14. We were born for l_____. It is the principle of e_____, and its only end.

15. To be free to s_____ the seven seas, we must make ourselves slaves to the c_____.

THOUGHT/DISCUSSION
Is a Key to Understanding

Answer these questions, either individually by journaling the answers or in a small discussion group.

1. How self-disciplined do you think you are? How important to you is the message of this chapter?

2. Describe a time when a lack of self-discipline brought significant pain into your life.

3. Describe a time when strong self-discipline brought significant good into your life.

DECISION TIME
Is a Key to Change

Answer these questions, either individually by journaling the answers or in a spiritual accountability group.

1. In what area of your life do you most need self-discipline? What will you do to improve in that area? What goal can you set to begin your improvement?

2. Do your friends and environment encourage or discourage self-discipline? What changes might you need to make in those areas?

3. What is the most important Bible verse for you regarding self-discipline? Commit to memorizing it deeply.

RECOMMENDED
Resource

Extreme Ownership, Jocko Willink

You won't live it until you believe it.

CHAPTER 16

THE SUBTLE POWER OF HUMILITY

We grow *up* into Christ by growing *down* into lowliness (humility). Christians . . . grow greater by getting smaller.[1]
—J. I. Packer

 CENTRAL PASSAGE: 1 Peter 5:5—"God is opposed to the proud, but gives grace to the humble."

Pride . . . is the mother of *all* sins," wrote C. S. Lewis.[2]
He did not mean merely that a superior and arrogant attitude was the source of all other sins. Rather, he meant that self—self-protection, self-fulfillment, and self-advancement—is the source of all other sins.

Scripture teaches that God opposes the proud but gives grace to the humble (1 Peter 5:5), validating humility and condemning pride. Humility is not seeing oneself as a human worm or social doormat, worth less than everyone else. Rather, true humility means, simply, seeing ourselves as God sees us. Each person has inherent and infinite value, but possesses no greater value than anyone else. And, as someone once said, this truth elevates us without inflating us and humbles us without debasing us.

It is bad theology to be prideful for these reasons:

- We have no greater value than anyone else (Acts 10:34).
- We have nothing but what God has given us (1 Corinthians 4:7).

- We can do nothing without Christ (John 15:5).
- We have no adequacy in ourselves, but only in God (2 Corinthians 3:5).

So, to be prideful is bad theology. Humility—seeing ourselves as God sees us, no more and no less—is the proper perspective. With this perspective, we will love God with all our hearts, souls, and minds, and our neighbors as ourselves.

The power of humility plays itself out in four key ways in life:

- Humility generates reciprocal submission.
- Humility generates repentance.
- Humility generates forgiveness.
- Humility generates true wisdom.

1. Humility generates reciprocal submission.

Humility generates r_____ s_____.

We naturally long for fulfillment in our personal relationships, and may be tempted to think that we can take what we want from a relationship. But we can't. God's way is that we must give to the relationship for the other person's sake, and then wait to see what we get back. Sometimes, when we grow most like Christ, the payback may be nothing, at least in this life.

If we could "get" by "taking," it would allow us to victimize others and come away satisfied and fulfilled, creating a world of happy predators. But, since we can only sustainably "get" from a relationship by "giving" to it, we are led to pursue unity and harmony in relationships, mirroring relationships within the Trinity.

This is the principle of "reciprocal submission," which the apostle Paul presents in Ephesians 5:21: "Be subject to one another in the fear of Christ." He then goes on in Ephesians 5–6 to describe reciprocal submission in three key relationships:

- husband/wife

- parent/child
- master/slave

In each of these three relationships, there is a clear authority and a clear subordinate. In the husband/wife relationship, the husband is the authority and the wife is the subordinate. In parent/child relationships, the parent is the authority and the child is the subordinate. In the master/slave relationship, the master is the authority and the slave is the subordinate.

50/50 relationships don't work. Eventually, the parties will come to an impasse that must be resolved. Neither do relationships work in which the dominant one abuses his or her authority, or in which the subordinate one rebels. The only relationships that work are those in which one is called to exercise godly authority out of selfless love and one is called to submit out of selfless love; each one must treat the other in the way he or she would want to be treated if the roles were reversed.

Husband/Wife Relationships

In husband/wife relationships, Ephesians 5:25 tells us that husbands are to submit to the needs of their wives by loving them as Christ loved the church and gave himself up for her. The authority of the husband is not the authority to abuse or dominate. Quite to the contrary, the husband is instructed to give himself up for the welfare of his wife. Ephesians 5:33 tells us that, in response, the wife is to respect her husband. Of course, there is nothing in Scripture to suggest that wives should check out and put all blame or responsibility on the husband. The Golden Rule ("Treat others the same way you want them to treat you," Luke 6:31) suggests that the wife should support and honor the relationship, contributing helpfully to it, while respecting and supporting the husband's spiritual leadership. Neither party can do their part without sacrificing self for the sake of the other.

Parent/Child Relationships

The same principle is true in parent/child relationships. Parents are to love their children and give them the nurture of the Lord.

Ephesians 6:4 tells us that parents are not to "provoke your children to anger; but bring them up in the discipline and instruction of the Lord." In return, Ephesians 6:1 instructs children to give their parents obedience.

Of course, this does not mean parents are not to discipline their children. Hebrews 12:5–11 makes it clear that good parents discipline their children for the purpose of godliness. But parents are, in the process, to respect their children. In the spirit of reciprocal submission, they should treat them the way they would want to be treated if the roles were reversed. Similarly, this does not mean that children will always find it easy to obey their parents or that their parents won't make mistakes; neither can children obey their parents in circumstances where it means disobeying Scripture. But children are, in the process of growing up, to honor their parents and willingly obey them as a way of growing in their ability to obey and honor God.

Master/Slave Relationships

Master/slave relationships in the New Testament Scriptures give us the principles that should govern employer/employee relationships, the primary place of application today.

The master is to give his slave justice and fairness, while the slave is to serve the Lord by serving his master. Of course, employees are not slaves, and in today's culture, an employee likely has the option of quitting. But the point of the principle is that as long as the employee chooses to work in a given situation, the employee should govern his service by these principles.

If these principles are observed by both parties, the workplace is harmonious and satisfying, usually becoming successful. If these principles are not observed, the workplace is contentious and often not successful.

Summary

Much damage is done by those who either distort and twist their biblical role on the one hand, or simply refuse to play it on the other; however, we cannot go into this. It lies outside the possible scope of this book. The desire in this book is simply to identify how God created relationships and intends them to work. We must start there.

When the one in authority is humble toward others (seeing everyone as God sees them), he/she will give him/herself to the welfare of those under his/her care. Those in submission to such individuals typically have little trouble playing their role of respect and response, which fosters harmony. That is how it's supposed to work.

2. Humility generates repentance.

Humility generates r_____.

The second way the power of humility plays itself out is in the power of repentance. Like reciprocal submission, repentance is not easy. "I was wrong. Please forgive me," is something that many find very difficult to say to God and almost impossible to say to others. Yet these are six of the most powerful words in the human language.

Repentance is necessary to keep our relationships with God and others whole and healthy.

- First, Scripture teaches us to repent in order to maintain our relationship with God. First John 1:9 says, "If we confess our sins, He is faithful and righteous to forgive us our sins and to cleanse us from all unrighteousness." When we repent, we restore our fellowship on a vertical level with God.
- Second, Scripture also teaches we must repent in order to maintain our relationships with others. In Luke 17:3, we see that when we repent it opens the door for the restoration of fellowship on a horizontal level.

There is no "undo" button for life. But when we sin against God or others, we can repent, and we can say those golden and healing words, "I was wrong. Please forgive me."

Being right with God and others is not a matter of never sinning. If it were, we would all be sunk. Rather, being right with God and others is a matter of ready repentance whenever we do sin.

3. Humility generates forgiveness.

*Humility generates f*_____.

The third way the power of humility plays itself out is in the power of forgiveness. Forgiveness is essential to sustaining relationships, because sooner or later the other person will do something that you must either forgive or the relationship will be broken.

We Must Forgive for Three Reasons
To Maintain Our Relationship with the Lord

Matthew 6:14–15 says, "For if you forgive others for their transgressions, your heavenly Father will also forgive you. But if you do not forgive others, then your Father will not forgive your transgressions." This does not mean that if we do not forgive others, we will not go to heaven (Ephesians 2:8–9; Titus 3:5). Rather, this means that our fellowship with God will be broken and hypocritical until we repent and forgive others who wronged us.

To Maintain Our Relationships with Others

We must forgive to restore relationships with others. Ephesians 4:32 says, "Be kind to one another, tender-hearted, forgiving each other, just as God in Christ also has forgiven you."

To Keep from Ruining Ourselves

We must forgive to keep from destroying ourselves. In Ephesians 4:26–27 we read: "Be angry, and yet do not sin; do not let the sun go down on your anger, and do not give the devil an opportunity." This teaches that if we do not forgive, we give the devil an opportunity to gain a spiritual warfare advantage in our lives.

The only way we can keep anger and other damaging sins from consuming us is to forgive.

Two Aspects of Forgiveness

Forgiveness involves relinquishing the right for revenge (Matthew 18). This does not mean, however, that fellowship is necessarily restored (especially in cases when there is real danger of ongoing abuse or harm) or that all consequences of the sin are removed when we forgive. We are called to forgive others unconditionally here on earth, but some of the relationships involved may never be reconciled or restored on this side of heaven.

There are two aspects to the Bible's teaching on forgiveness:

1. **In one place, the Bible teaches that we must forgive, with no conditions.** Matthew 6:14–15 says that we are to forgive, period. And it warns us that if we do not forgive others, our heavenly Father will not forgive us.

2. **In another place, the Bible teaches that we forgive with conditions.** Luke 17:3 says, however, "Be on your guard! If your brother sins, rebuke him; and if he repents, forgive him." *If* he repents?!? This teaches that we may, under certain circumstances, hold the offender accountable for his actions (we rebuke him), and only restore the relationship if he repents.

How do we harmonize these two passages? Forgiveness in Matthew 6 refers to giving up the right to exact revenge, while the Luke 17:3 passage refers to re-establishing fellowship. So, we can reconcile the passages by observing that we are to give up the right to revenge in all instances . . . we are to pardon. However, the steps of re-establishing fellowship (reconciliation and restoration) may be influenced by whether or not the other person repents.

Nevertheless, it seems that the times when Luke 17 would kick in would be rare and involve a rather serious issue because of Colossians 3:12–14, which says:

So, as those who have been chosen of God, holy and beloved, put on a heart of compassion, kindness, humility, gentleness and patience; bearing with one another, and forgiving each other, whoever has a complaint against anyone; just as the Lord forgave you, so also should you. Beyond all these things put on love, which is the perfect bond of unity.

This passage seems to suggest that normal things would simply be overlooked—forgiven. But there is apparently a level of severity at which the principle of Luke 17:3 kicks in and *fellowship* is not restored unless the offending party repents.

A final principle is that we are to "love [our] enemies and pray for those who persecute [us]" (Matthew 5:44). So, even if our forgiveness does not restore fellowship (because the offense is so great and the other person does not repent), we are still to respond in love toward our offenders whether or not they repent.

Here are the basic biblical principles to guide our lives:

1. We always forgive, in terms of giving up our resentment and desire for revenge (Matthew 6:14).
2. Fellowship may not be restored even if you do forgive another, as in the case of an egregious sin for which the other person does not repent or ask forgiveness (Luke 17:3; Matthew 18:15–20).
3. We are always to respond in love to our offender, whether or not he repents (Matthew 5:44).

In addition, experience suggests that forgiveness is sometimes a process. That is, we forgive as an exercise of our will; but the memory of the offense sometimes comes back, causing us to embrace the injury again and forcing us to either forgive again or reiterate our initial act of forgiveness.

4. Humility generates true wisdom.

Humility generates true w_____.

A fourth power of humility is the capacity for wisdom. James 3:14–17 says,

If you have bitter jealousy and selfish ambition in your heart, do not be arrogant and so lie against the truth. This wisdom is not that which comes down from above, but is earthly, natural, demonic. For where jealousy and selfish ambition exist, there is disorder and every evil thing. But the wisdom from above is first pure, then peaceable, gentle, reasonable, full of mercy and good fruits, unwavering, without hypocrisy.

This passage tells us that if we are prideful (selfish ambition), the wisdom produced by that pride is earthly, natural, and demonic.

On the other hand, humility can produce true wisdom, which is pure, peaceable, gentle, reasonable, full of mercy and good fruits, unwavering, and without hypocrisy.

This should be a stark warning to Christians that we must be wary of self-will in others, especially in ministry leaders. It leads to false wisdom that is destructive to all relationships and endeavors, whether in the home, the workplace, or ministry.

It should go without saying that it should also be a warning to us. We must be on guard against our own self-will. It generates wisdom that produces "disorder and every evil thing" (James 3:16).

Conclusion

There is great power in humility. It can lead to better relationships (reciprocal submission), greater integrity (repentance), greater freedom (forgiveness), and greater wisdom. The opposite is also true. Pride leads to broken relationships, loss of integrity, bondage to negative emotions, and destructive "wisdom."

Considering the benefits of humility and the damage of pride, it only makes sense that Christians would commit themselves to cultivating humility and suppressing pride.

REPETITION
Is the Key to Mental Ownership

Chapter Review

1. Humility generates r_____ s_____.
    a. H_____/w_____ relationships
    b. P_____/c_____ relationships
    c. M_____/s_____ relationships

2. Humility generates r_____.
3. Humility generates f_____.
4. Humility generates true _____.

The Christian Life in 1,000 Words—Review

(Only the last ten chapters will be displayed)

If something is important, you must repeat it until it changes you.

7. Spiritual growth requires a balance of G_____ part and o____ part.
8. There are three enemies of the Christian: the w_____, the f_____, and the d_____.
9. A p_____ mind will be spared the d_____ pull of negative input and be released to the u_____ pull of positive input.
10. We must make peace with the difficult fact that God is g_____ and, at the same time, his children s_____.
11. God wants f_____ and l_____ over anything else we might offer him.
12. God will often d_____ us in a manner that seems, initially, to d_____ us.
13. God's blessing in the Old Testament was the "fruit of the v_____"; in the New Testament, it is the "fruit of the S_____."
14. We were born for l_____. It is the principle of e_____, and its only end.
15. To be free to s_____ the seven seas, we must make ourselves slaves to the c_____.
16. In the Christian life, we r_____ by d_____.

THOUGHT/DISCUSSION
Is a Key to Understanding

Answer these questions, either individually by journaling the answers or in a small discussion group.

1. Do you think you have a balanced understanding of humility? Does this chapter's definition of humility change your perception of it?

2. Describe a positive example of reciprocal submission that you have seen.

3. Which is harder for you—repentance or forgiveness?

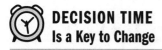

DECISION TIME
Is a Key to Change

Answer these questions, either individually by journaling the answers or in a spiritual accountability group.

1. How helpful do you think you are in your reciprocal submission relationships? Do you play your role well? Are there changes you need to make?

2. Are there things of which you need to repent in your relationships with others? Do you need to let them know?

3. Are there people you need to forgive? Will you forgive them? What has been holding you back?

RECOMMENDED
Resource

A Gentle Answer, Scott Sauls

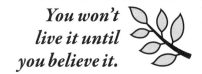

*You won't
live it until
you believe it.*

CHAPTER 17

THE MYSTERY OF PRAYER

[When we pray,] God will either give us what we ask or give us
what we would have asked if we *knew* everything he *knew*.[1]
—*Timothy Keller*

 CENTRAL PASSAGE: Philippians 4:6—"Be anxious for nothing,
but in everything by prayer and supplication with thanksgiving let your requests be made known to God."

Prayer can be a mystery. We pray for something, and don't get it.
We pray not to get something, and we do get it. We get something
good we didn't even pray about. The Bible says, "ask and you will
receive." But we have all asked for things we didn't receive. So, is the
Bible true? Is that promise real? Many Christians wish they understood prayer better.

Because this is not a book on prayer, we will have to stick with the
bare essentials of what we can know and understand about prayer.
After reading this chapter there will still be many things we don't
understand about prayer, but this will be a good foundation for gaining a better understanding down the road.

1. God is not a cosmic vending machine.

God is not a cosmic v_____ m_____.

God is not a cosmic vending machine: prayer in, answer out. He
is not a genie in the bottle: rub the bottle and get three wishes. He
is not a magician: "Alakazam!" and you've got what you want.

In fact, prayer is not really about getting what you want. Matthew 6:8 says, "Your Father knows what you need before you ask."

So, what is prayer about? In his book *Prayer: Does It Make Any Difference?*, Philip Yancey writes, "God wants to relate to [us] personally, to love and be loved."[2]

That is the point of prayer. God is a person, and he wants to have a personal relationship with us based on love. Just as parents do not want to be viewed as vending machines by their children, just as parents love their children and want a relationship with them, and just as parents want that relationship to grow from infancy to adulthood, so does God.

Prayer, at the core, is about the development of a relationship with God. The purpose of prayer is the cultivation of a love-based relationship between us and God, in which we make occasional requests of God and God makes occasional requests of us, both looking, as James Packer has said, for each to give the other his best.

Having said that, there are some biblical principles that guide us in our prayer.

God wants us to pray.

Philippians 4:6 says, "Be anxious for nothing, but in everything by prayer and supplication with thanksgiving let your requests be made known to God."

God w_____ us to pray.

God will answer some prayers.

1 John 5:14 says that if we ask anything according to his will, he hears us.

God will answer s_____ prayers.

God will not answer all prayers.

God doesn't answer prayers if . . .

- We ask with wrong motives (James 4:3).
- We willingly tolerate sin (Psalm 66:18).
- If a husband treats a wife badly (1 Peter 3:7).
- If we doubt God (James 1:5–6).
- If we reject God's Word (Proverbs 28:9).

In addition, some prayers go unanswered simply because they are trite or frivolous; others, because the prayer requests of multiple, sincere Christians would contradict each other. One Christian headed to a picnic prays for sunshine on a Sunday afternoon, and a farmer prays for rain. How would God answer both? Still other prayers may be answered, but on a timeline we don't get to know about and which may extend beyond our lifetimes. Other unanswered prayers are simply a mystery. We may never know why they were not answered.

God will n____ answer all prayers.

By definition, God cannot answer prayers that never get prayed.

So, knowing that God wants us to pray, knowing that he will answer some prayers, we pray. Not to pray at all would mean that no prayers would be answered.

The bottom line is that we must trust the character of God enough to pray either way: If he is who he says he is, all-powerful and all-good, and if he is our loving heavenly Father, we must trust him for whatever the answers are or are not. While God delights to give us good things, he requires that we view reality from his perspective and that we serve him rather than his serving us. Regardless of what we might get in response, we are to honor God by bringing our requests to him and trusting his wisdom.

By definition, God cannot answer prayers that n_____ get prayed.

2. We pray to enter a partnership with God.

We pray to enter a p_____ with God.

Again, in his book *Prayer*, Philip Yancey writes, "I understand prayer as partnership, a subtle interplay of human and divine that accomplishes God's work on earth."[3]

Prayer gives us the dignity of causality.

C. S. Lewis wrote, "'God,' said Pascal, 'instituted prayer in order to lend to His creatures the dignity of causality.' But not only prayer; whenever we act at all He lends us that dignity. It is not really stranger, nor less strange, that my prayers should affect the course of events than that my other actions should do so."[4]

This means that God honors us by allowing us to cause things to happen through prayer that otherwise may not have happened. Sometimes, we may see the answers to our prayers, while at other times we have no way of knowing (if we are praying for persecuted Christians on the other side of the globe, for example), but we can imagine the possibility of getting to heaven and hearing a litany of things that happened on earth because we prayed.

Prayer gives us the d_____ of c_____.

God allows us to partner with him in the Creation Mandate and the Great Commission.

Two overriding biblical charges to God's people in Scripture are the Creation Mandate and the Great Commission.

In the Creation Mandate, humans are to responsibly govern the created world according to God's intended design (Genesis 1:28). We are to oversee creation as God would and on his behalf. In the Great Commission, we are to take the message of the Gospel to the entire world (Matthew 28:18–20).

In the pursuit of these two charges, also, God gives us through prayer the dignity of causality, allowing us to cause things to happen that might not otherwise have happened if we had not prayed.

God allows us to partner with him in the C_____
M_____ and the G_____ C_____.

God nurtures us spiritually through prayer.

Revelation 3:20 says, "I stand at the door and knock; if anyone hears My voice and opens the door, I will come in to him and will dine with him, and he with Me."

This is an invitation to fellowship and communion with Christ through prayer. Prayer—though it is often draining, frustrating, and even an agony at times—is, in the long term, a powerful force for personal transformation, as God requires a reorientation of our priorities and values if prayer is to make any ultimate sense.

To reorder our lives means that we put God higher than anything we want from him. Thus, if he doesn't grant our request, we are not devastated because we still have him, and he is the most important thing.

Therefore, if we accurately assess all our petitions as we pray, we may find that the greatest need is for us to change our perspective. In this way, God uses prayer to transform our lives to a perspective that allows us the deepest level of fellowship with him and, therefore, our highest satisfaction.

God n_____ us spiritually through prayer.

Finally, God wants to change our perspective.

If our prayers were always answered easily, this would make us arrogant and entitled, like a spoiled child who gets everything he wants. By delaying answers to prayer, God . . .

- purifies our motives, helping us not pray foolishly or selfishly.
- clarifies our requests, so that our prayers are not so general that we wouldn't recognize an answer if we got it.
- highlights the fact that, when we do get an answer, it was God who answered and not just a stroke of good luck.
- saves us from the arrogance and ingratitude of a too-easy life.

Finally, God wants to change our p_____.

3. God invites us to hammer on heaven's door.

God invites us to h_____ on heaven's door.

Jesus prayed, in the Garden of Gethsemane, "O My Father, if it is possible, let this cup pass from Me." But he followed this with, "Not as I will, but as You will" (Matthew 26:39 NKJV). In the end, that is always the final perspective on prayer: God's will be done.

Having said this, there are two parables in the Gospels in which God invites us to hammer on heaven's door for the things we want.

- A man who hammers on his neighbor's door asking for bread to serve an unexpected guest. The neighbor acquiesces when the neighbor does not stop knocking (Luke 11:5–8).
- A woman who visits a judge repeatedly asking for legal protection. The judge agrees, fearing that if he doesn't she will wear him out (Luke 18:1–5).

Jesus taught this parable "to show that at all times they ought to pray and not to lose heart" (Luke 18:1).

But why would God invite us to importune him for the things we want?

- Do we have to wear him down?
- Do we have to inform him of things he might not know?
- Do we have to prove our devotion by this form of self-flagellation?

None of these things can be true! As we saw earlier, God wants to change us, and can use persistent praying to help. As we saw, through persistent prayer God . . .

- gives us the dignity of causality.
- allows us to partner with him in the Creation Mandate and the Great Commission.

- matures us spiritually.
- changes our perspective.

There is a final reason for God's inviting us to pray persistently to him:

4. God wants us to work with him in the family business.

God wants us to work with him in the f_____ b_____.

Imagine an earthly parent who owns a large and thriving business, who then brings a son and daughter into the family business to learn it from the ground up.

Perhaps this parent has the children sweep the factory floor, then learn to make widgets. Next, they learn shipping and receiving, followed by customer service. Finally, they are brought into the front office where they learn accounting, marketing, management, and leadership.

The goal is to equip the children to run the family business, not merely for financial reasons but, also, because of the joy of working with them and fostering the closest possible mutual destiny with them. It is often the highest aspiration of a business-owning parent.

In the same way, God wants us to learn his "family business." As his children, he grooms us for the position in which we can make the highest contribution to his Kingdom. As a result, when things do not come easily for us, when our prayers are not quickly and easily answered, or when God is "slow" to deliver us from a hard situation, we can come to God and hammer on his door for insight, for answers, and for strength.

Unless we know for certain that he has turned our request down, we are free to hammer on the door, believing that the hammering process will enable us to get to know him better, serve him more effectively, and more fully enjoy the pleasure of our mutual destiny with him.

5. Prayer can follow biblical examples.

Prayer can follow biblical e_____.

There is no one way that we should pray. There is no formula. There are no success principles. Prayer is simply a matter of us talking to our heavenly Father. Nevertheless, we can look to Scripture to see some of the characteristics of biblical prayers and use these to guide us in our own prayers.

Of course we have the example of the Lord's Prayer in Matthew 6, but this should not be understood as a prescription for how to pray at all times. Even Jesus didn't exclusively follow this exact pattern in his recorded prayers.

I have read many different, catchy headings for prayer, and, frankly, have found them helpful because they are so memorable. There are several different similar examples of this that can be found, but here is a list I created that I find helpful:

- Wow
- Sorry
- Help me
- Help them
- Can we talk?
- Thanks

Wow

This is a catchy word to summarize the idea of praise and adoration in prayer. We can begin by praising God for who he is and by expressing our appreciation for his character and his works. In the Lord's Prayer, Jesus said, "Our father who art in heaven, hallowed be thy name" (Matthew 6:9 KJV).

Sorry

This word summarizes the idea of confession, of repentance, and of getting anything out of the way that might be interfering in our relationship with the Lord. In the Lord's Prayer, Jesus said, "Forgive us our debts as we also have forgiven our debtors."

Help Me

This prayer summarizes the freedom we have to ask the Lord to meet our needs. In the Lord's Prayer, Jesus said, "give us this day our daily bread" (Matthew 6:11). Bread was a symbol for all our daily needs.

Help Them

This is the same idea, except we pray for others rather than ourselves.

Can We Talk?

This word captures the idea of simply talking with God. Of expressing to him whatever is on our mind. We might even imagine him as sitting across the table from us—and, as we imagine what it would be like if we could see his presence in that way, we talk to him about whatever is on our minds.

Thanks

Gratitude is a cardinal virtue, and thanking God for his love, his character, and his work of grace in our lives is an excellent way to end a time of prayer.

Again, there is no formula for prayer. The shortest prayer in the Bible is, "Lord, save me!" (Matthew 14:30). Recorded prayers in the Bible typically don't follow every element in this six-part classification; however, these categories are found in various prayers in the Bible and can help lead us into a balanced time of prayer with God when generally followed.

Conclusion

Much about prayer dissolves into mystery. We don't get good things we prayed for. We get bad things we prayed not to get. We get good things we didn't even pray for. It often does not seem to make any sense.

But as we deepen our understanding of prayer, we see that the issue with prayer is that we are cultivating a relationship with him as a basis for asking things from him. Prayer is much more than just asking, just as conversation with a parent is more than a child just asking the parent for things. As we look to him as a heavenly Father instead of as a celestial vending machine, prayer can become a vehicle for getting to know him better, serving him more effectively, and loving him more completely.

REPETITION
Is the Key to Mental Ownership

Chapter Review

1. God is not a cosmic v_____ m_____.
   a. God w_____ us to pray.
   b. God will answer s_____ prayers.
   c. God will n____ answer all prayers.
   d. By definition, God cannot answer prayers that n_____ get prayed.
2. We pray to enter a p_____ with God.
   a. Prayer gives us the d_____ of c_____.
   b. Prayer allows us to p_____ with God in the Creation Mandate and the Great Commission.
   c. God n_____ us spiritually through prayer.
   d. God changes our p_____ through prayer.
3. God invites us to h_____ on heaven's door.
4. God wants us to work with him in the f_____ b_____.
5. Prayer can follow biblical e_____.
   a. W____
   b. S_____
   c. Help m__
   d. Help t_____
   e. Can we t_____?
   f. T_____

The Christian Life in 1,000 Words—Review

(Only the last ten chapters will be displayed)

If something is important, you must repeat it until it changes you.

8. There are three enemies of the Christian: the w_________, the f_______, and the d_______.
9. A p___________ mind will be spared the d____________ pull of negative input and be released to the u______ pull of positive input.
10. We must make peace with the difficult fact that God is g_____ and, at the same time, his children s_________.
11. God wants f_________ and l_____ over anything else we might offer him.
12. God will often d__________ us in a manner that seems, initially, to d__________ us.
13. God's blessing in the Old Testament was the "fruit of the v_____"; in the New Testament, it is the "fruit of the S_________."
14. We were born for l_____. It is the principle of e______________, and its only end.
15. To be free to s_____ the seven seas, we must make ourselves slaves to the c___________.
16. In the Christian life, we r_____ by d_______________.
17. When we pray, God will either give us what we ask or give us what we would have asked if we k_____ everything he k_____.

THOUGHT/DISCUSSION
Is a Key to Understanding

Answer these questions, either individually by journaling the answers or in a small discussion group.

1. How well do you think you understand the biblical principles of prayer? Were there things in this chapter that surprised you or that you didn't know before?
2. Have you struggled in the past with prayer? What do you think is the most helpful thing in this chapter to aid your prayer life?
3. Which is the most helpful to you of the ways we enter into partnership with God?

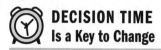

DECISION TIME
Is a Key to Change

Answer these questions, either individually by journaling the answers or in a spiritual accountability group.

1. Have you been guilty of viewing God as a celestial vending machine in the past? How comfortable are you with the idea of leaving it up to God to determine whether or not you get an answer to prayer?
2. Are there things in your life that are higher than God, and that make it difficult for you to sincerely tell God "your will be done"?
3. Does it appeal to you to help God run the family business? What ministry would you like to be able to do for/with God if you could?

RECOMMENDED
Resources

Before Amen, Max Lucado
Prayer: Does It Make Any Difference?, Philip Yancey
Prayer: Experiencing Awe and Intimacy with God, Timothy Keller

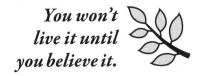

*You won't
live it until
you believe it.*

CHAPTER 18

THE POWER OF TRUST AND OBEDIENCE

If we believe, we obey. If we do not *obey*,
it is because we do not *believe*.

 CENTRAL PASSAGE: Hebrews 11:6—"Without faith it is impossible to please Him, for he who comes to God must believe that He is and that He is a rewarder of those who seek Him."

W hat we believe has a powerful impact on us. In fact, it is everything. We always act consistently with what we believe. Therefore, one of the great challenges of life is to be sure that what we believe is true.

It is not unusual for impressionable young boys to believe they can fly, especially after seeing a movie about Superman or another superhero. More than one youngster has climbed up into a tree with a sheet tied around his neck only to end up with a fat lip when he jumped.

It is not enough merely to believe something. What you believe must be true.

1. Faith is an all-powerful force.

Faith is an a____-p_____ force.

If we truly believe something is true, we act on that belief. If we don't, we don't act.

This is a powerful lesson for the Christian life, because it strips away all the confusion and brings us face to face with reality. If we do not obey God, it is because we do not believe him. And if we partially believe him, we partially obey him.

The governing principle is this: in everything God asks of us, he does so to give something good to us or to keep some harm from us. Therefore, the shortest distance between us and the life we long for is total obedience to God.

This can be an extremely helpful principle to realize, because with it in clear view we can go to work on our faith instead of going to work on our obedience.

We will not win the battle of obedience simply by hunkering down and trying to be more obedient. We must become convinced that happiness in God is superior to any happiness apart from God. When we become this convinced, obedience follows. And why not? It's the pathway to the happiness we long for in life.

2. Unbelief started with Adam and Eve.

U_____ started with Adam and Eve.

Faith is the main thing in the Christian life. Scripture says:

- "Without faith it is impossible to please Him, for he who comes to God must believe that He is and that He is a rewarder of those who seek Him" (Hebrews 11:6).
- "The righteous man shall live by faith" (Romans 1:17).
- "We walk by faith, not by sight" (2 Corinthians 5:7).

Faith is demonstrated in two ways:

1. Obeying God when there is something to <u>do</u> (e.g., *loving your neighbor as yourself*).
2. Resting in God when there is nothing to actually do, but there is something to <u>believe</u> (*my God will supply all your needs according to his riches in glory in Christ Jesus* [Philippians 4:19]).

We may know this, but at the same time there is often a gap between knowing it and complying with it. Incomplete obedience and incomplete peace are indications of this gap.

So why do we fall short in our faith in God? Going back to Adam and Eve, we tend to hold back from complete *obedience* and *resting* in God because *we are unsure of God's readiness to meet our needs.* So, instead, we try to make up the difference with self-effort.

This is the universal problem for all of God's children, seen first in the Garden of Eden in Genesis 3:

Step #1—Doubt: Satan came along and asked Eve, "Indeed, has God said, 'You shall not eat from any tree of the garden?'" (v. 1). His goal was to plant doubt in Eve's mind that God had her best interests at heart. He said that if she ate from the forbidden tree, "You surely will not die! For God knows that in the day you eat from it your eyes will be opened, and you will be like God . . ." (vv. 4–5).

Step #2—Take control: Eve took the bait. She accepted the insinuation that God did not have her full and best interests in mind. So, she decided she needed to take control of her own destiny. Eve ate the fruit, then gave it to Adam, and he ate.

Step #3—Pay the price: We cannot break the laws of God. We can only break ourselves against them when we violate them. So, Adam and Eve paid the price for their lack of faith, with horrific consequences following their decision.

In retrospect, we might be tempted to wonder how Adam and Eve could be so gullible. Yet this is the same pattern of deception that Satan uses with all of us, and we often fall for it just as Adam and Eve did. It is doubtful that they were any more gullible than we. After all, we have the teachings of Scripture and their example, and *still* fall for it.

1. We doubt that God really knows what we need to be happy.

2. We conclude that if we are going to be happy, we will have to take control of our own lives.

3. When we take control, we suffer the consequences.

Having inherited Adam and Eve's tendency toward doubt and self-protection in our own responses to God, we often struggle with five common problems in our efforts to live by faith. Understanding this gives us a foundation for correcting these problems. So, let's go to work on our faith, not our obedience.

3. There are five factors that erode our faith.

There are five factors that e_____ our faith.

Ignorance

Jesus said, "you will know the truth, and the truth will make you free" (John 8:32). Knowledge isn't everything, but everything rests on knowledge. To the degree that we do not know the truth, we are vulnerable to ignorance and deception. We cannot do something until we know or understand it. If we do not have a mature understanding of God's truth, it limits our capacity to live by faith.

I_____

Difficulty

It is easier to drift than to sail. It is easier to relax than to work. There is a natural tendency to want to take the easy way out. The hitch, of course, is that—in the end—drifting and relaxing are not the easy way out. They appear to be the easy way out at first, but down the road there's always a greater price to pay. Diligence is harder up front but easier down the road. Drifting and relaxing are easier up front but harder down the road.

D_____

Fear of the Unknown

We naturally fear the unknown. As Shakespeare said through Hamlet, "[We'd] rather bear those ills we have than fly to others that we know not of."[1] We wonder, what would God do to us if we gave ourselves over to doing whatever he might ask of us? Would he send us to some dreadful corner of the world to live a life of misery and deprivation? Would he afflict us with some dreadful malady? Would he make us into monks, missionaries, or misfits?

Fear of the u_____

Fear of the Known

It may not be a fear of the unknown, but of the *known* that holds back our faith. We might actually *know* that if we give ourselves fully to God, we would have to surrender something that we currently hold dear. It might be a moral issue, it might be an addiction, or it might be misplaced priorities—regardless, we don't want to give up the illusion of control.

Or, it may be otherwise harmless things we enjoy, but which become sin when we put them before service to God and others. We may be convinced that the things we want to hang onto will make us happier than our following the will of God. They won't, of course. But that's what we may believe, nevertheless.

Fear of the k_____

No Clear Strategy

We simply might not know what to do if we committed to pursuing God fully. What would it mean? How would we go about it? What's the plan? We may be uncertain about what we would do tomorrow if we gave ourselves fully to obeying and resting in God today.

Understanding these five factors that erode our faith clarifies our problems and enables us to focus on addressing them, repeatedly telling ourselves the truth—that we will be happier completely trusting and obeying God than not—and asking the Lord to "increase our faith" (Luke 17:5).

No clear s_____

4. Our natural strategy for happiness is faith in self.

Our natural strategy for happiness is faith in s_____.

By nature, we want God to make our lives on earth go better. We want to be nice and good, work hard, and be smart. As we go about all this, we call on God to bless our well-laid plans . . . so that, with our effort and a little help from him, our lives on earth will be healthy, prosperous, and happy.

But that plan never works. Things are always going wrong.

When things begin to go wrong, our instinct is to grab hold of things . . . to try to increase our control over life's circumstances and do for ourselves what God in his apparent "negligence" has failed to do for us.

God, of course, objects to such a response, and in his severe mercy begins to pry our controlling fingers off of that which we're clutching. And, as he does, we are left with one of three options . . .

1. Live in fear of him
2. Live in anger toward him
3. Submit completely to him

5. The supernatural strategy for happiness is faith in God.

The supernatural strategy for happiness is faith in G___.

When we submit completely to him, we discover that—hard as it might be—the option that we feared the most is actually the doorway to the life for which we long. Our greatest dread—giving up self-determination and willingly submitting to God—is the very doorway to the supreme treasure of life.

The Bible teaches this clearly, of course. But, instinctively, we resist believing it because self-protection, self-advancement, and self-fulfillment are the core motivations of our natural inclinations.

The apostle Paul spells it out in Romans 12:1: "Therefore I urge you, brethren, by the mercies of God, to present your bodies a living and holy sacrifice, acceptable to God, which is your spiritual service of worship."

Then he appeals: "And do not be conformed to this world, but be transformed by the renewing of your mind, so that you may prove what the will of God is, that which is good and acceptable and perfect" (Romans 12:2).

Becoming a living sacrifice leads to a renewing of the mind, which leads to a transformed life. That which we want most, a transformed life, begins with becoming a living sacrifice.

A living sacrifice is not killed. It chooses to die. Choosing to die goes against all natural inclinations. Just like when a person is rappelling off a high mountain cliff, the brain might reason that you are safe and that the rope will hold you. Your emotions, though, are screaming for you to turn around and run.

So it is in the Christian life. We understand the point of Romans 12:1; we just have a good deal of difficulty putting it into practice.

Yet it is the primary thing God is doing in our lives—bringing us, if we will come—to the point of offering ourselves as living sacrifices, which is an act of complete obedience based on complete faith.

Conclusion

We see in all of this that obedience is not a self-discipline or commitment problem. It is a faith problem. When we understand this and begin focusing on our faith rather than our obedience, our obedience begins to follow.

When we become convinced that we will be happier by being faithful and obedient to God than by following our own strategy, there is a surge in our power to turn from sin.

This is what God wants for us because he loves us and wants the best for us. Of this, C. S. Lewis writes:

> "Make no mistake," [God] says, "if you let me, I will make you perfect. The moment you put yourself in My hands, that is what you are in for. Nothing less, or other, than that. You have free will, and if you choose, you can push Me away. But if you do not push Me away, understand that I am going to see this job through."[2]

One of the great life lessons, then, is: don't fight God. We mustn't try to fight or shrink or hide from God. We must willingly submit to the refinement process through which he takes us. If we fight it, we will diminish our potential, reduce our joy, shrink our power, and decimate our impact.

Continuing his comments on this subject, Lewis writes: "[God] claims all, because He is love and must bless. He cannot bless us unless He has us. When we try to keep within us an area that is our own, we try to keep an area of death. Therefore, in love, He claims all. There's no bargaining with Him."[3]

This must be true! And if so, our only rational response is total obedience to him.

REPETITION
Is the Key to Mental Ownership

Chapter Review
1. Faith is an a____-p_____ force.
2. U_____ started with Adam and Eve.
3. There are five factors that e_____ our faith.
   a. I_____
   b. D_____
   c. Fear of the u_____
   d. Fear of the k_____
   e. No clear s_____

4. Our natural strategy for happiness is faith in s_____.

5. The supernatural strategy for happiness is faith in G____.

The Christian Life in 1,000 Words—Review

(Only the last ten chapters will be displayed)

If something is important, you must repeat it until it changes you.

9. A p_____ mind will be spared the d_____ pull of negative input and be released to the u_____ pull of positive input.

10. We must make peace with the difficult fact that God is g_____ and, at the same time, his children s_____.

11. God wants f_____ and l_____ over anything else we might offer him.

12. God will often d_____ us in a manner that seems, initially, to d_____ us.

13. God's blessing in the Old Testament was the "fruit of the v_____"; in the New Testament, it is the "fruit of the S_____."

14. We were born for l_____. It is the principle of e_____, and its only end.

15. To be free to s_____ the seven seas, we must make ourselves slaves to the c_____.

16. In the Christian life, we r_____ by d_____.

17. When we pray, God will either give us what we ask or give us what we would have asked if we k_____ everything he k_____.

18. If we believe, we obey. If we do not *o*_____, it is because we do not *b*_____.

THOUGHT/DISCUSSION
Is a Key to Understanding

Answer these questions, either individually by journaling the answers or in a small discussion group.

1. Explain in your own words the power of faith.

2. Explain in your own words why you think Adam and Eve sinned.

3. Explain in your own words why living by faith is so counterintuitive.

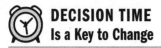

DECISION TIME
Is a Key to Change

Answer these questions, either individually by journaling the answers or in a spiritual accountability group.

1. Do you believe that everything God asks of you is to give something good to you or keep something bad from you?
2. Of the five factors that erode our faith, which one is the most troublesome for you?
3. Have you ever deliberately offered yourself as a living sacrifice to God? Are you prepared to live each day as a living sacrifice?

RECOMMENDED
Resource

Trusting God, Jerry Bridges

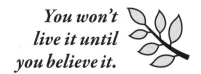

*You won't
live it until
you believe it.*

CHAPTER 19

THE FUNDAMENTAL IMPORTANCE OF GRATITUDE

We should be *grateful* for what the will of God gives
us rather than *ungrateful* for what it doesn't.

> **CENTRAL PASSAGE:** 1 Thessalonians 5:18—"In everything give
> thanks; for this is God's will for you in Christ Jesus."

Gratitude is a fundamental virtue. With it, many other virtues fall into place. Without it, the other virtues do not fall into place.

But why should we be grateful? Is nurturing gratitude simply a "don't worry, be happy" attitude toward life?

It can sometimes feel as though life beats the gratitude out of us. We try to be good people, work hard, treat others well, and do some good in the world, but what do we get for it? One disappointment after another. Failed endeavors, difficult people, broken health, and financial reversals!

Sure, if you're one of the lucky ones, be grateful. You got it all. If you're one of the unlucky ones, on what basis would you be grateful?!?

1. The Bible encourages gratitude.

The Bible encourages g_____.

The Bible says a great deal about gratitude and its twin, thankfulness:

- "Offer to God a sacrifice of thanksgiving" (Psalm 50:14).
- "Enter His gates with thanksgiving and His courts with praise. Give thanks to Him, bless His name" (Psalm 100:4).
- "Give thanks in all circumstances; for this is the will of God in Christ Jesus for you" (1 Thessalonians 5:18 ESV).
- "Do all things without grumbling or disputing" (Philippians 2:14).
- "Therefore as you have received Christ Jesus the Lord, so walk in Him, having been firmly rooted and now being built up in Him and established in your faith, just as you were instructed, and overflowing with gratitude" (Colossians 2:6–7).

Scripture says, "His divine power has granted to us everything pertaining to life and godliness" (2 Peter 1:3). So, if God has given us everything we need, gratitude is a reasonable response. For the Christian, this is a good place to start.

Being a grateful person can be a significant challenge, one that many people would be reluctant to take on if the Bible did not champion it. Our challenge is to be grateful for what the will of God gives us rather than be ungrateful for what it does not.

2. We should be grateful because, in the end, all will be more than well.

We should be grateful because, in the end, all will be more than w_____.

Yet, how do we build a "theology of gratitude"? Yes, we can aspire to gratitude simply because God says we should, but why does God say we should? Is there not a reason why he says we should?

Answer: Yes.

Life is made up of exchanges in which we give something now to get something better later.

Athletes, musicians, students, artists, entrepreneurs, and others who must do hard work over time in order to achieve their goals understand. You give up something now to get something better later. And often, the harder it is, the more rewarding it is. Olympians, Navy SEALs, or Nobel Prize winners are more grateful for their achievements than graduates of kindergarten, athletes who received a "participation" trophy, or singers who warble only in the shower; they are more grateful for their success because it was harder. Much harder.

The value of something we receive is assessed in terms of what it cost to get it.

So it is in our Christian life. The whole idea is that we give up something now to get something better later.

There is much personal sacrifice—on the surface, at least—in living the Christian life. Jesus said, "whoever loses his life for My sake will find it" (Matthew 16:25). But everything we sacrifice in this life is more than compensated for, either in this life, in the next, or both.

There are four benefits of sacrifice and trials in this life, and by focusing on the benefits rather than the trials, we cultivate gratitude.

Spiritual Transformation

James 1:2–4 says, "Consider it all joy, my brethren, when you encounter various trials, knowing that the testing of your faith produces endurance. And let endurance have its perfect result, so that you may be perfect and complete, lacking in nothing."

The road to transformation always goes through the tunnel of trials.

Just as greater physical exercise may result in greater physical strength, so greater spiritual exercise may result in greater spiritual strength.

A positive response to trials yields the priceless benefit of spiritual transformation!

Greater Impact in Ministry

Second Corinthians 1:3–4 (NIV) says, "Praise be to the God and Father of our Lord Jesus Christ, the Father of compassion and the God of all comfort, who comforts us in all our troubles, so that we can comfort those in any trouble with the comfort we ourselves receive from God."

No trial need ever be wasted! Not only will God use it to transform us, but if we let him, he will also use it to work through us to help others.

Eternal Reward

Romans 8:18 says, "I consider that the sufferings of this present time are not worthy to be compared with the glory that is to be revealed to us."

God gives us disproportionate eternal reward for every single response of faith and obedience. We cannot even give someone a cup of cold water in Jesus's name without receiving an eternal reward (Matthew 10:42). We cannot outgive God!

Deeper Fellowship

Philippians 3:10 says, "that I may know Him and the power of His resurrection and the fellowship of His sufferings."

Christ suffered for us more than we suffer for him, yet he didn't have to. Though we typically suffer because we have to, he voluntarily suffered for us because he loves us. When we grasp this, when we take this astonishing truth into our hearts, we develop deep appreciation and gratitude for what he has done in suffering and dying for us.

A bond of identity is forged with him through our mutual suffering, and we can enter into a level of fellowship with him that we cannot know without suffering.

These are four potential benefits of trials. To help us cultivate gratitude, we must burn these four benefits into our minds. In the end, all will be more than well. Like the athlete, the musician, or the farmer, Christians look forward to disproportionate reward. We get much more than we give up. We must focus on the future, when in the end all will be more than well.

3. We should be grateful because gratitude is good for us here and now.

We should be grateful because gratitude is good for us h_____ and n____.

Not only is gratitude good for us spiritually and for eternity, it is good for us practically, here and now. Today, as a result of a growing body of research information, even non-Christians recognize the remarkable benefits of thankfulness and gratitude.

Happiness: Even a cursory internet search reveals an abundance of research from Harvard Medical School, *Forbes* magazine, and *Psychology Today* touting the temporal benefits of gratitude.

Studies reveal that gratitude leads to a happier life. Its focus is on the present and appreciation for what we have now, rather than wanting more and more. Gratitude turns our mental focus to the positive, which compensates for our brain's natural tendency to focus on the threats, worries, and negative aspects of life. As such, gratitude creates positive emotions like joy, love, and contentment, which, research shows, can undo the grip of negative emotions like anxiety.

According to research, fostering gratitude can also broaden your mind and create positive cycles of thinking and behaving in healthy, beneficial ways.

Health: A similar search will reveal not just psychological and emotional benefits of gratitude, but also physical health benefits. Gratitude is a great stress buster, which is important because stress is linked to several leading causes of death, including heart disease and cancer, and claims responsibility for up to 90% of all doctor visits.

Gratitude helps you sleep better, boosts the immune system to help the body fight off both minor and major health issues, helps reduce the physical impact of extreme losses in life, and even helps people live longer.

Impact on others: Still further research reveals the impact that gratitude has on our influence over others. In the business arena, a grateful person is more attractive to others. Gratitude can give someone more influence in the workplace when speaking to crowds, or when relating personally to individuals. The internet is awash with studies revealing an impressive list of benefits that come to us through gratitude.

4. We can take helpful steps to cultivate gratitude.

We can take helpful steps to c_____ gratitude.

How can we become more grateful people? Here are a few suggestions.

Choose *to be more grateful.*

The Bible says that God will supply all our needs according to his riches in glory in Christ Jesus (Philippians 4:19). We may want more than we have, but we don't need more than we have.

In Hebrews 13:5, we read, "Make sure that your character is free from the love of money, being content with what you have; for He Himself has said, 'I will never desert you, nor will I ever forsake you.'"

Benjamin Franklin said, "Content makes poor men rich; Discontent makes rich men poor."[1]

If this is true about money, it is also true about other things we might want that the will of God is not currently giving us . . . relationships, accomplishments, reputation, etc.

We can make the conscious decision to be grateful for what we have rather than ungrateful for what we don't have.

C_____ to be more grateful.

Cultivate an eternal perspective.

As we mentioned earlier, there is nothing we do for God, nor any sacrifice we make for God, that he will not reward, many times over, in heaven. Paul said, "For I consider that the sufferings of this present time are not worthy to be compared with the glory that is to be revealed to us" (Romans 8:18).

Paul also wrote, in 2 Corinthians 4:16–18, "Therefore we do not lose heart, but though our outer man is decaying, yet our inner man is being renewed day by day. For momentary, light affliction is producing for us an eternal weight of glory far beyond all comparison, while we look not at the things which are seen, but at the things which are not seen; for the things which are seen are temporal, but the things which are not seen are eternal."

From this passage, we learn that if we focus on temporal things, we will lose heart. If we focus on eternal things, we will not lose heart. Therefore, our task is to cultivate an eternal perspective, training ourselves to view things from God's perspective, rather than our own limited perspective. It is to our advantage, both here and now, as well as for eternity.

As missionary Jim Elliot said, "He is no fool who gives what he cannot keep to gain that which he cannot lose."[2]

Cultivate an e_____ p_____.

Take practical steps.

Research has shown that there are simple, practical steps we can take to cultivate gratitude. Something as simple as consistently saying "please" and "thank you" has demonstrated statistically significant increases in a positive outlook on life.

Other very simple things we can do include:

- Smile at others.
- Write thank you notes/emails or give "thank you" gifts.
- Compliment others.
- Don't complain or criticize.
- Put pleasantness in your voice when you talk on the phone.
- Follow the Golden Rule: do unto others as you would have others do unto you.
- Apologize, if necessary.
- Forgive, if necessary.
- Choose to be a positive person.

Take p_____ steps.

Conclusion

Gratitude is always an option. When Matthew Henry, an 18th-century British minister and scholar, was accosted by thieves and robbed, the following prayer was attributed to him, "Let me be thankful, first because I was never robbed before; second, because, although they took my purse they did not take my life; third, because although they took my all, it was not much; and, fourth, because it was I who was robbed, not I who robbed."[3]

That's the trick—to find a reason to be grateful in all things. We can be ungrateful that roses have thorns, or grateful that thorns have roses. The latter expands and strengthens us; the former shrinks and weakens us.

If we don't like the food, we can be grateful that we do not have to go hungry. If we do not like our job, we can be grateful that we have a paycheck. If we have to relate to difficult people, we can be grateful thus: that God will disproportionately bless us for being gracious; that it gives us the opportunity to leave behind small attitudes, values, and behaviors and rise to great ones; and that God will use it to make us more like Christ.

If we live for earth's values, we get frustrated that we are surrounded by jerks, and we become resentful that we have to survive in such limiting conditions. We can feel alone and stuck in bad circumstances.

If we live for heaven's values, we can take encouragement that we are doing God's will, that eternal rewards are piling up as we speak, and that heaven's hosts are looking at us in admiration for the sufficiency of God's grace in our lives.

Without great problems, there can be no great deliverances; without great battles there can be no great victories; and with no great exertion there can be no great development of strength. If we embrace an eternal perspective and go through earth's challenges with a view toward heaven's rewards, this can strengthen us for the daily battle and give us increased capacity to love God with all our hearts, souls, and minds, and love our neighbors as ourselves (Matthew 22:37, 39).

Gratitude is a fundamental virtue. If we cultivate gratitude,

God is pleased, we are happier and healthier, we have greater influence on others, and many other virtues fall into place.

⟳ REPETITION
Is the Key to Mental Ownership

Chapter Review
1. The Bible encourages g_____.
2. We should be grateful because, in the end, all will be more than w_____.
3. We should be grateful because gratitude is good for us h_____ and n___.
4. We can take helpful steps to c_____ gratitude.
   a. C_____ to be more grateful.
   b. Cultivate an e_____ p_____.
   c. Take p_____ steps.

The Christian Life in 1,000 Words—Review
(Only the last ten chapters will be displayed)
If something is important, you must repeat it until it changes you.
10. We must make peace with the difficult fact that God is g_____ and, at the same time, his children s_____.
11. God wants f_____ and l_____ over anything else we might offer him.
12. God will often d_____ us in a manner that seems, initially, to d_____ us.
13. God's blessing in the Old Testament was the "fruit of the v_____"; in the New Testament, it is the "fruit of the S_____."
14. We were born for l_____. It is the principle of e_____, and its only end.
15. To be free to s_____ the seven seas, we must make ourselves slaves to the c_____.
16. In the Christian life, we r_____ by d_____.
17. When we pray, God will either give us what we ask or give us what we would have asked if we k_____ everything he k_____.

18. If we believe, we obey. If we do not *o*_____, it is because we do not *b*_____.

19. We should be g_____ for what the will of God gives us rather than u_____ for what it doesn't.

THOUGHT/DISCUSSION
Is a Key to Understanding

Answer these questions, either individually by journaling the answers or in a small discussion group.

1. Who is the most grateful person you know? Do you find that person winsome? What about that person would you like to emulate?

2. Which of the four benefits of trials do you find most appealing? Why?

3. Summarize in your own words what you see as the benefit of being a grateful person.

DECISION TIME
Is a Key to Change

Answer these questions, either individually by journaling the answers or in a spiritual accountability group.

1. Would you consider yourself to be a mostly grateful person or a mostly ungrateful person?

2. What do you assess is the greatest benefit of being a grateful person?

3. What is the most important thing you need to begin doing right away to cultivate gratitude?

RECOMMENDED
Resource

Choosing Gratitude, Nancy Leigh DeMoss

You won't
live it until
you believe it.
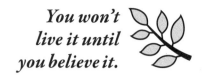

CHAPTER 20

FOUR TRADITIONAL MODELS FOR LIVING THE CHRISTIAN LIFE

We strive for righteousness, not to get God to love us, but in *gratitude* that he already does.

 CENTRAL PASSAGE: Ephesians 4:1—"I . . . implore you to walk in a manner worthy of the calling with which you have been called."

There are several "models" of living the Christian life that have arisen in the evangelical church in America. They include:

- The Exchanged Life Model
- The Spiritual Disciplines Model
- The Spirit-Filled Life Model
- The New Covenant Model

When these models are presented, it is possible to get the idea that you have to choose one view over the others. However, there is very helpful truth in each perspective, reflecting different emphases, and we get the greatest benefit not when we choose one over the others, but when we embrace and balance all four.

1. The Exchanged Life Model teaches that we are in Christ, and therefore enjoy the same standing before God that *Jesus* has.

The Exchanged Life Model teaches that we are in Christ, and therefore enjoy the same standing before God that J_____ has.

The Exchanged Life model of living the Christian life correctly observes that each of us is created with three deep longings:

- For *security* in unconditional love
- For a sense of belonging and inherent *significance*
- For awareness of innate *competence* to do something valuable

However, because we are imperfect people living in an imperfect world, these longings are never fully met. Through our parents, our peers, and society at large, we get feedback that convinces us of our deficiencies in all three areas:

- We feel *insecure* rather than unconditionally loved,
- We feel *inferior* rather than inherently significant, and
- We feel *inadequate* rather than innately competent.

As a result, we take steps to try to measure up in these areas:

- Appearance: We may try to earn a sense of love by looking as attractive and fashionable as we can, or to fit in with those with whom we identify, even if that means trying not to be attractive.
- Possessions: We may try to earn our sense of belonging by owning the "right stuff" that others with whom we identify also own.
- Accomplishments: We may try to earn a sense of competency by trying to accomplish things that those we identify with will think are important.

Our strategies don't work, however. Oscar Wilde once famously said in one of his plays, "In this world there are only two tragedies. One is not getting what one wants, and the other is getting it."[1]

If we don't get what we want, we are unhappy because we didn't get it. And if we do get what we want, we are unhappy because it didn't permanently satisfy.

This often applies to our strategies to earn a sense of self-worth through our own efforts. We simply cannot control circumstances completely enough to get what we want in each of the three areas. At times we may be able to achieve it temporarily, but we discover that it doesn't give us the sense of worth we hoped it would.

The solution is to rest in the fact that God has already met all our true needs.

- God meets our felt need for *security* by loving us infinitely and unconditionally. Because we are created in his image, we have inherent and infinite worth. He loves us so much that Jesus lived a very hard life and died a terrible death just to make it possible for us to be reconciled to God (Romans 5:8). We could not be more loved.
- God meets our felt need for *significance* by adopting us into his family (Ephesians 1:5), making us members of his inner circle. We belong to the most significant "group" there is . . . the family of God. He delights to call us his children.
- God meets our felt need for *competence* by preplanning good works that he wants us to do and sovereignly blessing our pursuit of them (Ephesians 2:10). And he has given us spiritual gifts (1 Peter 4:10) so that we are capable of doing them. We are utterly competent to do whatever God wants us to do.

When we act badly in life, it is often because something happens to make us feel insecure, inferior, or incompetent, and so we do something unhelpful (criticize, get angry, lie, cheat, ridicule, make fun of, act superior, etc.) in an attempt to cover up our feelings of intimidation.

As we transition from looking at ourselves the old way—the way the world does—and begin to look at ourselves the new way—the way God does—this can bring healing, strength, and hope to the soul. We no longer feel insecure, inferior, and inadequate, so we are less likely to strike out at others to cover our own negative feelings.

We are in Christ, and everything that is true of him is true of us.

If he is loved, we are loved. If he is significant, we are significant. If he is competent, we are competent. We must consciously embrace these truths, and count on them to be true for us, regardless of how we feel. As we do, the power of the truth transforms us, renewing our minds and our emotions (Galatians 5:22–23).

The more secure we are in "who we are in Christ," the better decisions we make and the better relationships we can have. The exchanged life, then, is not a matter of trying to do things *for* Jesus, but, rather, resting *in* Jesus.

2. The Spiritual Disciplines Model teaches that, in order to act "on the spot" as Jesus did, we must *prepare* ourselves as Jesus did before the "spot" got there.

The Spiritual Disciplines Model teaches that, in order to act "on the spot" as Jesus did, we must p_____ ourselves as Jesus did before the "spot" got there.

The Spiritual Disciplines model of living the Christian life teaches that we must observe the spiritual disciplines to grow spiritually.

It teaches that if we want to act "on the spot" as Jesus acted, then we must prepare ourselves as Jesus prepared himself before the "spot" got there. There is no value in asking, "What would Jesus do?" in a given situation unless we have cultivated our spiritual life as Jesus did in the period before the situation arrived.

We must engage in certain spiritual disciplines that prepare us mentally, spiritually, and emotionally for living as Jesus lived. Just as an athlete or a musician cannot hope to excel without preparation, so the Christian cannot hope to excel without preparation. Half-hearted measures always yield half-hearted results.

Some of the classic disciplines include:

- **Scripture** reading, studying the Bible regularly, memorizing and meditating on the Bible faithfully
- **Praying** faithfully, alone and with prayer partners

- Spending time in **solitude**, cultivating an eternal perspective
- **Fasting** occasionally to heighten spiritual sensitivity
- Sacrificial **service**, giving yourself and your resources unselfishly to the needs of others

The spiritual disciplines are not magic, but, rather, are a means to an end. These are disciplines that Jesus observed regularly and that prepared him to minister with power and worship with intimacy.

3. The Spirit-Filled Life Model teaches that, as we are *filled* with the Holy Spirit, we will be able to live a life pleasing to God.

The Spirit-Filled Life Model teaches that, as we are f_____ *with the Holy Spirit, we will be able to live a life pleasing to God.*

The Spirit-filled model of living the Christian life teaches that, as we are filled with the Spirit, we will be empowered to live a mature Christian life.

The Spirit-Filled Life model suggests that we cannot live the Christian life in our own power. Rather, as we rely on the power of the Holy Spirit within, we gain the power to live God-pleasing lives. In Ephesians 5:18, we are commanded to "be filled with the Spirit." As we give ourselves to faith and obedience of that command, we grow to spiritual maturity.

While there is more than one explanation for how we live the Spirit-filled life, the model based on Ephesians 5:18 requires some careful thinking if we hope to be true to the passage.

There are two different Greek words in the New Testament which have different meanings, but which are both translated "filled." This allows for potential misunderstanding.

One Greek word, *pimplemi*, is used in the context of extraordinary and miraculous short-term events centered in the book of Acts.

The other, *plerao*, is used by Paul to refer to long-term results related to personal character.

Comparison of the Two Words for "Filling"

Pimplemi	Plerao
Extraordinary results (miracles, etc.)	No extraordinary results
Used throughout book of Acts, but not used after Acts 19	Used only twice in New Testament, both after Acts 19
Did not last a long time (aorist tense)	Lasted a long time (present tense)
Intended to accomplish a task	Intended to change character

When Paul commanded us to be filled with the Spirit in Ephesians 5:18, he used the word *plerao*. Therefore, he was not commanding us to experience miraculous short-term events, but rather to submit to long-term governance by the Holy Spirit over the character and behavior of our lives.

Whatever interpretation one might have of the extraordinary results seen in the book of Acts, that interpretation cannot be applied to Ephesians 5:18 because of the differences in the Greek word used, as well as in the results described.

We are obligated/commanded to be filled with the Spirit in Ephesians 5:18. We are not obligated/commanded to be filled with the Spirit in the *pimplemi* basis of the word.

So, how do we obey the command in Ephesians 5:18? To discover the answer to that question, it is helpful to observe that the results of being "filled with the Spirit" in Ephesians 5:18 are essentially identical to "[letting] the word of Christ richly dwell within you" in Colossians 3:16. Notice the comparison in the following chart.

Comparison of the Results of "Being Filled with the Spirit" and "Letting the Word of Christ Richly Dwell Within You."

Ephesians 5:18—"Be filled with the Spirit"	Colossians 3:16—"Let the word of Christ richly dwell within you"
Speaking in psalms	Teaching with psalms
Singing	Singing

(continued)

Ephesians 5:18—"Be filled with the Spirit"	Colossians 3:16—"Let the word of Christ richly dwell within you"
Giving thanks	Thankfulness
Harmony between husbands & wives	Harmony between husbands & wives
Harmony between parents & children	Harmony between parents & children
Harmony between masters & bondservants	Harmony between masters & bondservants

Because of the striking parallel in the results described in these two passages, we have to ask ourselves if the two actions ("being filled with the Spirit" and "letting the word of Christ richly dwell in you") are not parallel causes for the same results.

That is, we have to ask ourselves if the way we are filled with the Spirit is by letting the word of Christ richly dwell within us.

This possibility is strengthened by looking at a comparison of the results in the two passages from another perspective:

Be filled (*plerao*) with the Spirit	Let the word of Christ richly dwell within you
No extraordinary results (miracles)	No extraordinary results (miracles)
Lasted a long time	Lasted a long time
A command to obey	A command to obey
Intended to change character	Intended to change character

From this, we might reasonably conclude that we can obey the command in Ephesians 5:18 "to be filled with the Spirit" by "letting the word of Christ richly dwell within us."

The point would be that we are to so immerse ourselves in the Scripture that the Holy Spirit is able to use the power of the Word to transform our thoughts, our deepest beliefs, our emotions, and our actions, with the result that we are controlled (filled) by the Holy Spirit.

The analogy of a speed limit sign is imperfect, but has helped me understand this a bit better. A speed limit sign controls me, but not directly. Rather, it is a sign that reflects a law, and if I choose to obey that law, I adjust my speed to reflect it. So, in that sense the speed limit sign controls and governs me.

When we are filled by the Holy Spirit in the *plerao* sense, the Holy Spirit does not take over my life, overcome my will, and exercise direct control. Rather, he convinces me of truth, convicts me when I violate truth, and helps me when I choose to obey truth. So, in that sense, he controls and governs me.

And when I read, study, memorize, and meditate on Scripture, so that the word of Christ richly dwells in me, the Holy Spirit is able to use the power of the Word (Hebrews 4:12) to bring about the spiritual change that he desires. He uses the Word to control the trusting and obedient heart and to gradually change that person into the character image of Jesus (Romans 8:29).

As we carry this understanding of being filled with the Holy Spirit into the next model, it helps us see the complementary teaching of models 3 and 4.

4. The New Covenant Model teaches that Jesus brought a New Covenant, superseding the Old Covenant; as a result, God himself is, or will supply, *everything* we need to live the Christian life.

The New Covenant Model teaches that Jesus brought a New Covenant, superseding the Old Covenant; as a result, God himself is, or will supply, e_____ *we need to live the Christian life.*

The New Covenant Model teaches that, with the coming of Jesus, the Old Covenant has fully passed away, having been supplanted by the work of Christ and the New Covenant he brought. It teaches that God himself is, or will supply, everything we need to live the Christian life. It is no longer a matter of God's children obeying an external law in their own power, but rather a matter of accepting the sufficiency of what Christ has done for us and of living consistently with that acceptance.

a. Christ has made possible an amazing spiritual transformation in the believer in Christ:

- The forgiveness of our sin (Ephesians 1:7)
- Our spiritual rebirth (1 Peter 1:23)
- Adoption into God's spiritual family (Ephesians 1:5)
- Direct access to God (Hebrews 4:15–16)
- God's laws written in our hearts (Romans 7:22)
- The Holy Spirit living within us (1 Corinthians 6:19)

Through these consequences of having received Jesus as our Savior, we have been removed from the lineage and heritage of Adam and have been placed into the lineage and heritage of Jesus. That which is true of Adam is no longer true of us, and that which is true of Jesus is now true of us.

b. We have a new nature, the "inner man," which we received from Christ, though we are still housed in an unredeemed physical body, still corrupted by the presence and power of sin (Romans 7:22–23).

c. Our great task in the Christian life is to begin living, in our physical body, like who we have become in the "inner man" (Ephesians 4:1).

d. The Holy Spirit is the power that enables us to live the Christian life. As we are filled with the Holy Spirit, we will increasingly make decisions consistent with our inner man (Galatians 5:16).

e. We walk in the Spirit by following these steps:

i. Examine our life for sin.

ii. Confess any known sin.

iii. Review who we are in Christ (see "A" earlier in this list).

iv. Allow ourselves to be filled with the Holy Spirit (choose/act as you believe he wants you to, trusting him to increasingly empower you as you let the word of Christ richly dwell within you, gradually changing you from the inside out).

v. Thank him.

Conclusion

In living the Christian life, there are four models that are **complementary**:

- The Exchanged Life Model
- The Spiritual Disciplines Model
- The Spirit-Filled Life Model
- The New Covenant Model

We do not have to choose among these four. There is no right one or wrong one. There is truth in each one, and it seems that a given model may appeal to some people more than others. Therefore, we can balance and harmonize all four, and in doing so we will have our most complete understanding of how to live the Christian life.

 **REPETITION**
Is the Key to Mental Ownership

Chapter Review

1. The Exchanged Life Model teaches that we are in Christ, and therefore enjoy the same standing before God that *J*_____ has.

2. The Spiritual Disciplines Model teaches that, in order to act "on the spot" as Jesus did, we must *p*_____ ourselves as Jesus did before the "spot" got there.

3. The Spirit-Filled Life Model teaches that, as we are *f*_____ with the Holy Spirit, we will be able to live a life pleasing to God.

4. The New Covenant Model teaches that Jesus brought a New Covenant, superseding the Old Covenant; as a result, God himself is, or will supply, *e*_____ we need to live the Christian life.

The Christian Life in 1,000 Words—Review

(Only the last ten chapters will be displayed)

If something is important, you must repeat it until it changes you.

11. God wants f_____ and l_____ over anything else we might offer him.

12. God will often d_____ us in a manner that seems, initially,
to d_____ us.

13. God's blessing in the Old Testament was the "fruit of the v_____";
in the New Testament, it is the "fruit of the S_____."

14. We were born for l_____. It is the principle of e_____,
and its only end.

15. To be free to s_____ the seven seas, we must make ourselves slaves
to the c_____.

16. In the Christian life, we r_____ by d_____.

17. When we pray, God will either give us what we ask or give us what
we would have asked if we k_____ everything he k_____.

18. If we believe, we obey. If we do not *o*_____, it is because we do
not *b*_____.

19. We should be g_____ for what the will of God gives us
rather than u_____ for what it doesn't.

20. We strive for righteousness, not to get God to love us, but in
g_____ that he already does.

THOUGHT/DISCUSSION
Is a Key to Understanding

*Answer these questions, either individually by journaling the answers or in
a small discussion group.*

1. Which of the four models for living the Christian life do you more
naturally understand and gravitate toward?

2. What do you see as some of the similarities of the four models?

3. What do you see as some of the differences?

DECISION TIME
Is a Key to Change

*Answer these questions, either individually by journaling the answers or in
a spiritual accountability group.*

1. Are these models new to you? What is the most helpful understanding you gained from reading the chapter?

2. Which of the spiritual disciplines do you think you need to focus on the most?

3. What do you think is the most important change you can make in your life as a result of reading this chapter?

 **RECOMMENDED**
Resource

Exchanged Life: *Lifetime Guarantee*, Bill Gillham
Spiritual Disciplines: *The Spirit of the Disciplines*, Dallas Willard
Spirit-Filled Life: *The Good Life*, Max Anders
The New Covenant: *Authentic Christianity*, Ray Stedman

A complete Christian needs to:
- Know what you need to know
- Become what you need to be
- Do what you need to do

PART 3

DO

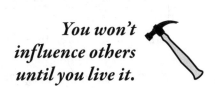

You won't influence others until you live it.

CHAPTER 21

THE REALITY OF SPIRITUAL WARFARE

You can't win a *battle* you don't know you're in.

 CENTRAL PASSAGE: Ephesians 6:12—"Our struggle is not against flesh and blood, but against the rulers, against the powers, against the world forces of this darkness, against the spiritual forces of wickedness in the heavenly places."

In the very place where you are right now, there are television signals, radio signals, internet signals, and smart phone signals. You can't see them, hear them, touch them, taste them, or smell them. But they're there!

In the same way, it is possible that there are angels and demons around where you are right now. You can't see them, hear them, touch them, taste them, or smell them, but they are quite possibly there!

The apostle Paul tells us in Ephesians 6 that we are all in the midst of an ongoing spiritual war. The apostle Peter tells us in 1 Peter 5 that we must be on the alert at all times for spiritual danger.

However, many Christians are clueless about spiritual warfare. Because we cannot see spiritual beings, many Christians are tempted to think it is "extreme" to assume the spiritual beings are waging war against them. If we are to take the Bible at face value, though, the Scriptures teach us that we are in a war and tell us how that war can be won.

1. Christians must recognize the reality of spiritual warfare.

Christians must recognize the reality of s_____ w_____.

The apostle Peter said, "Be of sober spirit, be on the alert. Your adversary, the devil, prowls around like a roaring lion, seeking someone to devour" (1 Peter 5:8).

We need to take this warning at face value. There is no advantage to being clueless in the Christian life.

NORAD, the North American Aerospace Defense Command, is a highly sophisticated early warning system for airspace around North America. It immediately detects anything that invades our airspace, and is designed to give us as much advance notice as possible if any missile, drone, or airplane were to be headed our way.

NORAD is a multi-billion-dollar system that we have put in place because we believe that there are hostile forces that would do us harm, if they had the chance.

Christians should do the same, spiritually. We are to have our spiritual radar on high alert to the potential of the enemy attacking us in an attempt to spiritually neutralize or defeat us.

C. S. Lewis said, "There is no neutral ground in the universe: every square inch, every split second, is claimed by God and counter-claimed by Satan."[1] One of the most important mental shifts a Christian must make is the shift from living for the American Dream to fighting the spiritual battle.

2. Christians must recognize the three types of spiritual conflict.

Christians must recognize the three types of spiritual c_____.

Dirty Tricks

One level of spiritual warfare can be called "Dirty Tricks," which are circumstantial opposition of evil spirits to God's people and will.

In the first chapter of Job, we see Job's life being devastated. One day, he was walking the earth with fabulous wealth, good health, and a large family. Virtually overnight, he lost it all.

The Sabeans attacked and took Job's oxen and donkeys which

were being used to farm his land, and killed the servants. Next, lightning killed his sheep and shepherds. The Chaldeans rustled his camels and killed the camel keepers. A great wind destroyed the house where his children were and killed them all. Finally, Job lost his health and ended up sitting in a garbage dump with his body covered from head to toe with excruciating boils.

Job had no way of knowing why these tragedies befell him. They could all be explained with earthly, natural explanations. However, the curtain of heaven is pulled back for those of us who read the account in the Bible, and we learn that all of the incidences were a result of spiritual warfare.

While the level of dirty tricks we will face is not likely to be as great at Job's, they can nevertheless seem very great to us when we endure them. As we are alert to them, we can more carefully and more biblically respond.

Mind Games

The second level of spiritual warfare is "Mind Games." Mind Games are a strategy of deception used by the devil to deceive and defeat Christians. Satan's name means "deceiver." Deception is his primary strategy. He is the great trickster, the great illusionist, the great con artist, and the great liar. Jesus said in John 8:44, "[The devil] was a murderer from the beginning, and does not stand in the truth because there is no truth in him. Whenever he speaks a lie, he speaks from his own nature, for he is a liar and the father of lies."

Satan plays games with our minds to get us to believe . . .

- that which is false is true
- that which is bad is good
- that which is wrong is right

Don't underestimate these mind games!

They may seem simple and obvious when we see them stated so simply, but Satan is very good at making them convincing in the moment. If you are not careful, you'll be tricked into thinking something is true which is actually false; that something is good which is actually bad; or that something is right which is actually wrong.

He's very good at it, which is why the Scriptures say, "Be strong in the Lord and in the strength of His might. Put on the full armor of God" (Ephesians 6:10–11).

Satan's strategy is the same with us as it was in the Garden of Eden with Eve and Adam: to deceive us into doubting God's character, his love for us, and his benevolent intentions toward us, and to prompt us to take control over our own lives. If we know Satan's mind games, we can be better prepared to resist them.

Hand-to-Hand Combat

Occasionally, the enemy comes out from behind his Dirty Tricks and Mind Games and engages God's people directly in Hand-to-Hand Combat. This is direct opposition by evil spirits to God's will and God's people (Luke 13:11). We see an example of this when Jesus was tempted by the devil in the wilderness. Satan spoke directly to Jesus and tried to deceive him and tempt him into sinning (Matthew 4).

Another example can be found in Acts 16, where a demon-possessed girl who could tell fortunes followed the apostle Paul around for days, interfering with him as he ministered. Paul finally turned to the demon and commanded it to come out of her—and it did. This was another example of Hand-to-Hand Combat.

There are many times in the Bible when we see direct confrontation with evil spirits, and such things are being seen more and more today as the light of the gospel dims in many parts of our developed world. On the other hand, one of the most frequent sources of these reports comes from missionaries who often do work amidst very primitive cultures where the gospel is spreading. Demons are always active in every culture, but they can be more or less concealed, depending on the culture's worldview and understanding. In the West, for example, where we prefer to explain things with science, demons often work in more subtle ways, content that we aren't mindful of

them. In cultures whose worldview accepts their presence, they may
be less concealed and more focused on direct confrontation.

We may not be sure, especially with Dirty Tricks and Mind
Games, when something is spiritual warfare or when it may be
accounted for by other means. After all, we live in a fallen world, and
bad things also happen simply as a result of the world in which we
live or even as trials sent by God to grow us.

However, in the Bible we see spiritual warfare behind a number
of life problems:

- Circumstantial upheaval (as in the book of Job)
- Physical maladies—doubled over, mute, deaf, seizures
  (such as in Luke 13:11)
- Mental instability in the life of King Saul (1 Samuel 16)
- Faulty thinking causing conflict & disorder (James 3:15–18)
- Thoughts raised up against God (2 Corinthians 10:4–5)

This is not a complete list, but it is a list of examples from
Scripture of the kinds of things the enemy does to wreak havoc in the
lives of people. As we are alert to these possibilities, we can be better
prepared to resist.

3. Christians must use three types of spiritual defenses.

Christians must use three types of spiritual d_____.

To offset the three types of spiritual conflict, the Bible makes it
clear that there are three levels of defense we have in spiritual warfare.

Alert

A_____

You can't win a battle you don't know you're in.

First, we must be alert to the reality of spiritual warfare. If we
aren't, we are vulnerable. If we are ignorant, careless, or unbelieving,
Satan will likely neutralize us, at best, and badly defeat us, at worst.

To remind you again of what the apostle Peter said: "Be of sober spirit, be on the alert. Your adversary, the devil, prowls around like a roaring lion, seeking someone to devour" (1 Peter 5:8).

There is no advantage to being clueless in the Christian life.

Armor

A_____

You must fight a spiritual war with spiritual weapons.

We must also put on spiritual armor, which is a metaphor for being prepared for spiritual warfare. The armor is found in Ephesians 6:14–17, and is introduced thus: "Put on the full armor of God, so that you will be able to stand firm against the schemes of the devil" (Ephesians 6:11).

The spiritual armor that Paul refers to in this passage is referring to the six pieces of armor that a Roman soldier had. If all six pieces were in place, the soldier was prepared and ready for successful warfare. If he was missing a piece, he was vulnerable in warfare.

When we put on the individual pieces of armor, here is what we are doing spiritually:

- Belt of truth: This means I accept the truth of Scripture and will follow it with integrity.
- Breastplate of righteousness: This means I will not harbor known sin and will strive to be like Christ.
- Shoes of peace: This means I believe God's promises and count on them to be true for me.
- Shield of faith: This means whenever I feel like doubting or sinning or quitting, I will reject those thoughts and feelings and tell myself the truth.
- Helmet of salvation: This means I rest my hope in the future and live in this world according to the values of the next.
- Sword of the Spirit: This means I will use Scripture to fend off attacks of the enemy and to advance the cause of Christ.

Having put on the armor of God, we are now ready for the final step in spiritual warfare, spiritual resistance.

Resist

R_____

Be spiritually shrewd. Don't take the enemy's bait.

Three different passages of Scripture tell us to resist the enemy:

- "Therefore, take up the full armor of God, so that you will be able to **resist** in the evil day, and having done everything, to stand firm" (Ephesians 6:13).
- "'God is opposed to the proud, but gives grace to the humble.' Submit therefore to God. **Resist** the devil and he will flee from you. Draw near to God and He will draw near to you" (James 4:6–8).
- "Be of sober spirit, be on the alert. Your adversary, the devil, prowls around like a roaring lion, seeking someone to devour. But **resist** him, firm in your faith" (1 Peter 5:8–9).

An image that can be helpful in strengthening one's capacity to resist the devil is the image of a fishing hook.

Satan may offer us something that, in and of itself, is not wrong, but the will of God is not giving it to us. If so, there is a hook in it. Like a worm offered to a fish, there is nothing wrong with the worm. But if there is a hook in it, it is dangerous. So it can be with the enemy's temptations. To strengthen your capacity to resist, picture a hook in the thing Satan is using to tempt you, and then don't take the bait.

When you are fishing, you may be tempted to marvel at how foolish the fish are in that they cannot tell the difference between food and bait. Yet, enemy spiritual forces must often marvel at the foolishness of some Christians who think they can get away with flirting with spiritual danger, only to end up hooked by it.

Don't be spiritually foolish. Don't take the enemy's bait.

Conclusion

Frederick Buechner once wrote, affirming his grandmother's wisdom: "Reality can be harsh, and . . . you shut your eyes to it only at your peril because if you do not face up to the enemy in all his dark power, then the enemy will come up from behind some dark day and destroy you while you are facing the other way."[2]

We are all in a spiritual war, and to be clueless about it is not an advantage! We must accept the reality that each of us is in a spiritual war and respond in three ways:

- Be alert! You can't win a war you don't know you are in.
- Wear spiritual armor: You must fight a spiritual war with spiritual weapons.
- Resist: Be spiritually shrewd. Don't take the enemy's bait.

REPETITION
Is the Key to Mental Ownership

Chapter Review

1. Christians must recognize the reality of s_____ w_____.
2. Christians must recognize the three types of spiritual c_____.
   a. D_____ T_____
   b. M_____ G_____
   c. H_____-to-H_____ C_____
3. Christians must use three types of spiritual d_____.
   a. A_____
   b. A_____
   c. R_____

The Christian Life in 1,000 Words—Review

(Only the last ten chapters will be displayed)

If something is important, you must repeat it until it changes you.

12. God will often d_____ us in a manner that seems, initially, to d_____ us.

13. God's blessing in the Old Testament was the "fruit of the v_____";
    in the New Testament, it is the "fruit of the S_____."
14. We were born for l_____. It is the principle of e_____,
    and its only end.
15. To be free to s_____ the seven seas, we must make ourselves slaves
    to the c_____.
16. In the Christian life, we r_____ by d_____.
17. When we pray, God will either give us what we ask or give us what
    we would have asked if we k_____ everything he k_____.
18. If we believe, we obey. If we do not o_____, it is because we do
    not b_____.
19. We should be g_____ for what the will of God gives us
    rather than u_____ for what it doesn't.
20. We strive for righteousness, not to get God to love us, but in
    g_____ that he already does.
21. You can't win a b_____ you don't know you're in.

THOUGHT/DISCUSSION
Is a Key to Understanding

*Answer these questions, either individually by journaling the answers or in
a small discussion group.*

1. Is the reality of spiritual warfare new to you? In just a few words,
   summarize your understanding of spiritual warfare.
2. Of the three types of spiritual combat, which one do you think is
   the most difficult to deal with?
3. Of the three types of spiritual defenses, which one seems easiest to
   use? Which one seems hardest?

DECISION TIME
Is a Key to Change

*Answer these questions, either individually by journaling the answers or in
a spiritual accountability group.*

1. How real does spiritual warfare seem to you? What do you think is the most important area of needed progress for you?
2. Do you think you are in a spiritual battle? If not, why do you think that is? If so, what do you think the battle is?
3. What do you think is the greatest weakness in your defenses for spiritual conflict? What do you think you need to do to shore up that weakness?

RECOMMENDED
Resource

What You Need to Know about Spiritual Warfare, Max Anders

*You won't
influence others
until you live it.*

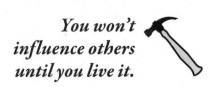

CHAPTER 22

THE CHALLENGE OF DISCERNING GOD'S WILL

The point of our lives is not to get smart or to get rich
or even to get happy. The point is to discover God's
purposes for us and to make them our *own*.
—*Cornelius Plantinga Jr.*[1]

 CENTRAL PASSAGE: Colossians 1:9—"We . . . ask that you may
be filled with the knowledge of His will in all spiritual wisdom
and understanding."

All earnest Christians want to know God's will. We instinctively want to please God. Plus, we want guidance when we make important decisions. We want the security of knowing we are doing what God wants us to do and that he will bless us for doing it.

But how do we get this guidance? We may be saying, "I have to decide which college I'm going to go to. I have to decide whom I am going to marry. I have to decide which job I'm going to take, whether or not to give money to a ministry that is asking me for it, or whether to put my kids in public school vs. Christian school. I have a million decisions I have to make. How can I have confidence that they are the decisions God wants me to make?"

The Bible leads us to seven principles that can guide us in discerning God's will.

1. Scripture helps us discern God's will.

S_____ *helps us discern God's will.*

The Bible is God's owner's manual for humanity. Just as car manufacturers put an owner's manual in each vehicle telling owners how to operate and maintain their new car, so God has given us the Bible, telling us how to operate and maintain ourselves.

The Bible does not speak directly to all of the specific decisions we have to make, but it is full of instructions and commands for many of life's decisions.

As examples, here's an incomplete but representative list of some things the Bible makes perfectly clear:

- Don't murder (Exodus 20:13).
- Don't commit adultery (Exodus 20:14).
- Don't lie, cheat, or steal (Exodus 20:15–16).
- Don't lust or covet (Exodus 20:17).
- Forgive others (Matthew 6:15).
- Work hard (Colossians 3:23).
- Be honest (Colossians 3:9).

In addition, in his book *The Mystery of God's Will*, Chuck Swindoll offers a specific list of things that are in God's will for every believer:

- Obey your parents (Ephesians 6:1).
- Marry a Christian (2 Corinthians 6:14).
- Work at an occupation (1 Thessalonians 4:11–12).
- Support your family (1 Timothy 5:8).
- Give to the Lord's work and to the poor (2 Corinthians 8–9; Galatians 2:10).
- Rear your children by God's standards (Ephesians 6:4).
- Meditate on the Scriptures (Psalm 1:2).
- Pray (1 Thessalonians 5:17).
- Have a joyful attitude (1 Thessalonians 5:16).

- Assemble for worship (Hebrews 10:25)
- Proclaim Christ (Acts 1:8)
- Set proper values (Colossians 3:2)
- Have a spirit of gratitude (Philippians 4:6)
- Display love (1 Corinthians 13)
- Accept people without prejudice (James 2:1–10)[2]

And the list goes on. There are hundreds of other clear instructions on God's will in Scripture. Nothing mysterious here! The better you know the Word of God, the less confusing the will of God will be.

Of course, these are general principles that fit many situations, rather than directives to our specific situations. But this we know: if any decision violates the principles of Scripture, it is a wrong decision.

2. Prayer helps us discern God's will.

P_____ helps us discern God's will.

Lewis Sperry Chafer, founder of Dallas Theological Seminary, once wrote, "His leading is only for those who are already committed to do as He may choose."[3]

God is not our genie in a bottle. Our wish is not his command. He is our God, and we are accountable to him for doing what he shows us and being willing to go where he leads us. As we submit to him and pray to him to guide us, we can rest in the confidence that he will.

Scripture teaches that we can pray to God for wisdom in decision making: "If any of you lacks wisdom, let him ask of God, who gives to all generously" (James 1:5).

Paul prayed for the Colossian believers that they might be "filled with the knowledge of His will" (Colossians 1:9).

Throughout Scripture, we see people praying to know God's will (Colossians 4:3; Philippians 4:6; James 1:5).

Prayer, along with a spirit of submission to God, is part of the process of determining God's circumstantial will.

3. Counsel helps us discern God's will.

C_____ helps us discern God's will.

Proverbs 11:14 says, "Where there is no guidance the people fall, but in abundance of counselors there is victory." James Packer once wrote, "Don't be a spiritual Lone Ranger; when you think you see God's will, have your perception checked. Draw on the wisdom of those who are wiser than you are. Take advice."[4]

Not only Scripture but also history and common sense tell us the wisdom of advice and counsel. The Old Testament kings had counselors, the presidents of the United States have counselors, the heads of large organizations have counselors . . . because they know, as the saying goes, "Two heads are better than one."

When seeking the will of God, go to those believers whose knowledge, whose wisdom, whose character, and whose spiritual maturity you trust. God will help guide you through them.

4. Wisdom helps us discern God's will.

W_____ helps us discern God's will.

God has given us a capacity for wisdom, and he expects us to use it. In Proverbs 2, King Solomon, the wisest man who ever lived, wrote:

> Make your ear attentive to wisdom,
> Incline your heart to understanding;
> For if you cry for discernment,
> Lift your voice for understanding;
> If you seek her as silver
> And search for her as for hidden treasures;
> Then you will discern the fear of the LORD
> And discover the knowledge of God.
> For the LORD gives wisdom . . . (vv. 2–6)

So, we see that wisdom can be gained by searching for it. It will keep us from many bad decisions, and will help us walk in God's moral will as well as his circumstantial will. With wisdom we combine what has been learned through Scripture, prayer, and counsel from others in order to make the best decisions we can.

5. Guidance helps us discern God's will.

G_____ helps us discern God's will.

Along with both counsel and wisdom, we take into account circumstances in which God may be guiding us. One cannot go through a closed door, so open and closed doors are sometimes the way God leads us and paces our progress on any given path. In 1 Corinthians 16:8–9, the apostle Paul wrote, "I will remain in Ephesus until Pentecost; for a wide door for effective service has opened to me ..."

In another example, Paul in 2 Corinthians 2:12–13 describes his arrival at the city of Troas and seeing how much work needed to be done. However, he then remarked, "I had no rest for my spirit, not finding Titus my brother." So, the circumstance of Paul's failure to find Titus gave him such a lack of inner peace that he changed his plans and went to Macedonia instead.

Wisdom requires that we include the reasonable avenues of potential leading from God before making a decision.

6. Freedom helps us discern God's will.

F_____ helps us discern God's will.

Not every decision has earthshaking consequences. Whether you wear a blue shirt or red shirt is not likely to have consequences. When no major consequences can be foreseen, you are free to do what you want.

For example, in 1 Corinthians 10:27, the apostle Paul wrote, "If one of the unbelievers invites you and you want to go, eat anything that is set before you without asking questions for conscience' sake."

This passage does not say, "If any unbelievers invite you to dinner, search the Scriptures, pray for days, seek the counsel of others, make a pros and cons list, and agonize sleeplessly." Rather, it says simply,

"If you want to go." Scripture gives us a measure of freedom to do what we want. Therefore, we should not strain to try to relate all decisions to spiritual significance or sovereign importance.

7. Love helps us discern God's will.

L_____ helps us discern God's will.

St. Augustine, a fourth-century believer, said, "Love [God], and do what thou wilt."[5] This might initially strike you as a shocking statement, suggesting that you can be completely unrestrained in the pursuit of your desires.

But with a closer look, we see that this is not the case. If we love God, we will do as he wants us to do. In John 14:15, the apostle John recorded Jesus's words, "If you love Me, you will keep My commandments." So, if we love God, we will not do anything that we understand to be wrong. In that spirit of submission and obedience, if we still do not know what God's will is—after consulting Scripture, praying, seeking guidance, and applying our best wisdom—Augustine is suggesting that God has given us the freedom to do as we would like to do.

This makes sense, if we assume that God, in his love, would not allow us to make a decision in this way that is not in his circumstantial will. There are times in life when we have no external verification of what God's will is, but we must make a decision anyway. In these circumstances, many have found Augustine's counsel to be very helpful.

Conclusion

Philip Yancey wrote this about discerning the will of God:

> I have a confession to make. For me, at least, guidance only becomes evident when I look backward, months and years later. Then the circuitous process falls into place and the hand of God seems clear. But at the moment of decision I feel mainly confusion and uncertainty. Indeed, almost all the guidance in my life has been subtle and indirect....

Looking back, the hand of God seems evident in those and many other choices. I had always thought of guidance as forward-looking. Yet in my own experience I have found the direction to be reversed. For me, guidance only becomes clear as I look backward. As for the present, my focus must be my relationship to God. Am I responding with obedience and trust?[6]

God does have a circumstantial will for us, but there will be times when we will not know what it is. In those times we can use Scripture, prayer, counsel, wisdom, and providential circumstances to make the best decision we are able to make, trusting God's leading in the process.

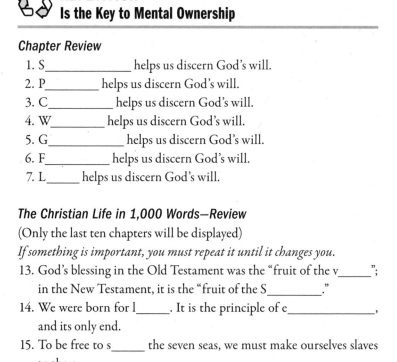 REPETITION
Is the Key to Mental Ownership

Chapter Review

1. S_____ helps us discern God's will.
2. P_____ helps us discern God's will.
3. C_____ helps us discern God's will.
4. W_____ helps us discern God's will.
5. G_____ helps us discern God's will.
6. F_____ helps us discern God's will.
7. L_____ helps us discern God's will.

The Christian Life in 1,000 Words—Review
(Only the last ten chapters will be displayed)

If something is important, you must repeat it until it changes you.

13. God's blessing in the Old Testament was the "fruit of the v_____"; in the New Testament, it is the "fruit of the S_____."
14. We were born for l_____. It is the principle of e_____, and its only end.
15. To be free to s_____ the seven seas, we must make ourselves slaves to the c_____.
16. In the Christian life, we r_____ by d_____.

17. When we pray, God will either give us what we ask or give us what we would have asked if we k_____ everything he k_____.

18. If we believe, we obey. If we do not o_____, it is because we do not b_____.

19. We should be g_____ for what the will of God gives us rather than u_____ for what it doesn't.

20. We strive for righteousness, not to get God to love us, but in g_____ that he already does.

21. You can't win a b_____ you don't know you're in.

22. The point of life is not to get smart or get rich or even get happy. The point is to discover God's p_____ for us and make them our o____.

THOUGHT/DISCUSSION
Is a Key to Understanding

Answer these questions, either individually by journaling the answers or in a small discussion group.

1. For which issue in your life are you seeking God's will right now? Which principle do you need to concentrate on in seeking it?

2. In your own words, summarize the role of Scripture in discerning the will of God.

3. Who are the people in your life to whom you feel most comfortable going for counsel?

DECISION TIME
Is a Key to Change

Answer these questions, either individually by journaling the answers or in a spiritual accountability group.

1. Which principle for discerning God's will do you find easiest to apply? Which one do you find the most difficult?

2. Lewis Sperry Chafer said, "His leading is only for those who are already committed to do as He may choose." Is discerning God's

will in your life impeded because you are not committed to doing as he may lead?

3. Explain whether Philip Yancey's observation in the conclusion about God's leading only being clear by looking backward encourages or discourages you.

RECOMMENDED
Resource

The Will of God, Charles Stanley

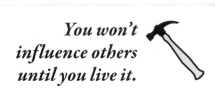

You won't influence others until you live it.

CHAPTER 23

THE IMPORTANCE OF GRIT

The most reliable predictor of success in life is grit.[1]
—*Angela Duckworth*

 CENTRAL PASSAGE: 1 Corinthians 15:58—"Be steadfast, immovable, always abounding in the work of the Lord, knowing that your toil is not in vain in the Lord."

True Grit is the title of a 1969 Western starring John Wayne in the role of U. S. Marshal Rooster Cogburn, who is hired by a young girl, Mattie Ross, to track down and bring to justice the man who murdered her father. Mattie hires Cogburn because she heard he had "true grit," which he demonstrates as the plot unfolds, accomplishing his mission.

"Grit" is defined as determination, perseverance, tenacity, fortitude, and courage. It is, simply, the refusal to give up. It is the spirit that Winston Churchill captured in a speech in 1941 in which he said: "Never give in, never give in, never, never, never, never—in nothing, great or small, large or petty—never give in except to convictions of honour and good sense."[2]

In education, the easiest thing to measure is IQ. However, those students with the highest IQ do not always do best in school, and certainly do not always do best in life. Psychologist Angela Lee Duckworth became intrigued with this seeming inconsistency and set out to understand what it was that most accurately foreshadowed success—both in academics and in life.

In a TED talk, Duckworth reported that she went to West Point to predict which cadets would stay in military training and which would drop out. She went to the National Spelling Bee to see if she could predict which students would go the farthest in competition. She studied which rookie teachers in demanding situations would still be there at the end of the school year, and who would be the most effective among these.[3]

Duckworth also partnered with businesses to see if they could determine which salespeople would keep their jobs and which would earn the most money.

In all those varied contexts, one characteristic emerged as a significant predictor of success. It wasn't social intelligence, it wasn't good looks, it wasn't physical health, and it wasn't IQ. "It was," she reported, "grit!"

Duckworth defined grit as "passion and perseverance for very long-term goals. Grit is having stamina; grit is sticking with your future, day in and day out, not just for the week, not just for the month but for years, and working really hard to make that future a reality. Grit is living life like it's a marathon, not a sprint."[4]

1. The Bible encourages grit.

The Bible e_____ grit.

The word "grit" does not appear in the Bible. But other synonyms do:

- **Endurance:** "Consider it all joy, my brethren, when you encounter various trials, knowing that the testing of your faith produces endurance. And let endurance have its perfect result, so that you may be perfect and complete, lacking in nothing" (James 1:2–4).
- **Steadfastness:** "Be steadfast, immovable, always abounding in the work of the Lord, knowing that your toil is not in vain in the Lord" (1 Corinthians 15:58).
- **Discipline:** "I discipline my body and make it my slave, so that, after I have preached to others, I myself will not be disqualified" (1 Corinthians 9:27).

- **Faithfulness:** "Be faithful until death, and I will give you the crown of life" (Revelation 2:10).

In addition, the Scriptures support the idea that grit can be encouraged:

- "Be strong and courageous! Do not tremble or be dismayed, for the LORD your God is with you wherever you go" (Joshua 1:9).
- "Be strong, act like a man" (David's charge to his son, Solomon, as David was about to die [1 Kings 2:2 NIV]).
- "Be strong and let your heart take courage, all you who hope in the LORD" (Psalm 31:24).
- "Be on the alert, stand firm in the faith . . . be strong" (1 Corinthians 16:13).

A Google search on "perseverance in the Bible" yields a treasure trove of passages that encourage us to have spiritual grit.

I agree, from reflecting on my own life as well as observing the lives of many people to whom I've ministered over the decades, that the single greatest predictor of spiritual success is "grit," a predisposition to simply never quit.

2. The Bible demonstrates grit.

The Bible d_____ grit.

Not only does the Bible teach grit, but it also demonstrates grit. Perhaps the four greatest examples of grit in the Bible are Joseph, Moses, David, and Paul.

The Example of Joseph

As a young man, Joseph was given dreams by God indicating that he would be a great leader. Yet, instead of becoming a great leader soon after the vision, Joseph's life went in what seemed to be the opposite direction.

Joseph's brothers sold him as a slave to Egypt, where he faithfully served Potiphar, the captain of Pharaoh's bodyguard, but he was nevertheless thrown into prison on false charges. He faithfully served the prison warden, but was forgotten for years. It seemed that Joseph was on the fast track in the opposite direction of being a great leader.

In spite of this, Joseph hung in there, never failing in his commitment to the Lord. When God's refining work in his life was done, he snatched Joseph out of the prison and made him Prime Minister of Egypt, fulfilling the initial promise.

The Example of Moses

God called Moses to go to Egypt to lead the Israelites out of slavery. Moses was extremely reluctant, but eventually went and appealed to Pharaoh to let the Israelites go. Instead, Pharaoh intensified the burden of slavery on the Israelites to backbreaking levels.

God used Moses to levy a series of ten plagues on Egypt that started out bad and got worse! Pharaoh finally relented and ejected the Israelites in exasperation, but soon afterward he changed his mind. He sent his army to get them back, so the Lord parted the Red Sea, enabling the Israelites to escape. On the other side of the sea, the Israelites ran out of food. Later, they ran out of water. Finally, the Amalekites attacked them.

The Israelites were so exasperated with this uninspiring deliverance that they wanted to kill Moses and go back to Egypt. Things were continually going from bad to worse.

In spite of this, Moses hung in there, never failing in his commitment to the Lord, and God eventually used him to lead the children of Israel to the borders of the promised land.

The Example of David

David was anointed by Samuel to be king over Israel. But instead of having a coronation ceremony the next day, David spent the next 15 years of his life running for his life from the current King Saul.

In spite of this, David hung in there, never failing in his commitment to the Lord. He eventually ascended to the throne of Israel, in fulfillment of God's prophecy and his symbolic anointing.

The Example of Paul

God revealed to Paul that he was going to be a missionary to the Gentiles, but for years Paul languished in obscurity and under opposition by church leaders.

Eventually, when Paul finally did begin his missionary work, he was beaten, shipwrecked, attacked by animals, imprisoned, robbed, and relentlessly deprived of the normal basics of life. But he hung in there, never failing in his commitment to the Lord, and he eventually was used as one of God's greatest servants.

Each of these individuals demonstrated grit . . . a stubborn refusal to give up on their purpose and calling in life.

3. The Bible rewards grit.

The Bible r_____ grit.

Not only does the Bible teach grit, and not only does it give examples of grit, but it also makes it clear that we will be rewarded for exercising grit!

- "Let us not become weary in doing good, for at the proper time we will reap a harvest if we do not give up" (Galatians 6:9 NIV).
- "He who sows sparingly will also reap sparingly, and he who sows bountifully will also reap bountifully" (2 Corinthians 9:6).
- "Well done, good and faithful slave. You were faithful with a few things, I will put you in charge of many things" (Matthew 25:21).
- "For I consider that the sufferings of this present time are not worthy to be compared with the glory that is to be revealed to us" (Romans 8:18).
- "For momentary, light affliction is producing for us an eternal weight of glory far beyond all comparison . . ." (2 Corinthians 4:17).

When you study grit on even just the secular level, the rewards of grit are clear. The internet is alive with websites touting grit and offering to help others develop grit. In addition, schools, both public and charter, are beginning to emphasize the value of "grit" over intelligence for academic success. Grit is such a popular idea that it has earned a place in modern culture. Why? Because culture is learning something God has woven into the fabric of his world: grit is a key to success in virtually any area of life.

Conclusion

To be foolishly and mindlessly gritty is not a virtue.

Nor is it true that we should never quit. While the criteria of when to quit are often very subtle, even people who possess great grit recognize that there are times when the right thing to do might be to quit something.

Nevertheless, there are many times when grit is exactly what is called for. In Ephesians 2:10, we read, "For we are His workmanship, created in Christ Jesus for good works, which God prepared beforehand so that we would walk in them."

When we are convinced that God has called us to a task, we all need grit to see it through.

Teddy Roosevelt, the personification of grit, once said:

> It is not the critic who counts; not the man who points out how the strong man stumbles or where the doer of deeds could have done them better. The credit belongs to the man who is actually in the arena, whose face is marred by dust and sweat and blood; who strives valiantly; who errs, who comes short again and again, because there is no effort without error and shortcoming; but who does actually strive to do the deeds; who knows the great enthusiasms, the great devotions; who spends himself in a worthy cause; who at the best knows in the end the triumph of high achievement, and who at the worst, if he fails, at least fails while daring greatly, so that his place shall never be with those cold and timid souls who neither know victory nor defeat.[5]

Grit is often the difference between success and failure, between reward and loss, between victory and defeat, and between really living or just sitting on the sidelines. It is often the difference of whether or not we are able to walk in the good works the Lord has prepared for us. If the Lord has called us to a task, we must respond with grit.

♻ REPETITION
Is the Key to Mental Ownership

Chapter Review

1. The Bible e_____ grit.
2. The Bible d_____ grit.
   a. The example of J_____
   b. The example of M_____
   c. The example of D_____
   d. The example of P_____
3. The Bible r_____ grit.

The Christian Life in 1,000 Words—Review

(Only the last ten chapters will be displayed)

If something is important, you must repeat it until it changes you.

14. We were born for l_____. It is the principle of e_____, and its only end.
15. To be free to s_____ the seven seas, we must make ourselves slaves to the c_____.
16. In the Christian life, we r_____ by d_____.
17. When we pray, God will either give us what we ask or give us what we would have asked if we k_____ everything he k_____.
18. If we believe, we obey. If we do not *o*_____, it is because we do not *b*_____.
19. We should be g_____ for what the will of God gives us rather than u_____ for what it doesn't.
20. We strive for righteousness, not to get God to love us, but in g_____ that he already does.
21. You can't win a b_____ you don't know you're in.

22. The point of life is not to get smart or get rich or even get happy. The point is to discover God's p_____ for us and make them our o____.

23. The most reliable predictor of success in life is g_____.

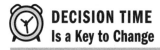

THOUGHT/DISCUSSION
Is a Key to Understanding

Answer these questions, either individually by journaling the answers or in a small discussion group.

1. Summarize in your own words what "grit" is.
2. Which of the biblical examples of grit do you find most inspiring, and why?
3. Which of the verses that talk about the reward of grit do you find most motivating?

DECISION TIME
Is a Key to Change

Answer these questions, either individually by journaling the answers or in a spiritual accountability group.

1. On a scale of 1–10, how "gritty" do you think you are? How gritty would you like to be?
2. Have you ever failed at something because you did not exercise grit? Have you ever succeeded at something because you *did* exercise grit?
3. Is there an area of your life right now that demands grit from you? Are you prepared to exercise the necessary grit? Might you need help and encouragement? If so, how could you get the help/encouragement you need?

RECOMMENDED
Resource

Grit, Angela Duckworth

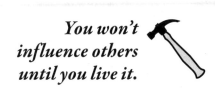

You won't influence others until you live it.

CHAPTER 24

THE IMPORTANCE OF SCRIPTURE

You must master the Bible so well that the Bible masters you.

> **CENTRAL PASSAGE:** Hebrews 4:12–"The word of God is living and active and sharper than any two-edged sword . . ."

There is a very close connection between God and his Word. Jesus himself is called *the Word of God* (John 1:1, 14; Revelation 19:13). To know God, you must know his Word; to honor God, you must honor his Word; and to be in touch with God, you must be in touch with his Word. Mighty promises are given to those who master the Bible so well that the Bible masters them.

- We are promised spiritual stability, fruitfulness, and true prosperity as we meditate on his Word day and night (Psalm 1:1–3).
- When the words of Jesus abide in us, our desires will be given to us according to God's will (John 15:7).
- Meditating on God's Word leads to prosperity and success in our spiritual endeavors (Joshua 1:8).
- We will have more wisdom than our enemies, more insight than our teachers, and more understanding than the aged (Psalm 119:97–100).
- We will have greater power over sin (Psalm 119:11).
- We will have comfort in affliction (Psalm 119:50).

- By drawing near to God, we have his promise that he will draw near to us (James 4:8).

These passages help us to realize how important the Bible is, and what remarkable potential we bring to our lives when we become serious students of Scripture.

There are four steps to mastering the Bible so well that the Bible masters you:

1. Read the Bible
2. Study the Bible
3. Memorize the Bible
4. Meditate on the Bible

Seems simple. Obvious, even, for those who have been Christians for a while. Yet very few people take all four steps. Many take one step. Some take two steps. A few take three steps. Very few take all four steps. As a result, very few people ever experience the full impact that the Bible offers.

1. Read the Bible for breadth of knowledge.

Read the Bible for b_____ of knowledge.

To begin a mastery of the Bible, you must read. This may seem self-evident to some, but it is groundbreaking to others who have never developed the habit. Some Christians do not read the Bible, or only read snippets that are attached to daily devotionals. This will not get you where you want to go. You must begin to read the Bible widely.

It is only by covering a lot of territory in Scripture that you gain a breadth of knowledge. If you never read the Old Testament, you will never have a general knowledge of it. If you only read the Gospels, or the Epistles, you will never have a basic grasp of the other sections of the Bible. As a result, your life will be untouched by important truth, plus your ability to connect the dots from various different Scripture passages—a critical component of a mature Christian experience—will be limited.

There is a simple way to read for breadth of knowledge. If you read the Bible for five minutes a day, you will read the Bible over thirty hours a year! (5 minutes × 365 days = 1,825 minutes divided by 60 minutes per hour = 30.4 hours!!!)

Think of it!!! Thirty hours a year! Perhaps no other discipline will provide a breadth of Bible knowledge more easily. If you want to master the Word so well that the Word masters you, begin by reading it.

Very early in my Christian experience, I was challenged to read the Bible at least five minutes a day. I took this challenge, and have not missed a day in over forty years. As a result, I have read the Bible for a couple thousand hours! And it was all done at the manageable pace of five minutes a day. There is no easier way I could have gained and maintained the breadth of knowledge of Scripture than by taking this simple step.

When you read, don't get bogged down by anything you don't understand. Just skip over it and read for the things you do understand. Otherwise, you will get bogged down. Also, underline everything that seems especially important.

Be sure to pick a readable translation. I read from the New Living Translation, which is more conversational, and I study from the New American Standard Bible, which is more literal. Most people read *and* study from the New International Version, which is more literal than the New Living Translation and more readable than the New American Standard Bible. But pick something that works for you. Then pick a time to read each day (I read in the evening before bed, but many people read first thing in the morning). And pick a plan. You can Google Bible reading plans for options. If nothing else, just read what interests you.

One helpful plan for beginners is to read only the historical books: Genesis, Exodus, Numbers (there might be some things in Exodus and Numbers that you could skip over to keep from getting bogged down), Joshua, Judges, 1 Samuel, 2 Samuel, 1 Kings, 2 Kings, Ezra, Nehemiah, Matthew, Mark, Luke, John, Acts. Those books give you the story of the Bible. Then you might finish the New Testament. After that, you might add Psalms and Proverbs to close out a high-altitude reading of the Bible.

2. Study the Bible for depth of knowledge.

Study the Bible for d_____ of knowledge.

Few of us can gain a depth of knowledge without sitting under skilled teachers. So, most people must sit under effective preaching of the Bible and get involved in a Bible study taught by an effective teacher. For maximum benefit, Bible study must have assignments that get you studying and interacting with the Bible on your own. To gain a depth of knowledge, you cannot be passive. You must become active in the process of deepening your knowledge. Crawl before you walk, and walk before you run, but deep, rich knowledge should be your goal. That is the only way you will progress to this destination.

If this is new to you, begin by attending a church that is committed to teaching the Bible, not only from the pulpit during sermons but also in small groups or Sunday school classes. You might also find helpful information in Christian bookstores or online. More seasoned Christians might also be able to give you valuable suggestions. Finally, if you are an avid reader, there is a wealth of knowledge available to you through good books available online or at Christian bookstores.

3. Memorize to master the Bible.

Memorize to m_____ the Bible.

It is through memorization of Scripture that the Bible begins to make a fuller impact in our lives. Until then, our knowledge of Scripture often lies dormant in our memory bank during the ups and downs of life, and may not impact our immediate thoughts and emotions.

The key is to memorize the Scripture deeply—so deeply that you can recite it without any struggle, so deeply you can recite it as easily as you can the Pledge of Allegiance. It is much better to have fewer verses memorized deeply than more verses memorized at a shallow level.

We should follow the example of Jesus. When he was tempted by the devil in Matthew 4, he quoted Scripture in response. When we know Scripture well enough to quote it immediately in response to life's challenges, the Bible begins to take on a power that it did not previously have in our lives.

Memorize whatever passages seem especially important to you for whatever season of spiritual life in which you find yourself. As you read the Bible, underline verses that jump out at you. Then spend time memorizing the ones most significant to you. You could also Google passages on subjects important to you (fear, anger, hope, faith, etc.), or ask friends.

The key, however, is to review your super-verses regularly. I review mine almost daily. When you add a new verse or passage, keep reviewing the old ones. If you have them memorized deeply, it doesn't take long to go through them all. It is amazing how many passages you can review at the speed of an auctioneer.

Memorize one verse so that you can say it without hesitation. Then memorize another, but add it to the first. Memorize a third one, but add it to the first two, and so on. Keep doing this for the rest of your life. Pretty soon, your command of Scripture will be a mile wide *and* a mile deep.

But don't bite off more than you can chew. If you memorize slowly but faithfully, it will eventually pay big dividends. Just as reading the Bible five minutes a day soon begins to accumulate impressive results, so does memorizing verses at a manageable pace. As we keep up this practice, adding verses that are important to us without dropping off the old ones, we find that we will eventually have many verses memorized deeply.

Be a spiritual tortoise, not a spiritual hare.

4. Meditate for the Bible to master you.

Meditate for the Bible to master y____.

To meditate on Scripture simply means to think about it over and over, repeatedly reciting it in an attempt to gain new insight from it.

Here, the goal is not just recalling the words, as one does in memorization, but really thinking about the contents of the passage with sustained focus. I do not always get new insights when I meditate on my verses. But when I do, they are like gold. Plus, the repetition and deep reflection have the added benefit of driving the truth more deeply into our hearts and subconscious mind, changing us from the inside out and resulting in additional insights down the road.

In his book *Change Your Heart, Change Your Life*, Gary Smalley makes a compelling case for meditating on Scripture.[1] He states that what we think about all day long, over long periods, eventually seeps into our heart as controlling beliefs. When we learn the right thoughts and mentally chew on them over and over, day after day, they lodge in our hearts as beliefs, and these beliefs become the controlling influences of our lives. If we do not think about Scripture enough, the truth of Scripture may be in our heads as knowledge, but not in our hearts as deep, controlling beliefs. I encourage you to get *Change Your Heart, Change Your Life* for additional help in pursuing this goal.

Conclusion

Most Christians are so busy that they have difficulty disciplining themselves to implement the four-step process of mastering the Bible so well that the Bible masters them. However, I encourage you to start, at least on a very small level.

1. Read: Begin to read the Bible 5 minutes a day.
2. Study: Attend a Bible study at a church or online for help in beginning to study the Bible.
3. Memorize: Choose one verse or brief passage to memorize. Just pick something that seems important to you. Memorize it so well that you can say it as fast as an auctioneer. To make this easy, read the verse/passage once a day for 30 days without trying to memorize it. By then, you will be so familiar with it that it will not take much more work to memorize the verse/passage deeply. Add a new verse/passage when you feel ready. Progress at a manageable pace.

4. Meditate: Review that verse/passage each day. Perhaps have a 3 × 5 in your Bible to remind you to review it when you read your Bible. When you are ready, add new verses while still reviewing old ones.

This will get you started on the four-step process, and once you get started it is easy to expand your efforts. *The key is just to start!* Then you can build on that foundation as you see fit. Major spiritual progress is yours when you master the Bible so well that the Bible masters you.

REPETITION
Is the Key to Mental Ownership

Chapter Review
1. Read the Bible for b_____ of knowledge.
2. Study the Bible for d_____ of knowledge.
3. Memorize to m_____ the Bible.
4. Meditate for the Bible to master y____.

The Christian Life in 1,000 Words—Review
(Only the last ten chapters will be displayed)
If something is important, you must repeat it until it changes you.

15. To be free to s_____ the seven seas, we must make ourselves slaves to the c_____.
16. In the Christian life, we r_____ by d_____.
17. When we pray, God will either give us what we ask or give us what we would have asked if we k_____ everything he k_____.
18. If we believe, we obey. If we do not o_____, it is because we do not b_____.
19. We should be g_____ for what the will of God gives us rather than u_____ for what it doesn't.
20. We strive for righteousness, not to get God to love us, but in g_____ that he already does.
21. You can't win a b_____ you don't know you're in.

22. The point of life is not to get smart or get rich or even get happy. The point is to discover God's p_____ for us and make them our o____.

23. The most reliable predictor of success in life is g_____.

24. You must m_____ the Bible so well that the Bible m_____ you.

THOUGHT/DISCUSSION
Is a Key to Understanding

Answer these questions, either individually by journaling the answers or in a small discussion group.

1. Are these four-fold steps new to you, or have you heard of each of them before? Have you ever seen them linked together before?

2. In your own words, describe this four-fold process.

3. Which one seems easiest for you? Which one seems hardest?

DECISION TIME
Is a Key to Change

Answer these questions, either individually by journaling the answers or in a spiritual accountability group.

1. How many of the steps to mastering the Bible are you currently taking? If you are not taking all four steps, why are you not?

2. Have you tried these steps before and failed? If so, why do you think you failed? Are you prepared to do all four steps now?

3. How much different do you think your life will be in five years if you do these four steps for five years, compared to if you do not?

RECOMMENDED
Resource

Change Your Heart, Change Your Life, Gary Smalley

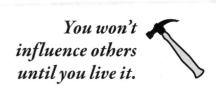

CHAPTER 25

SPIRITUAL FOCUS

To live well in the *world*, we must first live well with *God*.

CENTRAL PASSAGE: John 4:24—"God is spirit, and those who worship Him must worship in spirit and truth."

M any prisoners of war go into an elaborate inner world in order to survive. During the Vietnam War, for example, the outer world of the American prisoners of war was so horrifying, so inhumane and so meaningless, that to survive they had to escape into an inner world that they mentally created. The prisoners who successfully survived the POW experience were the ones who most effectively used their imagination to construct a vivid inner world to occupy their minds and protect their emotions.

Reportedly, one man built a house in his head in such detail that he could discuss with his cellmate the color of the tile on the bathroom floor. He later built that house in the Midwest exactly as he had imagined it in his mind. Another story is told of a man who scratched out a keyboard on the cement floor and imagined playing a piano for hours every day. He even composed new songs that he was able to play on the piano when he returned home.

Yet another prisoner is said to have mentally played golf courses he was familiar with. He imagined in exact detail which course he was on, seeing in his mind's eye each tee, each fairway, each bunker, and each green, and mentally rehearsed each shot. He reported being a better golfer after he was released than he was before. These people developed the ability to live in their "seen" world by mentally cultivating their "unseen" world. While these stories cannot be verified in all details, the principle of going into an inner world to develop the capacity to cope with the outer world is confirmed by John McCain from his own experience in his book *Faith of My Fathers*.[1]

Christians have a similar challenge! The physical world in which we live is so foreign, so hostile, and so counter to biblical values that we must create an inner, "unseen world" if we wish to prosper spiritually. Drawing on the reality of this inner world gives us the capacity to live well in the physical world. Almost like prisoners of war, we must spend large amounts of time . . .

- blocking out the physical world
- magnifying the spiritual world
- cultivating our understanding of biblical truth
- feeding our allegiance to biblical values
- mentally rehearsing biblical behavior

. . . so that, as we live in the physical world, we will think and act by heaven's values and not earth's.

This is, of course, extremely difficult. It is the very battleground of life. But the freedom to have a rich, Christian experience depends on exercising this considerable discipline.

1. The Bible teaches the importance of a vital inner life.

The Bible teaches the i_____ of a vital inner life.

The apostle Paul made this point clearly in 2 Corinthians 4:16–18, when he wrote:

Therefore we do not lose heart, but though our outer man is decaying, yet our inner man is being renewed day by day. For momentary, light affliction is producing for us an eternal weight of glory far beyond all comparison, while we look not at the things which are seen, but at the things which are not seen; for the things which are seen are temporal, but the things which are not seen are eternal.

Furthermore, in Colossians 3:1–2 Paul said, "Therefore if you have been raised up with Christ, keep seeking the things above, where Christ is, seated at the right hand of God. Set your mind on the things above, not on the things that are on earth."

Scripture is unambiguous. We must reorient our lives to reflect eternity if we are to experience the full blessing of God and if our lives are to be marked with the peace, power, and joy promised in Scripture. The only way to do this is to cultivate a vital inner life.

In addition, Jesus modeled the importance of a vital inner life.

While on earth, Jesus was continuously seeking solitude, prayer, and meditation to strengthen and cultivate his inner life and his connection with his Father.

Scripture gives us a number of clear instances of this:

- He spent time alone before major decisions (when he chose the twelve disciples—Luke 6:12).
- He spent time alone during a period of strenuous ministry (after feeding the five thousand—Matthew 14:21–23).
- He spent time alone while recovering from emotional trauma (upon learning of the beheading of his cousin, John the Baptist—Matthew 14:13).
- He spent time alone preparing for a great trial (on the night he was betrayed—Luke 22:41).
- Perhaps most emphatically, we see in Luke 5:16 that Jesus "would often slip away to the wilderness and pray." It was a normal part of his everyday existence.

So, we see a clear picture of Jesus nurturing a deep and strong inner life, modeling our need to do the same. The daily disciplines that gave Jesus his power and freedom are also the daily disciplines we need.

Dallas Willard made the point that we cannot behave "on the spot" as Jesus did unless we live the way Jesus did before the "spot" got there. It is futile to try to imitate Jesus in the difficult moments of life unless we adopt Jesus's overall lifestyle. What he did when he was alone is what enabled him to respond with spiritual success in the small and great moments of his life. The same must be true of us.[2]

2. Modern neuroscience enlightens us about a vital inner life.

Modern neuroscience e_____ us about a vital inner life.

Modern neuroscience is turning our understanding of the brain upside down. Instead of the brain being fixed and static as we used to think, we now know that it changes every day, and always changes in the direction of what we put into it.

In her book *Switch On Your Brain*, Christian neuroscientist Dr. Caroline Leaf explains that as we consciously direct our thinking, we can wire out toxic patterns of thinking and replace them with healthy thoughts. New networks begin to grow. We increase our intelligence and bring healing to both our brains and our physical bodies.

Dr. Leaf writes, "Five to sixteen minutes a day of focused, meditative capturing of thoughts shifts frontal brain states that are more likely to engage with the world. Research also showed that those same five to sixteen minutes of intense, deep thinking activity increased the chances of a happier outlook on life."[3]

Dr. Leaf further explains that when we direct our rest by introspection, self-reflection, and prayer; when we catch our thoughts; when we memorize and quote Scripture; and when we develop our mind intellectually, our brain function and our mental, physical, and spiritual health are greatly improved.

She goes on to write, "Regular meditators—by this I mean those who have adopted a disciplined and focused, reflecting thought life in which they bring all thought into captivity—show that their DMN (Default Mode Network) is more active and that there is more switching back and forth between networks. This means the brain is more active, growing more branches and integrating and linking thoughts, which translates as increased intelligence and wisdom and that wonderful feeling of peace. God also throws in some additional benefits such as increased immune and cardiovascular health."[4]

So, science is now showing us why what Scripture has been telling us for the last 2,000 years is so important. The brain needs a vital inner life if it is not to be held captive by the steady input of modern culture. That is why, as we saw in Chapter 6, we can only be living demonstrations of the fact that God's will is good and acceptable and perfect if we are transformed. And we will only be transformed as our minds are renewed (Romans 12:2).

3. There are three key components of a vital inner life.

There are three key c_____ of a vital inner life.

Prayer

First, of course, is prayer. As we saw in Chapter 17, prayer not only advances our relationship with God and brings the power of God to work on our behalf, but now we see that it also changes our brain. Prayer focuses our brain and improves its function, benefiting our mental, physical, and spiritual health. Prayer is part of our spiritual focus, and cultivating it will not only yield God's answers, but will also help bring the spiritual transformation for which believers long.

Scripture

Second is Scripture. As we saw in Chapter 6 (The Centrality of Mental Renewal to Spiritual Growth) and Chapter 24 (The Importance of Scripture), the Bible is central to everything in the Christian life. Unless we become serious students of Scripture, our minds will not have the spiritual strength and density necessary to have a vital inner life. We must begin the process of mastering the Bible so well that it masters us.

Focused Attention

The third category does not have a traditional name. It encompasses activities that are new to traditional evangelical Christianity.

Mental white space: Mental white space can be defined as a strategic pause between mental activities. It's really just intentional solitude. Our brains are kept so busy with the constant hailstorm of information and mental activity that if we don't give them down time, they become fatigued and are less effective, less creative, and less productive. If we do not let our brains slow down, wander, or even become bored, we pay a price—mental fatigue, mental fog, and impaired memory.

Jim Kwik in his book *Limitless* teaches that social media creates at least four dangers to the brain:

1. Digital deluge: with too much information to process, our brain gets overwhelmed and ceases functioning effectively.
2. Digital distraction: too much media burns brain calories, compromising mental and physical performance and causing us to feel alienated.
3. Digital dementia: short-term memory begins to deteriorate, like atrophy in unused muscles.
4. Digital deduction: we lose the ability to think critically.[5]

This is true for Christians and non-Christians alike. We cannot be mentally renewed to the point that our lives are transformed until we govern the impact of electronic media and social media on our brains. We must become effective at governing our exposure to electronic media and social media, thus giving our brains sufficient white space.

Mental rehearsal: while mental white space is important, in and of itself, it is also vital that we expand solitude to include neurological reconditioning.

The brain cannot tell the difference between a real and an imagined event. Therefore, mental rehearsal can be effective apart from actual rehearsal. And if mental rehearsal is added to actual rehearsal, the impact is even greater.

Therefore, it is important what we do with our minds, and we can use this feature of the mind to further our spiritual growth. We can mentally rehearse:

- Christlike behavior
- obeying Scripture
- ministry activity
- anything you want to be true of your spiritual life

As we envision ourselves doing these things, it changes our brains and makes it more likely that we will actually begin to act this way in the future.

We can also constructively use affirmations. An affirmation could be an attitude, value, habit, or action that is biblical but written as a statement rather than a Scripture verse. This has biblical precedent, I believe, in the life of David. He meditated not only on Scripture, but also on:

- Testimonies
- Statutes
- Precepts
- Decrees
- Ways
- Etc.

So, we might have an affirmation that is biblical, but not just a particular verse. Consider these possible examples:

- When people irritate, offend, or hurt me, I will take the high road.
- I will reflect the Lord's kindness to the people I meet.
- I will honor Christ in all that I think, say, and do.

- I will love my wife as Christ loved the church.
- I will do unto others as I would have others do unto me.

In repeating these (and potentially other) affirmations daily, the brain rewires itself and makes it easier to fulfill the affirmations in our behavior.

Mental refreshment: We can also do things that refresh us mentally:

- Work in a garden
- Play an instrument
- Take a walk in nature
- Read a good book
- Spend time with a valued friend
- Whatever truly refreshes your mind and makes it more receptive to the mental renewal process

The brain is a magnificent instrument that can be used to elevate us or defeat us. If we "love the Lord our God with all our mind," capitalizing on ancient traditions as well as modern discoveries, we can use the brain to turbocharge our spiritual progress.

Conclusion

If you put money in a vending machine for candy that costs more than you put in, nothing is going to come out. "Stupid machine!" you think, as you pound on the door and hammer the button. But, still, nothing comes out.

However, the problem is not that the machine is broken . . . the problem is that you haven't put enough money in.

Many Christians are frustrated with their spiritual lives, feeling that they have tried the Christian life and it hasn't worked. But in many cases, they are like people who put money into a vending machine in which everything costs more than they put in. When they don't get anything, they conclude that the Christian life is broken. It isn't broken; they just haven't put enough in!

We must spend sufficient mental time in the spiritual world so that we may live successfully in the physical world that is hostile to us. We will not have a normal or deeply satisfying Christian experience until we master this challenge.

REPETITION
Is the Key to Mental Ownership

Chapter Review

1. The Bible teaches the i_____ of a vital inner life.
2. Modern neuroscience e_____ us about a vital inner life.
3. There are three key c_____ of a vital inner life.
   a. P_____
   b. S_____
   c. F_____ A_____
      Mental w_____ s_____
      Mental r_____
      Mental r_____

The Christian Life in 1,000 Words—Review

(Only the last ten chapters will be displayed)

If something is important, you must repeat it until it changes you.

16. In the Christian life, we r_____ by d_____.
17. When we pray, God will either give us what we ask or give us what we would have asked if we k_____ everything he k_____.
18. If we believe, we obey. If we do not *o*_____, it is because we do not *b*_____.
19. We should be g_____ for what the will of God gives us rather than u_____ for what it doesn't.
20. We strive for righteousness, not to get God to love us, but in g_____ that he already does.
21. You can't win a b_____ you don't know you're in.
22. The point of life is not to get smart or get rich or even get happy. The point is to discover God's p_____ for us and make them our o____.

23. The most reliable predictor of success in life is g_____.
24. You must m_____ the Bible so well that the Bible m_____ you.
25. To live well in the w_____, we must first live well with G____.

THOUGHT/DISCUSSION
Is a Key to Understanding

Answer these questions, either individually by journaling the answers or in a small discussion group.

1. In your own words, how would you describe your understanding of a "vital inner life"?
2. Is neuroplasticity a new idea to you? How would you describe it in your own words?
3. What is the most important activity for your mind under the "Focused Attention" section?

DECISION TIME
Is a Key to Change

Answer these questions, either individually by journaling the answers or in a spiritual accountability group.

1. On a scale of 1–10, how vital do you think your inner life is? Where would you like it to be? What do you think you need to do to get it there?
2. How convinced are you of the value of applying the principles of neuroplasticity to spiritual growth?
3. What is the first step you will take from the "Focused Attention" section to encourage your spiritual growth?

RECOMMENDED
Resources

Switch on Your Brain, Dr. Caroline Leaf
Limitless, Jim Kwik

You won't
influence others
until you live it.
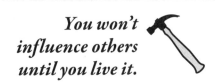

CHAPTER 26

THE "LITMUS TEST" OF GIVING

God doesn't want our *money*; he wants our *hearts*. The test of whether or not he has our *hearts* is if we give him our *money*.

>
>
> **CENTRAL PASSAGE:** Luke 16:13—"You cannot serve God and wealth."

King Solomon, the wisest man who ever lived, wrote, "Do not weary yourself to gain wealth, cease from your consideration of it. When you set your eyes on it, it is gone. For wealth certainly makes itself wings like an eagle that flies toward the heavens" (Proverbs 23:4–5). Later, he wrote, "He who loves money will not be satisfied with money, nor he who loves abundance with its income" (Ecclesiastes 5:10).

Money can be a wonderful servant, but is always a dreadful master.

The reason is that God created money to be an instrument. It was never intended to be an end in itself. Jesus himself said, "No servant can serve two masters; for either he will hate the one and love the other, or else he will be devoted to one and despise the other. You cannot serve God and wealth" (Luke 16:13).

There are four principles that guide us in becoming conduits for God's money:

- **The Stewardship Principle:** God owns everything we have. We are merely his asset managers.
- **The Treasure Principle:** We cannot take it with us, but we can send it ahead.

- **The Giving Principle:** The only thing we keep for eternity is what we give away on earth.
- **The Source Principle:** God wants us to view him as the source of all our money and to give accordingly.

1. The Stewardship Principle states that God owns everything we have. We are merely his asset managers.

The S_____ Principle states that God owns everything we have, and we are merely his asset managers.

In Matthew 25, Jesus teaches that when he gives us resources, we are to invest them in ways that produce a return on what he has given us. In Luke 12, he teaches that we are to lay up treasures in heaven, not on earth, because where our treasure is, there will our hearts be. We are held accountable for how we manage the things God gives us. Paul speaks to our stewardship responsibilities in 1 Corinthians 4 and says, "It is required of stewards that one be found trustworthy" (v. 2).

So, as stewards of the resources that God gives us, one of the things God asks us to do is to give back to him a portion of what he has given to us. Why would God make this request? The answer is that he does not need our money, but he wants our hearts. A primary way he has of testing our hearts is to ask for our money.

Haggai 2:8 tells us, "The silver is Mine and the gold is Mine." Deuteronomy 8:18 reminds us, "Remember the LORD your God, for it is he who gives you the ability to produce wealth" (NIV).

Giving generously keeps our heads clear and our hearts warm.

2. The Treasure Principle states that we cannot take money with us, but we can send it ahead.

The T_____ Principle states that we cannot take money with us, but we can send it ahead.

One of the primary ways we do things with God is to send our money ahead, investing it now in eternal things.

In his valuable book *The Treasure Principle*, Randy Alcorn tells a story that makes a powerful point on the wisdom of sending money ahead. He writes:

> Imagine you're alive at the end of the Civil War. You're living in the South, but you are a Northerner. You plan to move home as soon as the war is over. While in the South you've accumulated lots of Confederate currency. Now, suppose you know for a fact that the North is going to win the war and the end is imminent. *What will you do with your Confederate money?*
>
> If you're smart, there's only one answer. You should immediately cash in your Confederate currency for U.S. currency—the only money that will have value once the war is over. Keep only enough Confederate currency to meet your short-term needs.
>
> As a Christian, you have inside knowledge of an eventual worldwide upheaval caused by Christ's return. This is the ultimate insider trading tip: Earth's currency will become worthless when Christ returns—or when you die, whichever comes first. (And either event could happen at any time.) . . .
>
> There's nothing wrong with Confederate money, as long as you understand its limits. Realizing its value is temporary should radically affect your investment strategy. To accumulate vast earthly treasures that you can't possibly hold on to for long is equivalent to stockpiling Confederate money even though you know it's about to become worthless.
>
> According to Jesus, storing up earthly treasures isn't simply wrong. It's just plain stupid.[1]

Alcorn alludes to Jesus's words in Matthew 6:19–21, "Do not store up for yourselves treasures on earth, where moth and rust destroy, and where thieves break in and steal. But store up for yourselves treasures in heaven, where neither moth nor rust destroys, and where thieves do not break in or steal; for where your treasure is, there your heart will be also."

So, principle #2 of giving is that we cannot take money with us, but we can send it ahead.

3. The Giving Principle states that you only keep what you give away.

The G_____ Principle states that you only keep what you give away.

When we set our mind to give rather than accumulate, many good things happen.

The joy that comes from a life of giving is greater than the frustration of trying to get what we want from life. As usual, everything is backward. We think that getting what we want would give us happiness, while giving what we have would give us unhappiness, but the opposite is true.

Again, Randy Alcorn writes:

The act of giving is a vivid reminder that it's all about God, not about us. It's saying I am not the point, *He* is the point. He does not exist for me. I exist for Him. God's money has a higher purpose than my affluence. Giving is a joyful surrender to a greater person and a greater agenda. Giving affirms Christ's lordship. It dethrones me and exalts Him. It breaks the chains of [materialism] that would enslave me.

As long as I still have something, I believe I own it. But when I give it away, I relinquish the control, power, and prestige that come with wealth. At the moment of release the light turns on. The magic spell is broken. My mind clears, and I recognize God as owner, myself as servant, and other people as intended beneficiaries of what God has entrusted to me. . . .

Only giving breaks affluenza's fever. Only giving defies the spirit of entitlement. Only giving breaks me free from the gravitational hold of money and possessions. Giving shifts me to a new center of gravity—heaven.[2]

4. The Source Principle states that God wants us to view him as the source of all our money and to give accordingly.

The S_____ Principle states that God wants us to view him as the source of all our money and to give accordingly.

Christians, like non-Christians, tend to see their money as a reservoir out of which they draw to meet their needs. So, if a ministry need arises, they look at their reservoir and decide if they have enough money to meet the need. If they believe they do, they may give to the ministry need. If they believe they do not, they do not give to the need.

This is a safe way to live, and Christians can do a reasonable amount of good in this way if they manage their money carefully and are unselfish. However, there are times when God may call us to launch out in faith and give above and beyond our means.

In 2 Corinthians 8, the Macedonian Christians had experienced great suffering, with some of them apparently even being killed (1 Thessalonians 2:14–15). In the throes of this great suffering, they were also locked in deep poverty. Yet they begged the apostle Paul for the privilege of participating in the financial support of others in need, and gave generously. Paul writes that "according to their ability, and beyond their ability, they gave of their own accord" (2 Corinthians 8:3). They gave beyond their ability, something which Paul attributes to a work of grace that God had done in their lives.

If we see ourselves as conduits of God's reservoir of resources, we will be less inclined to hoard our resources and more inclined to pass them on, believing that God will take care of us as we do.

The principle from this passage is that if we view ourselves as conduits for his resources, he may funnel through us money that he wants to go to others' needs. In doing so, he meets the needs of others through us. He meets our needs as well. Our faith is stretched, and our joy is increased.

Conclusion

In 1888, Alfred Nobel, a Swedish chemist, was living in grand style off the fortune he made from inventing dynamite. As the story goes, when his brother died, a newspaper misunderstood and thought it was Alfred who had died. It published an article entitled "Merchant of Death Is Dead." Grieved that this would be his life legacy, Nobel made plans that, when he did pass away, he would leave 31 million Swedish kronor ($250 million in today's US dollars) to fund what has become known as the Nobel Prizes. Now, few people know who invented dynamite, but the whole world is aware of the Nobel Prizes.[3]

Alfred Nobel altered his legacy by investing his wealth in something of lasting value. We have the chance to do the same. Our obituary in heaven can be altered, no matter how old we are, when we invest our wealth, no matter how meager it might be, in eternal things. We can become a divine conduit through which God's resources flow.

REPETITION
Is the Key to Mental Ownership

Chapter Review

1. The S_____ Principle states that God owns everything we have, and we are merely his assets managers.
2. The T_____ Principle states that we cannot take money with us, but we can send it ahead.
3. The G_____ Principle states that you only keep what you give away.
4. The S_____ Principle states that God wants us to view him as the source of all our money and to give accordingly.

The Christian Life in 1,000 Words—Review
(Only the last ten chapters will be displayed)
If something is important, you must repeat it until it changes you.

17. When we pray, God will either give us what we ask or give us what we would have asked if we k_____ everything he k_____.
18. If we believe, we obey. If we do not *o*_____, it is because we do not *b*_____.

19. We should be g_____ for what the will of God gives us rather than u_____ for what it doesn't.
20. We strive for righteousness, not to get God to love us, but in g_____ that he already does.
21. You can't win a b_____ you don't know you're in.
22. The point of life is not to get smart or get rich or even get happy. The point is to discover God's p_____ for us and make them our o____.
23. The most reliable predictor of success in life is g_____.
24. You must m_____ the Bible so well that the Bible m_____ you.
25. To live well in the w_____, we must first live well with G____.
26. God doesn't want our m_____, he wants our h_____; and the test of whether he has our h_____ is if we give him our m_____.

THOUGHT/DISCUSSION
Is a Key to Understanding

Answer these questions, either individually by journaling the answers or in a small discussion group.

1. Which of the four principles do you find most motivating?
2. Which of the four principles do you find most challenging?
3. In your own words, what do you think it means that we only keep what we give away?

DECISION TIME
Is a Key to Change

Answer these questions, either individually by journaling the answers or in a spiritual accountability group.

1. Do you view your wealth as your own or God's? Are you struggling with this concept, or have you resolved it in your mind?
2. Are you currently "sending your wealth ahead"? Do you think you are sending enough?

3. What do you think is the most important decision you should make as a result of reading this chapter?

RECOMMENDED
Resource

The Treasure Principle, Randy Alcorn

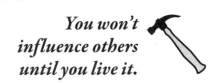

You won't influence others until you live it.

THE CHRISTIAN'S JOB

God gives each of us a *job* to do and *gifts* with which to do it.

 CENTRAL PASSAGE: 1 Peter 4:10—"As each one has received a special gift, employ it in serving one another as good stewards of the manifold grace of God."

God gives each of us a job to do and gifts with which to do it. This may be news to you, but as we look at key Scriptures each of us can learn what this job is, what the gift or gifts may be, and how we can enter into a life that is more full when each of us begins to understand and enter into this job and these gifts.

1. God has given each Christian a job to do.

God has given each Christian a j____ to do.

Ephesians 2:10 is a powerful passage with dramatic implications: "For we are His workmanship, created in Christ Jesus for good works, which God prepared beforehand so that we would walk in them."

From this passage, we understand that before we were even born, God planned good works that he wanted us to do. Amazing!

This is one of the keys to a rich and fulfilling life—to get involved doing the things God has called us to do. These things may not be big in the eyes of others, but if God has planned them for us, they are big to us. Understanding this can set us on a course of spiritual adventure to discover what it is that God has prepared for us that will fill our lives with deeper fulfillment.

We were created by God to live for something greater than self, and until we begin to live for something greater than self, we will squander our lives on things that do not matter for eternity.

Only when we rise above the gravitational pull of ordinary life and begin to live for things that are greater than self and beyond time will we be filled with a sense of meaning and purpose, having assurance that our lives count for something.

2. God has given us spiritual gifts with which to do our jobs.

God has given us spiritual g_____ with which to do our jobs.

Some individuals have extraordinary natural abilities. Mozart had remarkable musical abilities, Michael Jordan had remarkable athletic abilities, and Einstein had remarkable mental abilities.

Just as God has given some people extraordinary abilities to accomplish physical things, so he has given each Christian special abilities with which to accomplish spiritual things.

First Peter 4:10 says, "As each one has received a special gift, employ it in serving one another as good stewards of the manifold grace of God." This passage gives us the raw material for a working definition of spiritual gifts: a spiritual gift is a special capacity given to a believer by God with which the believer is to serve others.

Spiritual gifts are necessary because natural talent does not produce spiritual change. For example, Jesus said in John 15:5, "apart from Me you can do nothing." But what did he mean? The answer is given to us in the context, which is that of *bearing fruit*. In John 15, the entire first part of the chapter is talking about abiding in Jesus in order to be able to bear spiritual fruit. So, in the context of bearing spiritual fruit we can do nothing without Jesus.

In another example, Jesus said in John 6:44, "No one can come to Me unless the Father who sent Me draws him." We cannot lead anyone to Jesus. Only God can.

Finally, the apostle Paul wrote in 1 Corinthians 2:12–13, "Now we have received, not the spirit of the world, but the Spirit who is from God, so that we may know the things freely given to us by God, which things we also speak, not in words taught by human wisdom, but in those taught by the Spirit, combining spiritual thoughts with spiritual words."

The point of these three passages is that humans do not have the inherent capacity to effect spiritual change in the lives of others. Only God can produce spiritual change in the lives of others.

However, God has chosen to use us as instruments to help execute his will in the lives of others; one way he does this is through giving us spiritual gifts. Our spiritual gifts may not seem as amazing as Mozart's musical capacity, but on the spiritual level they are equally amazing. As we use our spiritual gifts, God works through us to accomplish spiritual change in the lives of others (something we could not do on our own). In this process he enriches us, in that we inherently enjoy using our spiritual gifts and are gratified with the results.

3. There are seven spiritual gifts for "service" in the church.

There are seven spiritual gifts for "s_____" in the church.

There are a number of teachings on spiritual gifts as a whole in Scripture about which there are a number of credible positions (Romans 12:6–8; 1 Corinthians 12:7–10; Ephesians 4:11–12), but there is common agreement on the "service" gifts in Romans 12:6–8, which this chapter focuses on.

Romans 12:6–8 lists seven gifts that seem specifically suited for serving and ministering to others on an ongoing basis in the church. There is widespread agreement that these gifts should be functioning in the church, and they are helpful in guiding us to what the "good works" are that God has prepared for us to do.

There are no definitions of spiritual gifts in Scripture, but over the years various possible definitions have been created to give general guidance in understanding the subject.

a. Prophecy: Christians with the gift of prophecy are likely to display a strong sense of right and wrong, along with the urgency to compel people to do what is right. Because none of the other gifts in Romans 12 are spectacular or miraculous gifts, this concept of prophecy probably does not include the miraculous ability to tell the future or to receive direct messages from God, which many believe to be the meaning of prophecy in the list of sign gifts given in 1 Corinthians 12:7–10. Rather, it likely focuses on the other, less spectacular aspects of prophecy, which are used simply to confront people with the truth of Scripture and urge them to obey.

b. Service: Christians with the gift of serving may have a strong desire to help others. Their mission in life may be to come alongside others to help them out of problems or to help them be successful in something they have undertaken. The Greek word for "service" comes from the root word used to describe "waiting" on tables. People with this gift may have difficulty understanding what their gift is, because they are often willing to do pretty much anything as long as it involves helping others with their needs.

c. Teaching: Christians with the gift of teaching may feel compelled to help others understand the truth of Scripture, believing that it is easier to obey Scripture if you understand it. Therefore, their gift might include not only the compulsion to help people understand the truth of Scripture, but also a better-than-normal ability to communicate the truth in ways that help people to understand.

d. Exhortation: Christians with the gift of exhortation may have a keen desire to encourage others. The Greek word for "exhortation" has a broad range of meanings including to appeal to, to exhort, to comfort, to cheer, or to encourage others. It comes from a word that means "to come alongside to help." Christians with this gift may find meaning in helping others who are struggling in life and need someone to come alongside them to give them moral and practical support.

e. Giving: Christians with the gift of giving are often strongly motivated to contribute to the practical physical needs of others. They may be abnormally aware of the financial needs of others and of the value or importance of financial assistance. In addition, they may be more inclined to help others financially than most, and may also encourage others who do not have the gift of giving to share their finances with those in need or to put those finances to a worthy goal.

f. Leading: Christians with the gift of leading may be inclined to step out into the future and have the ability to persuade others to follow. Some spiritual gift inventories call this the gift of "administration or managing." However, the Greek word means "to be at the head, to rule, to lead." A person with this gift may be a good administrator, or might not be. A good leader might be a poor administrator, and a good administrator might be a poor leader. The broader concept of being at the head of something might best be defined broadly as "leading," with no sense of the more specific abilities a leader might have.

g. Mercy: Christians with the gift of mercy might show a greater-than-normal sensitivity to the needs of others, especially to those who are hurting. Whereas the gift of "service" might tend to target the practical needs of others, the gift of "mercy" might tend to target the spiritual and emotional needs of others.

Do you see yourself in any of these descriptions? Many people see themselves with more than one spiritual gift, though one might seem greater than others.

At the same time, some people do not see any one of these gifts as being more pronounced than others in their lives. But it often takes "getting involved" in order for Christians to learn, through experience, what their gifts might be.

4. God rewards faithfulness, not results.

God rewards f_____, not r_____.

One potential danger with gifts is the possibility of feeling that your gifts are either inferior or superior to others' gifts. This is not the case. God is the one who gives spiritual gifts, and he does so according to his overall sovereign plan. Therefore, no one should feel inferior or superior to anyone else. We do not choose our gifts, and all gifts are equally important in God's plan.

On top of this, God is the one who determines the results of our spiritual gifts. We have already seen that no human can save another person or open their heart and eyes to spiritual truth. Only God can do this. Therefore, the results of our spiritual gifts are accomplished by God, not us. We can take no credit for anything positive that happens.

We are not responsible for results. We are only responsible for faithfulness to use our spiritual gifts.

The apostle Paul wrote in 1 Corinthians 4:2, "Moreover, it is required of stewards that they be found faithful" (ESV). It is not required of stewards that they be found successful. It is required that they be found faithful.

In a parable in Luke 19, Jesus praised the stewards who invested their master's money but scolded the steward who did nothing with his master's money. He praised their faithfulness rather than the degree of their success.

The good news with this is that each of us can be equally faithful. You may be given a gift that is small in the eyes of people, but you are 100 percent faithful to it. Others may be given gifts that are great in the eyes of people, and they are 100 percent faithful to their gifts. Both you and they will be equally rewarded by God for 100 percent faithfulness.

For this reason, we need not feel inferior or superior for our gifts. We need to just be focused on serving God with what he has given us, and God will reward us accordingly.

Francis Schaeffer wrote a book titled *No Little People*. In it, he makes the case that there are no little people, no little places, and no little jobs. Everyone is important to God. All places are important to God. And all jobs are important to God.

Conclusion

It is a profound privilege that God uses us to accomplish his will in the lives of others. When we get involved using our spiritual gifts, this can give us a sense of meaning and purpose in life that we cannot have otherwise. We are to be faithful to whatever he gives us to do each day, leaving the results to him. He rewards faithfulness, not success.

REPETITION
Is the Key to Mental Ownership

Chapter Review
1. God has given each Christian a j____ to do.
2. God has given us spiritual g_____ with which to do our jobs.
3. There are seven spiritual gifts for "s_____" in the church.
4. God rewards f_____, not r_____.

The Christian Life in 1,000 Words—Review
(Only the last ten chapters will be displayed)
If something is important, you must repeat it until it changes you.

18. If we believe, we obey. If we do not o_____, it is because we do not b_____.
19. We should be g_____ for what the will of God gives us rather than u_____ for what it doesn't.
20. We strive for righteousness, not to get God to love us, but in g_____ that he already does.
21. You can't win a b_____ you don't know you're in.
22. The point of life is not to get smart or get rich or even get happy. The point is to discover God's p_____ for us and make them our o____.
23. The most reliable predictor of success in life is g_____.
24. You must m_____ the Bible so well that the Bible m_____ you.
25. To live well in the w_____, we must first live well with G____.
26. God doesn't want our m_____, he wants our h_____; and the test of whether he has our h_____ is if we give him our m_____.
27. God gives us a j____ to do and g_____ with which to do it.

THOUGHT/DISCUSSION
Is a Key to Understanding

Answer these questions, either individually by journaling the answers or in a small discussion group.

1. In your own words, describe what you understand a spiritual gift to be.
2. Was it news to you that, even before you were born, God prepared good works for you to do? Describe how this makes you feel.
3. In your own words, describe what it means to you to know that you cannot effect spiritual change in anyone else; that God must do it.

DECISION TIME
Is a Key to Change

Answer these questions, either individually by journaling the answers or in a spiritual accountability group.

1. Do you have an idea of what your God-given job is in life? Are you doing it? If not, are you willing to do it?
2. Do you wish you had a bigger/better spiritual gift? Do you battle with disappointment over not having greater gifts? How content are you with your job and gift?
3. How faithful do you believe you are to your job and gift? 10 percent? 50 percent? 75 percent? 100 percent? What would have to be true for you to be more faithful?

RECOMMENDED
Resource

Spiritual Gifts Inventory (learn your spiritual gift) https://gifts.church growth.org/spiritual-gifts-survey/

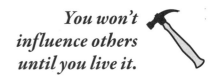

*You won't
influence others
until you live it.*

CHAPTER 28

THE CHRISTIAN DEFINITION OF SUCCESS

Success is being faithful to what God asks of us,
and leaving the results to him.

 CENTRAL PASSAGE: 1 Corinthians 4:2—"Now it is required that those who have been given a trust must prove faithful" (NIV).

Many Americans are preoccupied with success, which is often interpreted as being #1. Sports teams and athletes are rarely satisfied with being #2. The old adage is, "No one remembers who came in second."

Beyond that, each year *Fortune* magazine publishes the Fortune 400, a list of the 400 richest individuals in the United States. Is being on that list "success"? One of my alma maters sends out a regular mailing that lists the achievements of its graduates, and there are many stories of that institution's alumni having done well. Is that success?

Just what is success? Often, it is described as "getting what we want." Typically, we feel that if we get what we want, we are successful. But, of course, that may depend on what we want. We will explore the answer to these questions in four parts:

1. Success doesn't permanently satisfy, because after we have gotten what we want, we typically want something more.

Success doesn't permanently satisfy, because after we have gotten what we want, we typically want something m_____.

The Bible says that the eyes of man are never satisfied (Proverbs 27:20). And so it is. The world's concept of success can be a carrot on a stick. When you take a step toward it, it moves a step farther away. So, we have to decide whether or not we're going to be the donkey.

The old saying is often true: "You climb the ladder of success only to discover that it's leaning against the wrong wall."

It is certainly all right to have goals, and it is certainly all right to have vision for one's life. It is certainly all right to work hard to accomplish things. That may be God's will for your life. Determination can guide and motivate us to achieve good things we might not otherwise achieve. However, *needing* to be a success in earthly terms in order to be happy is a subtle trap, and the enemy can use it to discourage and defeat us if we let him.

2. Success is not necessary, because God loves us for who we are, not for what we accomplish.

Success is not necessary, because God loves us for who we are, not for what we a_____.

One of the greatest things to learn in life is that, by God's definition, earthly success is not necessary for us on any level or for any reason. Each of us has inherent, infinite worth because, and only because, we are created in the image of God.

A newborn baby has done nothing to earn the love of its parents. The love of the parents for the baby comes from within the hearts of the parents, not from anything the baby has done to earn their love. The same is true with us and God. The love that God has for us comes not from anything we have done to earn his love; rather, it comes from the heart of God.

We are his creations, his children, his adopted heirs, ones for whom he died. God created us so that he could have a relationship with us, so he could be kind to us forever, and so he could prove to the world, through us, that he is who he says he is . . . omnipotent, omniscient, omnipresent, loving, kind, and good. He wants to prove to the universe, through us, that he is all these things.

If we insist on pursuing earthly success as a measure of our worth, then two unpleasant things may happen:

First, circumstances may thwart us. We cannot control people, possessions, and circumstances well enough to guarantee success.

Second, God may pry our stubby little fingers, one at a time, off the thing we think will satisfy, so that we will learn that only he can satisfy.

God loves us too much to allow us to go through life blindly trying to find satisfaction in anything other than himself. He is the only One who can satisfy us completely and unendingly. In fact, he may induce failure in our earthly schemes so that we will learn to transfer our affections to him.

3. We can achieve true success by being faithful to God and leaving the results to him.

We can achieve true success by being faithful to God and leaving the r_____ to him.

When it comes to producing spiritual results that are pleasing to God, all we can do is be faithful. God produces the results. The apostle Paul wrote in 1 Corinthians 3:6, "I planted, Apollos watered, but God was causing the growth." This reinforces the words of Jesus who said in John 15:5, "Apart from Me you can do nothing." Why? Because bearing fruit is beyond our ability. Just as a flamethrower will not stop the flood, and just as a flashlight will not stop a forest fire, so human effort cannot produce divine results.

Only God can bring forth spiritual fruit. But he will use us to produce his fruit if we are faithful to him.

In Joshua 1:8, God tells us what it takes to succeed:

"This book of the law shall not depart from your mouth, but you shall meditate on it day and night, so that you may be careful to do according to all that is written in it; for then you will make your way prosperous, and then you will have success."

If we work this passage backward, we see that we can have good (spiritual) success if we will do according to all that is written in God's Word. And, to do all that is written in God's Word, we must meditate on it. So, biblically, our spiritual success is tied to our readiness to master the Bible so well that the Bible masters us.

Even then, it is not we who produce spiritual results, but God produces the results as we are faithful and obedient to him.

4. Divinely induced temporal failure can produce eternal success.

Divinely induced t_____ failure can produce e_____ success.

Sometimes our earthly "failures" may be divinely induced in order to create eternal rewards.

James 1:2–4 says, "Consider it all joy, my brethren, when you encounter various trials, knowing that the testing of your faith produces endurance. And let endurance have its perfect result, so that you may be perfect and complete, lacking in nothing."

The apostle Paul reinforced that idea when he said, "For momentary, light affliction is producing for us an eternal weight of glory far beyond all comparison . . ." (2 Corinthians 4:17)

Inherent within these passages is the implication that there are times when things are not going to go the way we want them to. There are going to be times when we will fail. But these times can produce in our lives rich spiritual fruit: personal transformation here on earth and disproportionate eternal reward.

Think of Job. His life fell apart. He experienced seemingly unending failure. And there was nothing he could do about it. All he could do was remain faithful.

Think of Joseph. His life fell apart. He experienced failure after failure. And there was nothing he could do about it but remain faithful.

There is a similar example of Moses. He plummeted from the

royal halls of Egypt to the desert sands of Midian, and there was nothing he could do but remain faithful.

So, what do we do when it feels like we are failures, and when God doesn't seem to be doing anything to help us? Or, worse, when it feels as though God is working against us?

First, evaluate with eternal values, not temporal values.

We must understand that, ultimately, success is determined by eternal values and not temporal values. The world's values will lead us in the wrong direction every time.

Jesus said in Mark 10:42–45 that if we want to be great, we must become servants.

Well, a servant doesn't look successful in the eyes of the world, but a servant does look successful in the eyes of God; and such a servant will be richly rewarded for faithfulness. So, while we cannot become so heavenly minded that we are no earthly good—by being careless, lazy, and uncaring about how we do things on earth—we must nevertheless transfer our value system to heaven and recognize that failure from earth's perspective is not usually failure at all from heaven's perspective.

Second, account for divine training sessions.

We must understand that God takes us through training sessions, and during these we may feel that we have been taken out of the game.

Basketball players are made in the summers and displayed in the winters. In the summers (offseason), it's running, lifting weights, calisthenics, shooting free throws, and no basketball games. It's a time of preparation for the games, which come later, in the winter (during basketball season).

God may do the same with us, putting us through periods of preparation before he uses us.

Third, factor in eternal rewards.

Jesus said, "I glorified You on the earth, having accomplished the work which You have given Me to do" (John 17:4). Jesus glorified the

Father by completing the work the Father had given him to do. We glorify God by completing the work he has given us to do. So, whether or not we think the work is befitting our potential, if it is what he has given us to do . . . and if we do it . . . we glorify him. And in doing so, we receive disproportionate eternal reward (Romans 8:18).

So, our continuous challenge is to serve God, even if that service makes us look like failures on earth. If we are doing what he has asked us to do, we are certainly not failures in heaven. We must understand we are "heavenlings," not earthlings.

Fourth, welcome divinely-induced failures as instruments of spiritual transformation.

We should not resent failures; rather, we should welcome them as instruments through which God will shape us into his image.

God takes us through trials, as we learned in James chapter 1, in order to make us into the kind of people he wants us to be. So, we should not resent the trials but should welcome them as the instruments through which God will shape us further into his image and make us more like Christ.

Conclusion

In conclusion, we must let God be God, we must let him be boss, and we must understand that he loves us and would never squander his investment in us. And if we focus on faithfulness rather than success, God can use us however he chooses, in ways more important than we realize. We will thus continue racking up eternal rewards that will astonish us when we get to heaven.

Understanding how to process failure when we do things wrong, as well as when we do things right, helps us to transform earthly failure into heavenly success and makes failure become a rich and valued friend.

Like people looking at the messy underside of a tapestry, we must imagine in our minds the beauty that must be forming on the top side. We must focus on faithfulness rather than success, taking joy from an eternal perspective rather than frustration from a temporal one. Someday, when the weaving is done, we will get to see the beauty on the other side.

 REPETITION
Is the Key to Mental Ownership

Chapter Review

1. Success doesn't permanently satisfy, because after we have gotten what we want, we typically want something m_____.
2. Success is not necessary, because God loves us for who we are, not for what we a_____.
3. We can achieve true success by being faithful to God and leaving the r_____ to him.
4. Divinely induced t_____ failure can produce e_____ success.

The Christian Life in 1,000 Words—Review

(Only the last ten chapters will be displayed)

If something is important, you must repeat it until it changes you.

19. We should be g_____ for what the will of God gives us rather than u_____ for what it doesn't.
20. We strive for righteousness, not to get God to love us, but in g_____ that he already does.
21. You can't win a b_____ you don't know you're in.
22. The point of life is not to get smart or get rich or even get happy. The point is to discover God's p_____ for us and make them our o____.
23. The most reliable predictor of success in life is g_____.
24. You must m_____ the Bible so well that the Bible m_____ you.
25. To live well in the w_____, we must first live well with G____.
26. God doesn't want our m_____, he wants our h_____; and the test of whether he has our h_____ is if we give him our m_____.
27. God gives us a j____ to do and g_____ with which to do it.

28. Success is being f_____ to what God asks of us and leaving the r_____ to him.

THOUGHT/DISCUSSION
Is a Key to Understanding

Answer these questions, either individually by journaling the answers or in a small discussion group.

1. In your own words, describe what you understand success to be.
2. How might you have described success before reading this chapter?
3. Can you think of a time when you did not succeed, and it turned out to be for the best?

DECISION TIME
Is a Key to Change

Answer these questions, either individually by journaling the answers or in a spiritual accountability group.

1. Can you think of a time when you succeeded in something that felt good but didn't last?
2. How hard do you find it to be faithful to God and leave the results to him?
3. Do you have an example of divinely induced failure in your life? Do you think you handled it well?

RECOMMENDED
Resource

Take the Stairs, Rory Vaden

You won't
influence others
until you live it.
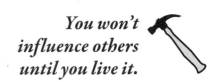

CHAPTER 29

THE PRIORITY OF EVANGELISM

We must share the gospel, not only because *others* need
to hear it, but also because *we* need to share it.

 CENTRAL PASSAGE: Matthew 28:19—"Go therefore and make
disciples of all the nations . . ."

Being born again is the single greatest privilege of human existence.
It does two things. First, it saves you *from* the worst imaginable
fate. Second, it saves you *to* the best imaginable fate.

The worst imaginable fate is to be eternally separated from God.

The best imaginable fate is to be eternally united with God without
any encumbrance from sin, living together forever with him and
all his children, and enjoying the glories and pleasures of heaven.

If being born again is the single greatest privilege of human existence, sharing the message of salvation is the single greatest responsibility of human existence. How could we, as Christians, possess this
eternally significant knowledge and not be dedicated to sharing it
with the world?

Those who have grasped the importance of the gospel have gone
to tremendous lengths to share it with others. Missionaries have
sacrificed their lives to take the gospel to those who have never
heard. Perhaps the best known of such stories is the tale of Nate
Saint and Jim Elliot. Along with three of their friends, they traveled
to the Ecuadorian jungle with the hope of sharing Christ with the
Huaorani Indians. Instead, the missionaries all died on the banks of
the Curaray River from the spears of the Huaorani.

For Christians in the Western world, it is difficult to imagine having to pay such a price. In our place and time in history, sharing the gospel is typically easier and less dangerous; however, it is no less important! When we grasp the importance of sharing the gospel, we need to be committed to paying whatever price God might ask us to pay for the sake of taking the message of salvation to those who have not heard.

In his providence some pay a great price, while others pay a lesser price. But we all must be prepared to pay the price God calls us to pay.

1. The Bible says that we are commanded to evangelize.

The Bible says that we are c_____ to evangelize.

Jesus's teaching about evangelism centers on Matthew 28:19–20, which is called the Great Commission:

> "Go therefore and make disciples of all the nations, baptizing them in the name of the Father and the Son and the Holy Spirit, teaching them to observe all that I commanded you; and lo, I am with you always, even to the end of the age."

This passage makes it clear that the evangelization of the world is a prime directive for Christians.

This command does not refer only to overseas evangelism; it means evangelism of the whole world wherever there is need of the gospel. The gamut is covered in Acts 1:8, where Jesus told his disciples (and by implication, us as well) that they were to be witnesses to him in Jerusalem (the city in which they lived), Judea and Samaria (the surrounding countries), and the remotest part of the world. Conceptually it is a target, with Jerusalem as the bull's-eye, Judea and Samaria as the next two rings, and the remotest part of the world as the outermost ring. We are to be committed to all four rings.

A complete view of evangelism would mean, then, that well-rounded Christians would be concerned about supporting international missions with both prayer and finances. At the same time, they would be concerned about being involved in personal evangelism in their own "Jerusalem." It is obvious that we would be interested in reaching our own "world" (neighborhood, family, workplace, etc.). But in today's diverse world, there are many opportunities even in the United States to do "cross-cultural" missions with international students, immigrant groups, etc.

The Great Commission contains several principles:

- We are given the commission both collectively and individually. No one is exempt.
- We are commanded to go. It is not an option.
- We are to baptize converts.
- We are to teach and make disciples of them, not merely evangelize.

Obviously, not all can go to the remotest part of the earth, nor can we all remain in "Jerusalem." Some remain in Jerusalem while others go to Judea and Samaria, while still others go to the remotest part of the earth. The commission can be fulfilled as all Christians join together in pursuing it.

2. Christianity has a history of evangelism.

Christianity has a h_____ of evangelism.

The Early Church: Christianity's track record on evangelism is impressive, indeed. The disciples of Jesus came out of the blocks evangelizing, eventually carrying the message to Judea and Samaria, Greece, Asia Minor (modern Turkey), and Italy.

The Spread of Christianity to Europe: Upon the legalization of Christianity under the Roman emperor Constantine in 313, Christianity began to spread rapidly throughout Europe, where it continued to gain ground for the next one thousand years.

Courageous missionaries such as Saint Patrick and others like him took the gospel to the relatively pagan areas of northern Europe, where Christianity eventually took hold in spite of corruption and strife. Eventually, all of Europe fell under the influence of Christianity.

The Spread of Christianity to America: Christians migrated to America for religious freedom. As was always the case, the spread of Christianity to new parts of the world involved significant personal sacrifice. The dangers of travel, the potential of accident or illness, and the lack of cultural amenities all made pioneering an undertaking only for the heartiest—both physically and mentally.

The Spread of Christianity around the World: As Christianity became established in the United States, major effort was undertaken early on to take the gospel to the rest of the world. China, Africa, and the South Sea Islands were special targets for strong missionary outreach. Emphasis was placed not only on evangelism but also on Bible translation and church planting.

Summary: This survey establishes the level of commitment the church has had to world evangelism throughout its entire history. Christians in our day can take instruction and inspiration from this level of commitment, exercising an equal level of commitment to the ultimate cause of world evangelism. If we are not to shrink when placed beside our spiritual ancestors, we must take up the challenge of world evangelism and support it—not, perhaps, in the same ways as our spiritual forefathers, but certainly to the same degree.

3. Modern Avenues of Evangelism

The world is a vastly different place than it was two thousand years ago, one thousand years ago, or even one hundred years ago. The world has shrunk. Communication with others on the other side of the globe can be nearly instantaneous. News and information are disseminated worldwide. Walls of protection and isolation have evaporated as people, even in remote places, carry access to the internet in their pockets. As a result, worldviews are evolving, values are shifting, and cultures are merging. The speed of change is continually increasing.

These dramatic changes have created, at the same time, enormous obstacles in evangelism as well as tremendous opportunities. As Christians ponder their obligation to be involved in world evangelism, a host of options open up to them. Examples include:

Personal Evangelism

Each person has the opportunity and responsibility to be involved in personal evangelism. Some people have the spiritual gift of evangelism, which spurs them on to energetic evangelism involvement. Others have gifts that make evangelism more challenging. That is, if someone is spending large amounts of time in his study getting ready to teach an important class because he/she has the gift of teaching, that person must work harder at being involved in evangelism. Evangelism may take a teacher away from his primary gift, while it takes the evangelist toward his primary gift. While the person with the gift of evangelism may be responsible for greater evangelistic involvement than the person with the gift of teaching, we are all responsible for being involved in personal evangelism.

Personal evangelism includes what is commonly called "friendship evangelism," in which a Christian cultivates relationships with others in the hopes of being able to share the gospel with them. It also includes taking spontaneous opportunities to share one's faith while going about normal life activities. Sharing with someone on a plane, at a conference, or in a neighborhood are all examples of spontaneous, personal evangelism.

Event Evangelism

In addition to personal evangelism, a Christian might also participate in event evangelism. This is participating in events that have been planned for the purpose of sharing the gospel with those who attend. A typical example might be a Christmas or Easter special event, a picnic, a sporting event, or other outreach events planned by your church (or even your small group or family). You could help put on the event in some way and/or invite someone to the event.

Ministry Evangelism

Ministry evangelism includes involvement with a parachurch ministry that is dedicated to evangelism. This might include such activities as being a counselor at an evangelistic meeting. It could include helping with setup and tear-down or following up on those who made decisions for Christ at another evangelistic event such as a music concert by Christian artists or a program put on by Christian illusionists. It might involve participating in evangelistic outreach at a prison, retirement center, halfway house, or other such ministries. Ministry evangelism could also include personal involvement, financial or prayer support, or any combination of other types of involvement.

Missionary Evangelism

Missionary evangelism includes cross-cultural evangelistic ministry. It could include inner-city evangelism, evangelism on Native American reservations, or evangelism to recent immigrant populations or international students, etc. It also includes overseas evangelism—helping take the gospel to those in other countries who have never heard. This might be pursued by someone who is a career missionary, a short-term missionary, or someone behind the scenes who does not actually go into the field but makes it possible for others to go. Involvement in missionary evangelism could also include personal involvement, financial or prayer support, or a combination.

Internet Evangelism

Internet evangelism is not really a separate category, but is rather a medium that spans all the previous categories. Through the internet, one can engage in personal evangelism in one's own culture or cross-culturally. In fact, the internet has become the greatest platform for evangelism in history, with historically traditional evangelism ministries (such as the Billy Graham Evangelistic Association or Cru) seeing many times more people coming to Christ through their internet ministries than ever came to Christ through their traditional ministry methods.

It is not just organizations who can leverage the internet for evangelism; individuals can also have tremendous internet evangelistic reach through question-and-answer internet sites, information sharing internet sites, and other social media sites.

Conclusion

The great challenge in becoming involved in evangelism is not only a matter of obligation—it is also a matter of opportunity. Certainly, we are obligated to evangelize. Christ commands it. But it is also our opportunity. Everything God asks of us is commanded because he wants to give something good to us or keep something bad from us. He asks us to evangelize, not only for the sake of the lost, but also because it is only as we enter into complete obedience to him that we gain the fullness of life that God has for us.

We must recognize and accept that we have been hardwired by God for ministry, and this includes evangelism. Our spiritual gifts, our temperament, and our personalities all combine to prepare us for evangelistic involvement. God has prepared good works that he wants us to walk in, and this includes the area of evangelism. When we get involved in evangelism in the way for which God has hardwired and prepared us, we will take great meaning in evangelism.

God doesn't *need* us to be involved in evangelism. He *wants* us to be involved in evangelism. God can get the message of salvation to others even if we are not obedient to the call. For example, he has saved millions of people through visions and dreams in Muslim countries where it is difficult or impossible to evangelize.

No, God doesn't need us. But he wants and commands us to do this good work, and he has given us the privilege of being used by him to take the message to others.

A well-known missionary story relates that when James Calvert sailed to the island of Fiji to evangelize the cannibal natives, the captain of the ship on which he was sailing tried to talk him out of landing. "You'll lose your life and the lives of those with you if you go among those savages."

Calvert's magnificent reply was, "We died before we came here."[1]

It is as Dietrich Bonhoeffer said, "When Christ calls a man, he bids him come and die."[2]

That is the challenge for each believer—to die to self, and then do whatever the Lord asks of us, knowing that this is our doorway to a life of ultimate meaning and purpose in him.

REPETITION
Is the Key to Mental Ownership

Chapter Review

1. The Bible teaches that we are c_____ to evangelize.
2. Christianity has a history of e_____.

The Christian Life in 1,000 Words—Review
(Only the last ten chapters will be displayed)
If something is important, you must repeat it until it changes you.

20. We strive for righteousness, not to get God to love us, but in g_____ that he already does.

21. You can't win a b_____ you don't know you're in.

22. The point of life is not to get smart or get rich or even get happy. The point is to discover God's p_____ for us and make them our o____.

23. The most reliable predictor of success in life is g_____.

24. You must m_____ the Bible so well that the Bible m_____ you.

25. To live well in the w_____, we must first live well with G____.

26. God doesn't want our m_____, he wants our h_____; and the test of whether he has our h_____ is if we give him our m_____.

27. God gives us a j____ to do and g_____ with which to do it.

28. Success is being f_____ to what God asks of us and leaving the r_____ to him.

29. We must share the gospel, not only because o_____ need to hear it, but also because w__ need to share it.

THOUGHT/DISCUSSION
Is a Key to Understanding

Answer these questions, either individually by journaling the answers or in a small discussion group.

1. How did you become a Christian? Did someone go out of his or her way to share the good news of the gospel with you?

2. Have you ever led anyone else to Christ? Do you know how? (See the following resources.)

3. Can you think of a time when you did not succeed, and it turned out to be the best thing you needed?

DECISION TIME
Is a Key to Change

Answer these questions, either individually by journaling the answers or in a spiritual accountability group.

1. Do you think you are as sensitive to the responsibility to evangelize as you should be?

2. Are you involved in evangelism on any level (sharing your faith, praying, or financially supporting evangelistic ministries)? Are you as involved as you think you should be?

3. If you could do anything you wanted to in evangelism and knew that you would be successful, what would you do? Is there any way you could do it?

RECOMMENDED
Resources

This chapter has been a very tight summary. If you would like to learn more about this subject, please consider these resources.

https://evangelism.intervarsity.org/resource/6-conversational
    -evangelism-tips-master-himself

https://evangelismexplosion.org

https://peacewithgod.net

The Master Plan of Evangelism, Robert Coleman

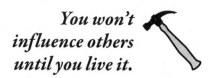

You won't influence others until you live it.

CHAPTER 30

THE PRIORITY OF HUMANITARIANISM

People will not care how much we *know* until they know how much we *care*.

> **CENTRAL PASSAGE:** Luke 6:31—"Treat others the same way you want them to treat you."

If you were in urgent need, would you want someone to help you?

If you had lost your home to a tornado, if you were out of money and could not buy food, or if you were homeless—would you want someone to help you?

If you were a refugee from a war-torn region of Africa, if your village well had dried up and you had to walk a mile to get fresh water, or if there were an epidemic sweeping your region and there was no medicine to combat it—would you want someone to help?

Of course you would!

Therefore, we ought to help others when we can.

But it can be a daunting task. There are so many needs that we cannot meet them all. It is easy to become so overwhelmed with the magnitude of the need that we throw up our hands in exasperation and stop trying to meet any needs.

However, that is not an option for Christians. Just because we cannot meet all needs does not mean that we cannot, or need not, meet some.

1. Jesus taught that we should be humanitarian.

J_____ taught that we should be humanitarian.

Jesus taught the Golden Rule in Luke 6:31, "Treat others the same way you want them to treat you." If we would want others to help us in our need, we should help others in their need.

Furthermore, in Luke 10, where Jesus had just taught on the command to love your neighbor, a lawyer to whom he was speaking wished to justify himself and asked Jesus, "Who is my neighbor?" (v. 29).

Jesus responded with the parable of the good Samaritan. A Jewish man traveling on a deserted highway was accosted by highwaymen who robbed him, beat him, and left him for dead. Jewish leaders passed by and did not help. But a Samaritan, who would normally have significant antipathy toward Jews, and vice versa, stopped and helped at significant personal expense—both in time and money.

From the parable of the good Samaritan, we learn several principles. I was taught these principles in seminary by Dr. Charles Ryrie, author of the *Ryrie Study Bible*:

The Jewish traveler had a genuine need. It was not merely a want; it was a need. Someone might have a want, preference, or desire that is so strong he believes it is a need, but that doesn't make it so. What parent hasn't heard his child express a "want" in the form of a "need"?

The traveler was in trouble through no fault of his own. There are times when people have been chronically irresponsible, and in those situations there might be instances when it is not best to help them out of their problems because it would be aiding and abetting their self-destructive behavior. That was not the case in this story.

The Samaritan's life naturally intersected with the traveler's. We cannot help everyone. The Samaritan had not given up his regular job and gone wandering the wilderness looking for victims. God might call someone to such a ministry, but that is not the point of this parable. The parable reflected the intersection of two people's lives in the normal course of everyday circumstances.

The traveler could not meet his own need. If someone can meet his own need, he might be expected to do so—even if he might not want to do so, or if it would be difficult.

The Samaritan had the ability to meet his need. He paid for the traveler's recovery expenses. Had there been a hundred people robbed and injured, the need might have exceeded the Samaritan's ability to meet it. If we do not have the ability to meet a person's need, we are not morally obligated to do so.

We might summarize by saying that if, in the living of everyday life, we come across a person who has a genuine need through no fault of his own that he cannot meet for himself, and if we have the ability to meet this need, we should consider that it might be God's intent for us to do so.

2. The Bible teaches that we should be humanitarian.

The B_____ teaches that we should be humanitarian.

In addition to Jesus's teaching on humanitarianism, the rest of the New Testament speaks strongly to the subject. The book of James, for example, speaks clearly and forcefully: "Pure and undefiled religion in the sight of our God and Father is this: to visit orphans and widows in their distress . . ." (1:27).

Later in the same letter, the apostle James wrote:

If a brother or sister is without clothing and in need of daily food, and one of you says to them, "Go in peace, be warmed and be filled," and yet you do not give them what is necessary for their body, what use is that? Even so faith, if it has no works, is dead, being by itself. (2:15–17)

The apostle Paul gave instructions in 1 Timothy 5 on how to take care of widows in the church—they were a group of people who were unable to care for themselves in that culture.

So, in addition to the teaching of Jesus and of the common-sense implications of Scripture that we need to care for those who cannot care for themselves, we see passages in the Gospels and Epistles that speak directly to the Christian responsibility to be humanitarian toward others' needs.

3. Christianity has historically been humanitarian.

Christianity has h_____ been humanitarian.

Believers who have taken scriptural teachings to heart have made a striking impact on the history of the world. In a powerful and enlightening volume titled *What If Jesus Had Never Been Born?*, D. James Kennedy and researcher Jerry Newcombe have presented compelling documentation for the impact Christians have made in the world.

> **Poverty:** The late Yale historian Kenneth Scott Latourette wrote that Christianity brought significant innovations in the use of money, including the idea that giving was an obligation for all who claimed Christianity. Even more important was the idea that this giving was extended to those outside the Christian faith. Emperor Julian, a pagan, was impressed with the church's care for its own poor and for outsiders as well. He wrote: "For it is disgraceful that, when no Jew ever has to beg and the impious Galileans [Christians] support both their own poor and ours as well, all men see that our people lack aid from us."
>
> From the time of the early church until today, Christians have been consistent in generously giving money to help relieve poverty.[1]
>
> **Health Care:** Christianity has been the driving force in history, not only in terms of helping the poor, but also in health care for the masses. Before Jesus, there were, essentially, no hospitals.

Medical treatment was considered a privilege for the wealthy. When Jesus came, again, everything changed. Christians began establishing hospitals and became a driving force behind medical advancement.[2]

Education: Taking education to the masses in early history was almost the exclusive province of Christianity. Inspired by a driving passion to see the Bible in everyone's language, Christians have devoted themselves to elevating unwritten languages into written languages, to the translation of the Bible into every major language of the world, and to literacy campaigns so that people can read the Bible in their own language. Not only has this had the eternal benefit of getting the Word of God to untold millions, but it also has had the temporal benefit of bringing literacy and education to much of the world. This has raised the standard of living and quality of life of an uncalculated number of people in the last two thousand years.[3]

Civil Rights: Finally, Christianity has been the driving force behind the abolition of slavery in the civilized world; the upholding of the value and rights of women, children, and minorities; and the humane treatment of prisoners. The Christian faith has been a major influence in the establishment of democracy around the world. Even many institutions that make no claim to Christianity, and which do not even realize their indebtedness to Christianity, are living off the borrowed stability afforded them by the influence of Christianity on the world.[4]

What if Jesus had never been born? It would probably be a very cruel world—just as it was in pagan Rome. But Jesus *was* born, and history is rich with examples of Christians showing care and compassion for the poor and needy as a result.

4. Modern Avenues of Humanitarianism

There are a number of categories of humanitarianism in which a Christian today might be involved:

Hunger Relief: More than one billion people around the world live on less than a dollar a day. Poverty has robbed these families and their children of hope, and threatens to steal their future. Many larger denominations and Christian relief organizations are involved, not only in trying to make sure these families have food for a given day, but also in trying to provide for them clean water, health care, education, and more.

Disaster Relief: Disasters have a life. They come and go with varying duration, intensity, and lasting impact. Hurricanes, tsunamis, earthquakes, and floods are common disasters that visit our planet—often without warning.

These are situations in which Christians have an opportunity to meet earthly needs while making a statement for the gospel—often in lands foreign to the gospel.

Housing: While abject poverty and disasters may present an acute need, inadequate housing presents an ongoing need with a crushingly negative impact. There is a direct correlation between sub-standard housing and sub-standard achievement in life. There are places where there might be enough food to survive, but the negative influence of inadequate housing often destroys the human spirit and potential.

Medical Treatment: Few things are as heartbreaking as acute medical needs that cannot be met. When this involves children, it is even more heartbreaking. Many of the needs that Jesus met in the Gospels were related to physical health.

Today, Christian medical missions often have a dramatic influence in people's lives because the gratitude for healing is so great. Medical missions are a vital need in today's world and are a ministry that Christians can support with full confidence.

Conclusion

People in the United States and other advanced countries are often so insulated from the devastating realities of life in other parts of the world that they do not know of the needs that exist. A Christian may be informed of critical humanitarian needs, but may forget and lose sight of them in the press of everyday life. A reminder can often rekindle a flame of concern and involvement.

Still, at other times it is simply a matter of obedience. Christians need to stop long enough to let the truth of Scripture penetrate, let the reality of the need penetrate, and then make the decision to be involved.

REPETITION
Is the Key to Mental Ownership

Chapter Review
1. J_____ taught that we should be humanitarian.
2. The B_____ teaches that we should be humanitarian.
3. Christianity has h_____ been humanitarian.

The Christian Life in 1,000 Words—Review
(Only the last ten chapters will be displayed)
If something is important, you must repeat it until it changes you.

21. You can't win a b_____ you don't know you're in.
22. The point of life is not to get smart or get rich or even get happy. The point is to discover God's p_____ for us and make them our o___.
23. The most reliable predictor of success in life is g_____.
24. You must m_____ the Bible so well that the Bible m_____ you.
25. To live well in the w_____, we must first live well with G____.
26. God doesn't want our m_____, he wants our h_____; and the test of whether he has our h_____ is if we give him our m_____.
27. God gives us a j____ to do and g_____ with which to do it.
28. Success is being f_____ to what God asks of us and leaving the r_____ to him.
29. We must share the gospel, not only because o_____ need to hear it, but also because w__ need to share it.
30. People will not care how much we k_____ until they know how much we c_____.

THOUGHT/DISCUSSION
Is a Key to Understanding

Answer these questions, either individually by journaling the answers or in a small discussion group.

1. Have you ever directly helped someone in humanitarian need? How did this make you feel?
2. Have you ever been in a situation in which you needed humanitarian help? Did anyone help you? How did you feel about this?
3. What need in the world is the one that draws you most naturally to help meet?

DECISION TIME
Is a Key to Change

Answer these questions, either individually by journaling the answers or in a spiritual accountability group.

1. Do you think you are as sensitive as you should be to the needs of others? Elaborate.
2. Do you currently give time and/or money to help meet humanitarian needs? Do you think you are giving enough?
3. What more would you like to do if you could? Do you think there is any way you could begin?

RECOMMENDED
Resources

This chapter has been a very tight summary. If you would like to learn more about this subject, please consider these resources.

https://www.samaritanspurse.org
https://www.opendoorsusa.org

THE CHRISTIAN LIFE IN A THOUSAND WORDS

This section reduces the entire book to one thousand words in an attempt to make the information even more readily understood and grasped. To do so, I have taken the brief phrases under each chapter title that summarize the content of the chapters and have linked them all together in paragraph form. In some cases, I used transitional phrases to help the flow.

I have used the same divisions that are in the chapters. Also, I have written the chapter summary statements in italics and the transitional words in regular font. As you read the paragraphs and recall the content of the chapters you have completed, this overview of the Christian life will help you see the "whole" and increase your grasp of this very large subject.

KNOW: There are some things so vital to the Christian life that unless you know them, you cannot become a complete Christian.

You were created by God, for God, and will only be happy as a Christian who is growing in God. As we pursue God as the source of our happiness, *we must live in this visible, temporal world according to invisible, eternal realities.* As we do, we focus on the fact *that the main thing God gets out of your life is the person you become. The main thing you get out of your life is the person you become. Therefore, the greatest thing you can do with your life is to become the greatest person you can become in God's eyes before you die.* As we strive to become all we can be before we die, we remind ourselves that *a Christian is not merely someone who has turned over a new leaf, but, rather, is someone who has turned over a new life. Spiritual growth is the process of the redeemed inner man gaining dominion over the unredeemed outer man. Spiritual growth requires a balance of God's part and our part.* As we grow spiritually, *there are three enemies of the Christian: the world, but flesh, and the devil.* As we face these three enemies, *a protected mind will be spared the downward pull of negative input and be released to the upward pull of positive input.* During the battle, *we must make peace with the difficult fact that God is good, and at the same time, his children suffer.*

BE: In the Christian life we are gauged not merely by what we know or do, but by who we become.

God wants faith and love over anything else we might offer him. As we strive to live for him, *God will often deliver us in a manner that seems, initially, to destroy us.* But, *God's blessing in the Old Testament was the "fruit of the vine." In the New Testament, it is the "fruit of the Spirit."*
To guide our relationship with God, we focus on the fact that *we are all born for love. It is the principle of existence and its only end*, and we dedicate ourselves to the reality that, *in order to be free to sail the seven seas, you must make yourself a slave to the compass.* In our reorientation process of life, we accept that things are often backward, and that *in the Christian life, we rise by descending.* As we further dedicate ourselves to a life of prayer, we must accept that *God will either give us what we ask or give us what we would have asked if we knew everything he knew.* At the same time, we give ourselves to trusting and obeying God, accepting that *if we believe, we obey. If we do not obey, it is because we do not believe.* As we live a life of faith and obedience, we learn to be *grateful for what the will of God gives us, rather than ungrateful for what it doesn't,* and *we strive for righteousness, not to get God to love us, but in gratitude that he already does.*

DO: God calls on Christians to manifest their knowledge and character by doing the things he calls and gifts them to do.

As we set out to do the things God has for us to do, we start by accepting the reality of spiritual warfare and recognizing that *you can't win a battle you don't know you're in.* Beyond that, we accept the central point of God's will, that *the point of our lives is not to get smart or to get rich or even to get happy. The point is to discover God's purposes for us and to make them our own.* As we pursue God's will, we come to grips with the fact that *the most reliable predictor of success in life is grit!* Since Scripture is a key to doing all this, we realize that *we must master the Bible so well that the Bible masters us.* This helps us realize that *to live well in the world, you must first live well with God.* Then, we see that *God doesn't want our money; he wants our hearts. The test of whether or not he has our hearts is if we give him our money.* After we give God our money, we then give God our time, embracing the fact that *God gives us a job to do and gifts with which to do it,* realizing that *success is being faithful to what God asks of us, and leaving the results to him.* In our work for the Lord, we accept our two primary responsibilities to the world: that *we must share the gospel, not only because others need to hear it, but also because we need to share it,* and that we must be sensitive to people's tangible needs, realizing that *people will not care how much we know until they know how much we care.*

There is much more to the Christian life that we must know, be, and do, but this very tight summary will help us get some of the essentials in our minds and help establish a foundation of knowledge upon which we can build a lifetime of future learning.

⚗ HOW TO HAVE A PROFITABLE SPIRITUAL FOCUS TIME

I n several of the chapters, we have looked at the necessity of mastering Scripture (24), praying (17), renewing the mind (6), and having spiritual focus (25). To those ends, a vital spiritual discipline for Christians is to spend time regularly in these pursuits. Traditionally, this time has been called "devotions," or a "quiet time."

Spiritual Focus Time

Because these terms are not automatically known by those not steeped in traditional Christian practices and terminology, and because—if someone *is* steeped in those practices and terminology—they may misunderstand the larger concept of "spiritual focus," I prefer to use the term "Spiritual Focus Time," taken from the concept presented in chapter 25. It is a new term to everyone, and therefore can be infused afresh with all the various necessary components.

As I said earlier in this book, the idea is that to live well in the world, we must first live well with God. The physical world in which we live is so foreign, so hostile, and so counter to biblical values that, if we are going to prosper spiritually, we must create an inner spiritual world that magnifies biblical reality. We must draw on that reality to gain capacity to live well in the physical world. Almost like prisoners of war, we must spend large amounts of time cultivating this biblical perspective so that, as we live in the physical world, we will think and act by heaven's values and not earth's.

A Starting Template for Spiritual Focus Time

While Christians can enjoy much creativity and flexibility in their spiritual focus time, it can be helpful to have something concrete with which to start, even though you might let it evolve into something else more helpful to you as time goes on.

If you already have a system that you use and are happy with, by all means continue. If you do not, here is a potential template that you might start with and experiment with as you develop your own approach to your time of spiritual focus.

1. Read your Bible.

- Five minutes a day. Remember, that's over 30 hours a year.
- Read these books:
    Genesis
    Exodus (skip the non-history parts, focusing on the story)
    Numbers (skip the non-history parts, focusing on the story)
    Joshua
    Judges
    1 Samuel
    2 Samuel
    1 Kings
    2 Kings
    Ezra
    Nehemiah
    Matthew
    Mark
    Luke
    John
    Acts
  (The previous list of books gives you the chronological story of the Bible.
  Then continue with . . .)
    The remainder of the New Testament
    Psalms
    Proverbs

- Repeat until you have another approach you would rather take.
- Use a version of the Bible with which you are comfortable. The most popular Bible version is the New International Version. A popular, more informal version is the New Living Translation. I use the rather academic New American Standard Version when I study and the less formal New Living Translation when I read. The best version is the one you prefer. Go to www.biblegateway.com for samples. Choose any chapter and read in any version.

2. Pray.

It can be helpful to break your prayer up into components that are commonly found in prayers in the Bible. The categories are often given rather formal names (adoration, confession, supplication, etc.). I have found the rather informal categories helpful to remember them (wow, sorry, help me, etc.).

WOW (adoration): Begin with words of respect and honor to God.

SORRY (confession): Confess any sins the Lord brings to your mind.

HELP ME (supplication): Pray for the things that are of interest and concern to you.

HELP THEM (intercession): Pray for others who are of interest and concern to you.

CAN WE TALK (communion): Pray and talk with the Lord about anything else that is of interest and concern to you. Talk to him as a Heavenly Father, as though he were physically present.

THANKS (thanksgiving): Thank the Lord for his blessings and goodness to you.

Feel free to adjust this pattern however it may be helpful to you. If this is completely new to you, I recommend you get the book *Before Amen*, by Max Lucado. It's a simple but excellent book on prayer. His categories of prayer are a little different, but you will likely find it very helpful.

3. Review Bible verse(s).

I consider a superverse to be any verse (or verses) that seems especially important to you. Your list of superverses might be very different from my list. That's okay. The only thing that matters is that they are important to you.

- Pick at least one verse that seems especially important to you.
- Read it every day for 30 days to get familiar with the verse, then memorize it so well you can say it without hesitation.
- Review it every day and other times your mind is free, especially when you wake up and go to sleep.
- It's a hefty commitment, but if you don't have another verse/ passage you'd rather memorize, and if you feel up to the task, you might do 1 Corinthians 13:4–7. It has been a life-changing passage for me and many others.

4. Review affirmation(s).

Affirmations are scriptural truths that are not strictly verses, but which summarize significant truths that you would like to be true of you.

- Create a statement of the most important change you would like to make in your life. If you don't have another preference, you might use this one until you find one you like better: *I leave behind small attitudes, values, and behaviors, and I rise to great ones.*
- You can add affirmations so that you have more than one, if you'd like. I have about 24 that I review, one set on M-W-F and another set on T-Th-Sa. I don't usually review them on Sunday.

5. Read this book again, after you have finished it for the first time, at the pace of one chapter a day for 30 days.
- No need to re-do the written exercises unless you want to. Just read a chapter a day.

- Repeat twice for a total of three months (your initial read of this book counts for the first month). Repeat even more if you are so inclined.
- Read the book every January thereafter to refresh your mastery of it.
- That's what I'm going to do, and I wrote it. Because if something is important, it must be repeated until it changes you, and to live well in the world you must first live well with God. Let the truth of this book soak deeply into your mind and heart.

Feel free to expand, adjust, and experiment with this basic idea of Spiritual Focus, and include anything else you think would help you spend time focusing on the Lord and his truth.

If you would like further help in cultivating your Spiritual Focus Time, visit www.thechangezone.com.

NOTES

Chapter 1: The Key to Happiness

1. Blaise Pascal, *Pensées*, trans. W. F. Trotter (Seattle, WA: Pacific Publishing Studio, 2011), 51.
2. C. S. Lewis, *The Weight of Glory* (Grand Rapids: Eerdmans, 1965), 1–2.
3. Pascal, *Pensées*, 51.
4. John Piper, *Desiring God* (Colorado Springs, CO: Multnomah Books, 2011), 18.
5. Piper, *Desiring God*, 19.
6. John Piper, *Battling Unbelief* (Colorado Springs, CO: Multnomah Books, 2007), 143–44.
7. Timothy Keller and Kathy Keller, *The Meaning of Marriage* (New York: Penguin, 2011), 124.

Chapter 2: The Necessity of an Eternal Perspective

1. C. S. Lewis, Mere Christianity (New York: HarperOne, 1980), 49.
2. Randy Alcorn, *The Treasure Principle: Unlocking the Secret of Joyful Giving* (Colorado Springs, CO: Multnomah, 2001), 45.

Chapter 3: The Necessity of an Eternal Purpose

1. Charles Colson, *Loving God: The Cost of Being a Christian* (Grand Rapids, MI: Zondervan, 2018), 92.
2. Kay D. Rizzo, *Over the Top* (Hagerstown, MD: Review and Herald, 2013), 55.

Chapter 4: Embracing Your True Spiritual Nature

1. John MacArthur, *The MacArthur New Testament Commentary: Ephesians* (Chicago: Moody Press, 1986), 164 (emphasis mine).

2. MacArthur, *Ephesians*, 178–179, emphasis mine.

Chapter 6: The Centrality of Mental Renewal to Spiritual Growth

1. Kitty Harmon, *Up to No Good: The Rascally Things Boys Do* (San Francisco: Chronicle Books, 2000), 41.
2. Caroline Leaf, *Switch On Your Brain: The Key to Peak Happiness, Thinking, and Health* (Grand Rapids, MI: Baker Books, 2013), 123–124.
3. Leaf, *Switch On Your Brain*, 128.
4. Barry Gordon, "Can We Control Our Thoughts? Why Do Thoughts Pop into My Head as I'm Trying to Fall Asleep?," *Scientific American*, March 1, 2013, https://www.scientificamerican.com/article/can-we -control-our-thoughts/.
5. Benedict Carey, "Who's Minding the Mind?," *New York Times*, July 31, 2007, https://www.nytimes.com/2007/07/31/health/psychology /31subl.html.
6. Leaf, *Switch On Your Brain*, 132.
7. Leaf, *Switch On Your Brain*, 79.

Chapter 9: The Power of a Protected Mind

1. Blake alluded to this concept multiple times; for example, see William Blake, *Jerusalem: The Emanation of the Giant Albion* (1804–1820), Plate 65, especially lines 75 and 79.
2. Gary Smalley, *Change Your Heart, Change Your Life: How Changing What You Believe Will Give You the Great Life You've Always Wanted* (Nashville: Thomas Nelson, 2007), 26.
3. Smalley, *Change Your Heart, Change Your Life*, 29.

Chapter 10: The Challenge of Pain, Suffering, and Evil

1. Stephen Fry, "Stephen Fry on God," RTÉ One, January 28, 2015, https://www.youtube.com/watch?v=-suvkwNYSQo.
2. This statement is a smoother version of the original phrase, which can be found in Fyodor Dostoevsky, *The Brothers Karamazov*, trans. Richard Pevear and Larissa Volokhonsky (New York: Farrar, Straus and Giroux, 1990), 589.

3. D. James Kennedy and Jerry Newcombe, "Christ and Civilization," in *What If Jesus Had Never Been Born?*, rev. ed. (Nashville: Thomas Nelson, 2001), 1–8.

Chapter 11: Understanding Why the Christian Life Doesn't Work Any Better Than It Does

1. James Dobson, *When God Doesn't Make Sense* (Carol Stream, IL: Tyndale House, 2012), 52.

Chapter 12: The Role of Trials in Christian Growth

1. This is paraphrased from Daniel Defoe, *The Life and Strange Surprizing Adventures of Robinson Crusoe* (London: W. Taylor, 1719), 299.

2. A. W. Tozer, *The Root of the Righteous* (Chicago: Moody Publishers, 2013), 165.

Chapter 14: The Primacy of Love

1. Benjamin Disraeli, *Sybil* (1845; repr., Oxford: Oxford University Press, 2017), 261 (emphasis added).

Chapter 15: The Necessity of Self-Discipline

1. Oscar Wilde, *Lady Windermere's Fan* (New York: Samuel French, 1893), 7.

2. Jim Rohn, "The Key to Getting All You Want? Discipline," *Success*, January 31, 2016, https://www.success.com/rohn-the-key-to-getting -all-you-want-discipline/.

3. Jesse Owens, Goodreads, https://www.goodreads.com/quotes /563376-we-all-have-dreams-but-in-order-to-make-dreams.

4. Theodore Roosevelt, Goodreads, https://www.goodreads.com /quotes/889686-with-self-discipline-most-anything-is-possible.

5. Michael Hyatt, "How to Beat Your Brain and Succeed," Michael Hyatt & Co., April 28, 2017, https://michaelhyatt.com/disciplined -mind/.

6. Jocko Willink and Leif Babin, *Extreme Ownership* (New York: St. Martin's Press, 2017), 14.

7. Peter Hollins, *The Science of Self-Discipline* (self-pub., CreateSpace, 2017), 126.

8. Hollins, *Science of Self-Discipline*, 108.

9. "What Is Grit?," FAQ on Angela Duckworth's website, accessed December 23, 2020, https://angeladuckworth.com/qa/.

10. One version of this story, as well as its background, can be found at Matt Carlson, "The Joke," https://www.carnegiehall.org/Explore /Articles/2020/04/10/The-Joke.

Chapter 16: The Subtle Power of Humility

1. J. I. Packer, *Rediscovering Holiness: Know the Fullness of Life with God* (Grand Rapids: Baker, 2009), 110.

2. C. S. Lewis, *Yours, Jack: Spiritual Direction from C. S. Lewis* (New York: HarperOne, 2008), 11.

Chapter 17: The Mystery of Prayer

1. Timothy Keller, *Prayer* (New York: Penguin, 2016), 228 (emphasis mine).

2. Philip Yancey, *Prayer: Does It Make Any Difference?* (Grand Rapids: Zondervan, 2006), 103.

3. Yancey, *Prayer*, 113.

4. C. S. Lewis, *The World's Last Night* (San Francisco: HarperOne, 2017), 8.

Chapter 18: The Power of Trust and Obedience

1. William Shakespeare, *Hamlet*, ed. Barbara A. Mowat and Paul Werstine (New York: Washington Square Press, 2004), 3.1.89–90.

2. C. S. Lewis, *Mere Christianity* (New York: HarperOne, 2001), 202.

3. C. S. Lewis, *The Weight of Glory* (New York: HarperOne, 2001), 190.

Chapter 19: The Fundamental Importance of Gratitude

1. Benjamin Franklin, "Poor Richard Improved, 1749," in *Autobiography, Poor Richard, and Later Writings* (New York: Library of America, 1997), 512.

2. Elisabeth Elliot, ed., *The Journals of Jim Elliot* (Grand Rapids: Revell, 2002), 174.

3. Billy Graham, *Unto the Hills: A Daily Devotional* (Nashville: Thomas Nelson, 2010), November 24 entry. For the actual entry which Henry wrote in his diary about the robbery, see J. B. Williams, *Memoirs of the Life, Character, and Writings of the Rev. Matthew Henry* (London: B. J. Holdsworth, 1828), 187–188.

Chapter 20: Four Traditional Models for Living the Christian Life

1. Oscar Wilde, *Lady Windermere's Fan* (New York: Samuel French, 1893), 38.

Chapter 21: The Reality of Spiritual Warfare

1. C. S. Lewis, *A Mind Awake* (San Francisco: HarperOne, 2017), 191.
2. Frederick Buechner, *A Crazy, Holy Grace* (Grand Rapids: Zondervan, 2017), 40.

Chapter 22: The Challenge of Discerning God's Will

1. Cornelius Plantinga Jr., *Not the Way It's Supposed to Be: A Breviary of Sin* (Grand Rapids: Eerdmans, 1996), 37 (emphasis mine).
2. Charles Swindoll, *The Mystery of God's Will* (Nashville: Thomas Nelson, 1999), 30.
3. Lewis Sperry Chafer, *He That Is Spiritual* (Grand Rapids: Zondervan, 1967), 92.
4. J. I. Packer, *Knowing and Doing the Will of God* (Ann Arbor, MI: Vine Books, 1995), 401.
5. St. Augustine, "Homily VII on the First Epistle of John," trans. H. Browne, NPNF1 (Grand Rapids: Eerdmans, 1994), 7:504.
6. Philip Yancey, *Grace Notes* (Grand Rapids: Zondervan, 2009), 37–38.

Chapter 23: The Importance of Grit

1. Angela Lee Duckworth, "Grit: The power of passion and perseverance," TED, April 2013, https://www.ted.com/talks/angela _lee_duckworth_grit_the_power_of_passion_and_perseverance ?language=en.
2. "Winston Churchill, "Never Give In, Never, Never, Never" (speech, Harrow School, United Kingdom, October 29, 1941), America's

National Churchill Museum, https://www.nationalchurchillmuseum
.org/never-give-in-never-never-never.html.

3. Duckworth, "Grit."

4. Duckworth, "Grit."

5. Theodore Roosevelt, "The Man in the Arena" (speech, Paris,
France, April 23, 1910), Theodore Roosevelt Center, https://www
.theodorerooseveltcenter.org/Learn-About-TR/TR-Encyclopedia
/Culture-and-Society/Man-in-the-Arena.aspx.

Chapter 24: The Importance of Scripture

1. Gary Smalley, *Change Your Heart, Change Your Life: How Changing
What You Believe Will Give You the Great Life You've Always Wanted*
(Nashville: Thomas Nelson, 2012).

Chapter 25: Spiritual Focus

1. John McCain with Mark Salter, *Faith of My Fathers: A Family Memoir*
(New York: Random House, 1999), 206.

2. Dallas Willard, *The Spirit of the Disciplines* (New York: HarperCollins,
1991), 7.

3. Caroline Leaf, *Switch On Your Brain: The Key to Peak Happiness,
Thinking, and Health* (Grand Rapids, MI: Baker Books, 2013), 75.

4. Leaf, *Switch On Your Brain*, 84.

5. Jim Kwik, *Limitless: Upgrade Your Brain, Learn Anything Faster,
and Unlock Your Exceptional Life* (Carlsbad, CA: Hay House, 2020),
22–30.

Chapter 26: The "Litmus Test" of Giving

1. Randy Alcorn, *The Treasure Principle* (New York: Multnomah, 2001),
13–14.

2. Alcorn, *The Treasure Principle*, 57.

3. For one perspective on the provenance of the obituary story, see
Colin Schultz, "Blame Sloppy Journalism for the Nobel Prizes,"
Smithsonian Magazine, October 9, 2013, https://www.smithsonian
mag.com/smart-news/blame-sloppy-journalism-for-the-nobel-prizes
-1172688/.

Chapter 29: The Priority of Evangelism

1. One source for this story (among others) is Emily Foreman, *We Died before We Came Here: A True Story of Sacrifice and Hope* (Colorado Springs, CO: NavPress, 2016), 186.

2. Dietrich Bonhoeffer, *The Cost of Discipleship* (New York: Touchstone, 1995), 89.

Chapter 30: The Priority of Humanitarianism

1. D. James Kennedy and Jerry Newcombe, "Compassion and Mercy," in *What If Jesus Had Never Been Born?*, rev. ed. (Nashville: Thomas Nelson, 2001), 28–39.

2. Kennedy and Newcombe, "Healing the Sick," in *What If Jesus Had Never Been Born?*, 141–156.

3. Kennedy and Newcombe, "Education for Everyone," in *What If Jesus Had Never Been Born?*, 40–56.

4. Kennedy and Newcombe, "Government of the People, for the People, by the People," in *What If Jesus Had Never Been Born?*, 57–76.